Business Guide to EU Initiatives 2001/2002

THE EU COMMITTEE
OF THE AMERICAN CHAMBER OF COMMERCE IN BELGIUM

Providing a unique business perspective on current initiatives and developed with the input of experts in each particular field, the ***Business Guide to EU Initiatives 2001/2002*** is an indispensable reference point for both specialists and newcomers. Being selective rather than comprehensive in scope, this publication includes essential information on the issues identified by the EU Committee's members as being of primary importance.

As the key organization that represents the views of European companies of American parentage to the European Union, the EU Committee of the American Chamber of Commerce has over the years provided substantial input into the European legislative process. Its member companies are drawn from a broad cross-section of the European business community and are typically based in most Member States of the EU. As such, the EU Committee represents some of the earliest and most committed business supporters of the European ideal and, in particular, the single market concept.

The editors of the ***Business Guide to EU Initiatives*** would like to express their thanks to all the members of the the EU Committee and their associates who have contributed to this edition. This publication incorporates the expertise of many business professionals, whose time and cooperation is highly valued. Thanks also goes to past and present EU Committee staff members including Chantal den Broeder, Peter Lee and Gillian McGrath for their help.

Susan Danger
Communications & Operations Manager

Anthony Smith
Senior Communications Officer

Marcelle Holloway
Communications Officer

Marc Limon
Communications Officer

Pamela Thomson
Assistant Communications Officer

Bénédicte Walter
Press & Marketing Officer

Carol Dannevoye
Marketing & Operations Assistant

The contents of this publication have been assembled and edited in good faith and are accurate according to the most recent sources available. Since EU legislation is in constant motion, refer to the *Business Guide Supplement* for more details on recent developments. Unless stated otherwise, statistics used in this guide are from EU institutions and Eurostat sources.

Brussels,
June 2001

THE EU COMMITTEE
OF THE AMERICAN CHAMBER OF COMMERCE IN BELGIUM

Table of Contents

The past year has witnessed a number of major developments for the European Union, from the drafting of a EU Charter of Fundamental Rights to the signing of a new EU Treaty in Nice. In addition, yet more significant developments, such as the Commission's White Paper on Governance, are in the pipeline. These changes show great promise and business remains a strong supporter of these and other attempts to drive forward the ideal of European integration.

In fact, all of the major developments mentioned above can be seen as part of a wider debate about the very future of the EU itself. A principal *raison d'etre* of the Treaty of Nice was, of course, to prepare the EU for enlargement by resolving some of the issues leftover from the Treaty of Amsterdam. Enlargement will, without doubt, alter the very fabric of the EU both on a geopolitical and an economic level. In the face of such upheaval, however welcome it may be, the Nice Treaty should be seen not as a *denouement* designed to solve a few outstanding institutional issues before admitting up to twelve new applicant states, but more correctly as the starting point of a debate, which is likely to continue for years to come, regarding the very nature of the EU and the future form it should assume.

This debate was stimulated by a speech from Joschka Fischer, Germany's foreign minister, who proposed a supranationalist strategy for the EU which would include a written constitution, an approach that was recently supported by German Chancellor Gerhard Schröder who called for a federalist Europe based on the German model. These comments have in turn drawn alternative visions of the future of the EU from France's President Jacques Chirac, UK Prime Minister Tony Blair and most recently French Prime Minister Lionel Jospin, who have instead advocated a more cautious approach to integration stressing the continued importance of the Member States. Against this background the Commission is preparing its own ideas on the future of an enlarged Union which will be contained in its eagerly awaited White Paper on Governance. The debate is likely to be concluded at a new intergovernmental conference planned for 2004, after which the future shape of the EU should become more clearly discernable.

These developments will have a long-lasting impact on the functioning of the European Union and as a committed supporter of the European ideal, the EU Committee will continue to seek to participate in policy development in its traditionally constructive and positive manner. The EU Committee's priorities for 2001 include the need for greater competitiveness in Europe, building consumer confidence, promoting coherency in Europe's environmental policy, ensuring the success of enlargement, driving forward the digital economy, and furthering open and global trade. These factors constitute, in our opinion, the European Union's greatest assets for maintaining global competitiveness. Efforts must be maintained to secure progress in each of these key areas.

This latest edition of the ***Business Guide to EU Initiatives*** will help the reader navigate through the often confusing and complicated world of EU policy-making and is, therefore, a vital tool for all those concerned with European affairs. The Business Guide is unique in its coverage of pending and recently adopted Community legislation, providing both the general and specialist reader with concise, straightforward summaries of the most important European legislative issues. Each entry provides an overview of the issue and summarizes the purpose of the proposal, before ending with a business perspective written by an expert in that field.

A companion publication is produced to complement the information provided in the ***Business Guide to EU Initiatives. Business Guide Supplement*** is published in print and on-line ten times a year and provides thorough, accurate and constantly updated information on new EU legislative proposals. The Supplement is a tracking guide for preparatory and developing Community legislation, and follows approximately 500 issues from their conception in the Commission through the Parliament and the Council. It provides complete references and relevant institutional contacts for each issue, a listing of upcoming initiatives awaiting publication, a table of all adopted legislation in each sector and titles and dates of EU Committee position papers where applicable.

The ***Guide*** and the ***Supplement*** are essential for everyone following Community legislation and needing an overview of activity sector by sector. I am sure you will agree that now, more than ever, the EU Committee offers you the best source of information on a range of policy initiatives with a real impact on business.

Maja Wessels
Chair of the EU Committee

THE EU COMMITTEE
OF THE AMERICAN CHAMBER OF COMMERCE IN BELGIUM

Instruments & Implementation

THE EU COMMITTEE
OF THE AMERICAN CHAMBER OF COMMERCE IN BELGIUM

1. The European Union Treaties

The Treaty on European Union

Title: The Treaty on European Union (TEU)
Published: Official Journal C 224 August 31, 1992
Status: Entered into force November 1, 1993

The Treaty on European Union, known as the Maastricht Treaty, represented the most important step towards an integrated Europe, since the Single European Act (SEA) of 1987. The Treaty founded a European Union, based on the Treaties of the European Communities (European Community (EC), Euratom and the European Coal and Steel Community (ECSC)), for which the main objectives are to establish:

- an economic and monetary union, ultimately introducing a single currency;
- a citizenship, attributing EU citizens the right to vote and to stand for European and municipal elections in the country where they reside;
- a common foreign and security policy (CFSP), ensuring European security and defending common values such as democracy and human rights; and
- cooperation on justice and home affairs, ensuring the internal security of the Union.

Other existing policy areas were also expressly included in the Treaty such as education, culture, public health, consumer protection, trans-European networks, and industry.

The Treaty asserts the principles of subsidiarity, proportionality, transparency and openness and economic and social cohesion. The latter involves a transfer of financial resources from more affluent regions (mainly in Germany, the Netherlands, Austria and Sweden) to less developed regions (mainly in Greece, Portugal, Ireland and Spain).

The Treaty of Amsterdam

Title: The Treaty of Amsterdam (ToA)
Published: Official Journal C 340 November 10, 1997
Status: Entered into force May 1, 1999

Signed on October 2, 1997, the Amsterdam Treaty made further amendments to the previous Treaties at both the policy and the institutional level. This Treaty was designed to prepare the Union for the challenges of the 21st century, including enlargement and economic and monetary union, and to make the European Union more relevant to its citizens. Institutionally, it brought important changes to the decision-making procedures within all three pillars of the Union and gave the European Parliament considerably more powers.

Despite changes brought about by the Treaty, a further Intergovernmental Conference (IGC) was started in 2000 in order to address a number of institutional issues left unresolved by the Amsterdam Treaty (the 'Amsterdam leftovers'), including Member States' voting weights in the Council, the extension of qualified majority voting and the future make up of the Commission. This new IGC ended with the Treaty of Nice.

The Treaty of Nice

Title: The Treaty of Nice
Published: Official Journal C 80 March 10, 2001
Status: Pre-ratification.

The Treaty of Nice was signed on February 26, 2001, the principal objective of the new Treaty being, as with the ToA, to prepare the Union for the challenge of enlargement. In preparation for enlargement three main areas, collectively known as the 'Amsterdam leftovers', were addressed in the Treaty discussions: a re-weighting of votes in the Council, the extension of qualified majority voting, and Commission reform.

Despite the decisions made in Nice, a declaration in the Treaty states that a 'deeper and wider debate about the future of the European Union' will still have to take place. The Swedish and Belgian Presidencies along with the Commission and the Parliament will orchestrate discussions involving all interested stakeholders including candidate countries and members of the public (see page 86). A report will be drawn up and presented in June 2001 for the European Council in Gothenburg and a declaration on how the process should continue will be put forward at the European Council meeting in Laeken, Brussels to be held in December 2001. There are four issues to be addressed:

- the distribution of powers bewteen the EU and Member States in accordance with the subsidiarity principle;
- the status of the Charter of Fundamental Rights;
- a simplification of the Treaties; and
- the role of national parliaments.

When these negotiations are concluded a new IGC will be convened in 2004 under the leadership of the German Presidency.

2. The Three Pillars of the EU

Union Temple

Schematically, the European Union may be depicted as a structure supported by three pillars. Each pillar fortifies the Union, yet each is also independent, in terms of competences and powers attributed to the institutions of the Union. The first pillar comprises the European Community, founded by the Treaties of Rome (TEC) and Paris, including economic and monetary union, citizenship and several other competences based around the single market. The second pillar represents the common foreign and security policy, and the third symbolizes justice and home affairs. The two latter pillars differ from the first in their decision-making, and the instruments applied have an intergovernmental character. Accordingly, as opposed to the first pillar, the Member States (through the European Council and the Council of Ministers) have the primary right to take initiatives; and the decisions taken have a largely political, rather than a legal, value as they are not binding before the European Court of Justice.

The First Pillar: EC Affairs and Additional Competences

The Treaties of Maastricht and Amsterdam have brought about important changes under the EU's first pillar. These include:

Citizenship
Articles 17-22 EC, introduced by the Maastricht Treaty, established European citizenship. Every national of a Member State becomes a citizen of the Union, which implies the right to:

- move and reside freely within the territory of the fifteen Member States;
- vote and stand as candidates at municipal and European elections where they reside in the Union;
- receive diplomatic and consular protection of the authorities of any Member State; and
- raise a petition to the Parliament and to the Ombudsman.

Free Movement of Persons
Following ratification of the Amsterdam Treaty, a range of areas concerned with the free movement of people were taken out of the intergovernmental sphere and made Community competences. However, the Commission's sole right to initiate legislation will not take effect for five years (ie, in May 2002). This holds for all aspects of visas and immigration, external border controls, judicial cooperation on civil matters and closer administrative cooperation in these areas.

Changes to Decision-Making
The Amsterdam Treaty effectively reduced the number of decision-making procedures from four to three (co-decision, assent and consultation) by eliminating the cooperation procedure from all policy areas except economic and monetary affairs, and extended the use of the co-decision procedure from 15 to 38 policy areas.

Also following the entry into force of the Amsterdam Treaty, unanimity is required in the Council on matters related to the right to move or reside anywhere in the Union (Article 18 EC), social security (Article 42 EC) and self-employed persons (Article 47 EC).

Under the Treaty of Nice profound changes will be brought in concerning voting in the Council (see pages 7, 87).

New Competences
The following areas have for the first time gained legal status following the ToA

- employment (Arts. 125 to 130);
- customs cooperation (Art. 135);
- general principles for transparency (Art. 255);
- countering fraud (Art. 280);
- statistics (Art. 285); and
- advisory authority on data protection (Art. 286)

Economic and Monetary Union (EMU)
Of special interest in the first pillar of the Union is the establishment of an economic and monetary union (EMU). Under the specific conditions laid down in the TEU, the third stage of EMU began on January 1, 1999 when the national currencies of the eleven participating countries were irrevocably locked into a monetary union and a single European currency, the euro, was introduced. Monetary policy for the euro-12 area (comprised of participating states - the last entrant, Greece, joined the other 11 in June 2000) is set by the independent European Central Bank. The euro is currently only used for electronic payments. Euro notes and coins will be introduced in January 2002.

Second Pillar: Common Foreign & Security Policy (CFSP)

Title V of the TEU sets down the parameters of the European Union's foreign and security policy (Articles 11-28 EU). Three main elements make up the common policy:

- initiation of a Europe-wide defense policy, which has led to the incorporation of the Western European Union (WEU) into the CFSP (with special arrangements for non-WEU Member States);
- cooperation on all areas of foreign and security policy with the objectives of consolidating and developing democracy and common values and preserving peace; and
- Member States are obliged to inform and consult one another within the Council on any matter of general interest.

A major change ushered in by the Amsterdam Treaty concerned the establishment of the new post of High Representative for the CFSP, who will also act as secretary general of the Council. The High Representative will have a Policy Planning and Early Warning Unit at his/her disposal, which will ensure coherence and continuity in the formulation of the CFSP. The first appointee to the post was Javier Solana, secretary general of NATO from 1995-1999.

The traditional 'troika' of past, present and future presidencies of the Council that represents the Union in affairs of international importance was replaced by the current Presidency with the assistance of the Secretary General of the Council (ie, the High Representative). The Commission is fully associated with the task of representation of the Union and the presidency may call on the assistance of the Member State that holds the next presidency in line.

The European Council defines the principles and general guidelines of the CFSP, for which a number of different instruments are available (Article 12 EU). These include joint actions, common positions, systematic cooperation and an instrument called the 'common strategy', which was introduced by the Amsterdam Treaty. The European Council adopts a common strategy on the recommendation of the Council in areas where the Member States have important interests in common. Once adopted the Council can agree joint actions and/or common positions by a qualified majority. Unanimity is required where no common strategy is reached.

Another feature of the ToA is the 'constructive abstention' principle concerning voting within the Council. If a decision requires unanimity, the abstention of one or more Member State(s) will not prevent its adoption. However, those countries that abstain are required not to take any action that may impede Union action based on the adopted decision. If the number of Member States opposing a decision, however, accounts for one third (or more) of the weighted votes in the Council, the decision will not be adopted. Where Member States intend to oppose a policy for 'important and stated reasons' of national policy, the Council may refer the matter by a qualified majority to the European Council where unanimity is then required.

More recent developments have also led to the framing of a Common European Security and Defense Policy (CESDP). Due to the inadequacies of Europe's military contribution to NATO operations during the Kosovo crisis in mid-1999, the Union has determined a course to allow the Council to take decisions on a range of conflict prevention and crisis management tasks. One of the key results of the Helsinki European Council in December 1999 was to set an objective to provide the Union with sufficient military and non-military capabilities to intervene in humanitarian and rescue tasks, peace-keeping and crisis management (the so-called Petersburg tasks). Member States have committed themselves to being able to deploy 60,000 persons capable of these tasks by 2003 and to sustain them for at least a year.

At a pledging conference on November 20, 2000 the Member States offered a total of 100,000 troops, 400 aircraft and 100 ships for crisis management operations. Belgian Foreign Minister Louis Michel promised a renewed effort to finalize plans for an EU rapid reaction force and a bigger EU diplomatic presence in the Middle East and Africa during Belgium's upcoming Presidency of the Union starting in July 2001.

The Third Pillar: Cooperation in the Field of Justice and Home Affairs (JHA)

The Treaty on European Union aimed to institute cooperation between the Member States within the following areas considered to be of common interest:

- common rules governing the crossing by persons of the external borders;
- policy regarding nationals from third countries, including an asylum and immigration policy;
- combatting drug addiction and fraud;
- judicial cooperation in civil and criminal matters; and
- customs and police cooperation.

An important element of the Amsterdam Treaty was the inclusion of the first specific objective in the area of JHA: Article 2 EU instructs the Union to establish 'an area of freedom, security and justice' in which the free movement of persons can be developed and maintained alongside 'appropriate measures with respect to external border controls, asylum, immigration and the prevention and combating of crime'.

This actually entails the transfer of a range of third pillar (ie, intergovernmental) competences to the first pillar (ie, Community) and the inclusion of a new Title (Articles 61-69 EC) on 'visas, asylum, immigration and other policies related to the free movement of persons' in the Treaty of Rome (TEC). This has effectively blurred the distinction between the first and third pillars. Under a transitional arrangement, the new Title retains some of the intergovernmental character of the third pillar. For a five year period from the date of entry into force of the ToA, individual Member States, as well as the Commission can initiate proposals in most of the areas covered by the Title. The proposals then follow the standard consultation procedure (see page 9). When the transitional period comes to a close, the co-decision procedure will apply to some aspects of visas, refugees and immigration policy. On additional aspects in these areas and on issues concerning borders, third country nationals, asylum, illegal immigration and judicial cooperation on civil matters the Council must decide by unanimity at the end of the transitional phase whether or not to give the Community full competence in these areas. In connection with the implementation of the Title on the free movement of persons, the Schengen Agreement concerning the opening of internal borders has been incorporated as a new protocol into the TEC. Denmark, Ireland and the UK opted out of the agreement, although the UK is currently negotiating its partial implementation. Applicant countries to the EU will be required to fully implement the Schengen provisions without exception.

In the areas of police and judicial cooperation on criminal matters, policy developments remain within the legal framework of the third pillar. Nevertheless, the ToA also introduced some new features to this sphere:

- the Commission can initiate proposals in all JHA areas though it shares this responsibility with Member States;
- the Parliament must be consulted (and give an opinion within a Council-defined time limit) on all measures, except common positions; and
- a limited role for the European Court of Justice (ECJ).

In JHA a common position sets down the EU's approach on a specific issue, after which a number of other instruments may be applied. Decisions or Framework Decisions, both introduced by the ToA, can be used for the purposes, respectively, of cooperation on criminal matters and of the approximation of laws in these areas. Another existing option is the use of Conventions, standard instruments of international law which may or may not come under the jurisdiction of the ECJ, depending on the Council's decision. The Council may also adopt a variety of Resolutions, Recommendations, Declarations or Conclusions which are not legally binding.

The scope of Europol's activities has been widened by the ToA. The Council is required to promote Europol, giving it more investigative powers, particularly in combating cross-border and organized crime. This includes establishing a research, documentation and statistical network on cross-border crime.

Both the third pillar and the TEC Title related to the free movement of persons contain safeguard clauses which Member States can invoke if measures encroach on their responsibilities for the maintenance of law and order and internal security.

3. Changes Under the Treaty of Nice

The following changes will occur when the Treaty of Nice comes into force:

Voting in Council - under the Treaty of Nice the number of Council votes has beeen re-distributed in anticipation of membership of the Union growing to 27. The number of votes allocated to each country is as follows:

• Germany, Italy, France, UK	29
• Spain and Poland	27
• Romania	14
• Netherlands	13
• Belgium, Greece, Portugal, Hungary, Czech Republic	12
• Austria, Sweden, Bulgaria	10
• Denmark, Ireland, Finland, Slovakia, Lithuania	7
• Luxembourg, Latvia, Estonia, Slovakia, Cyprus	4
• Malta	3

Extension of QMV - there will be a total number of 237 votes in the Council, and it will be possible to secure a decision with 169 votes under the new system. The threshold for QMV will be adjusted as new countries join the EU and will range from a minimum of 71.4% to a maximum of 73.4% of the votes cast.

Commission reform - each Member State will have one Commissioner from 2005 and this allocation will be frozen once the Union reaches 27 members. A system of rotation will be agreed upon and a cap of the number of Commissioners which will be installed. Members of the Commission including the President will be chosen by the Council using QMV. The President will also have increased powers, for example, s/he will be able to ask individual Commissioners to resign.

Parliamentary reform - in the Parliament candidate countries have been allocated seats ahead of accession which means the number of representatives will amount to 732 starting at the beginning of the 2004 - 2009 term. Germany will be able to keep its 99 MEPs, whilst France, Italy and the UK have settled for an 18% reduction in the number of seats.

Enhanced cooperation - the enhanced cooperation or flexibility agreement signed in Nice allows Member States in groups of eight or more to move ahead with closer integration in certain policy areas as long as the projects do not adversely affect single currency issues or exclude other Member States wishing to join later. Under the first pillar, the Council must approve the request with QMV, under the second pillar closer cooperation projects are permitted within the foreign policy area (excluding defense).

The Charter of Fundamental Rights - this was adopted as a non-legally binding political declaration by the President of the Council, the President of the Parliament and the President of the Commission. It is addressed to the institutions and bodies of the EU, and to the Member States only when they are acting in the field of Union law.

The Charter constitutes the first text of fundamental rights in which the indivisibility of rights is really proclaimed. The integration of social rights in the Charter will allow the Union to be equipped with a complete and balanced instrument for the protection of fundamental rights. The status of the Charter will be reviewed during the next reform negotiations.

The European Community's Legislative Role

Within the European Union, the European Community (EC) is responsible for proposing and adopting legislation which is relevant to the internal market. In the EU, all internal market legislation falls within the scope of the Treaty of Rome (TEC), and is, therefore, the responsibility of the EC. When acting as a legislator, the Community has at its disposal a wide range of legal instruments which determine how Member States should act regarding the implementation of European law. Based on the TEC, the proposal, adoption and implementation of each measure is determined by the legal basis. The following procedures and acts used by the Community refer only to areas which fall under pillar I of the Union (different procedures and acts come into play when decisions are made in the areas of CFSP and JHA). As the ***Business Guide to EU Initiatives*** is primarily concerned with the internal market, we concentrate on the legislative role of the EU in pillar I only.

Adoption of a Proposal by the Commission
Traditionally, the Commission has the sole right to initiate legislation in the domain of Community affairs, and particularly the internal market. Under transitional arrangements, Member States share this responsibility on matters related to the free movement of persons (see page 6). Legislation appears in its earliest stage once the relevant Directorate-General prepares a draft text and circulates it within the Commission. At this stage, the proposal is published as a Commission working document, with a SYN or SEC reference or an internal number. Once agreement on the proposed text has been reached (proposal is 'adopted') within the Commission, it is then published as a COM document, showing a year and date of issue (eg, COM (95) 547 November 14, 1995). This is the first public stage for the proposal. The COM document usually contains an explanatory memorandum which sets out the Commission's aim. At any moment throughout the procedure, the Commission may withdraw or amend its proposal.

European Parliament readings, ESC and CoR opinions
After a short interim period, and after translation into the eleven official languages of the Union, the proposal is then published in the "C" series of the Official Journal. It simultaneously seeks the opinion of the Economic and Social Committee (ESC) and/or the Committee of the Regions (CoR) and endorsement by the European Parliament, before being approved by the Council of Ministers. The Treaty of Rome lays down four decision-making procedures:

- **consultation** means that one opinion from the Parliament is required;
- **assent** means that the Parliament must approve or oppose a proposal but cannot make amendments;
- **cooperation** means that two readings by the Parliament are given; before the second, the Council adopts a common position (used only for economic and monetary affairs) (Article 252 EC);
- **co-decision** was introduced by the TEU and is based on Article 251 EC. This procedure grants extensive powers to the Parliament, giving it the right to oppose, amend or veto (by an absolute majority) a Council common position. In this event, the Council may call a Conciliation Committee (50% Council members and 50% EP members - 24 members in total) to explain its position. If the point of contention remains unresolved after talks in the Committee, Parliament can veto the proposal. The ToA introduced a "simplified co-decision" procedure which reduces the duration of the procedure by cutting the number of Parliament hearings from three to two. Additionally, a proposal which has been endorsed by both the EP and the Council without any amendments may be adopted after only one reading.

Adoption of Legislation by the Council
Within the Council, a measure can be adopted after the opinions above have been given. In cases where the Parliament has given the first of its two opinions, the Council adopts a common position; this is a political agreement followed by final adoption or rejection after the second Parliamentary reading. The Council has different voting options: (a) unanimity; (b) simple majority (8 out of 15) of the Member States; or (c) qualified majority (62 votes out of 87). In the case of issues not proposed by the Commission (notably, CFSP, JHA), these 62 votes have to represent the wishes of at least 10 Member States. In the event of between 23 and 27 votes (blocking minority) against an issue, there will be a reasonable delay during which the Council will do whatever it can to help secure a qualified majority. Once the proposal is formally adopted, it is published in the "L" series of the Official Journal, with full details of the legislation's implementation and scope. All COM documents and Official Journals are published by the Office for Official Publications located in Luxembourg, and are publicly available on subscription, or on demand.

Decision-making Procedures for Community Legislation

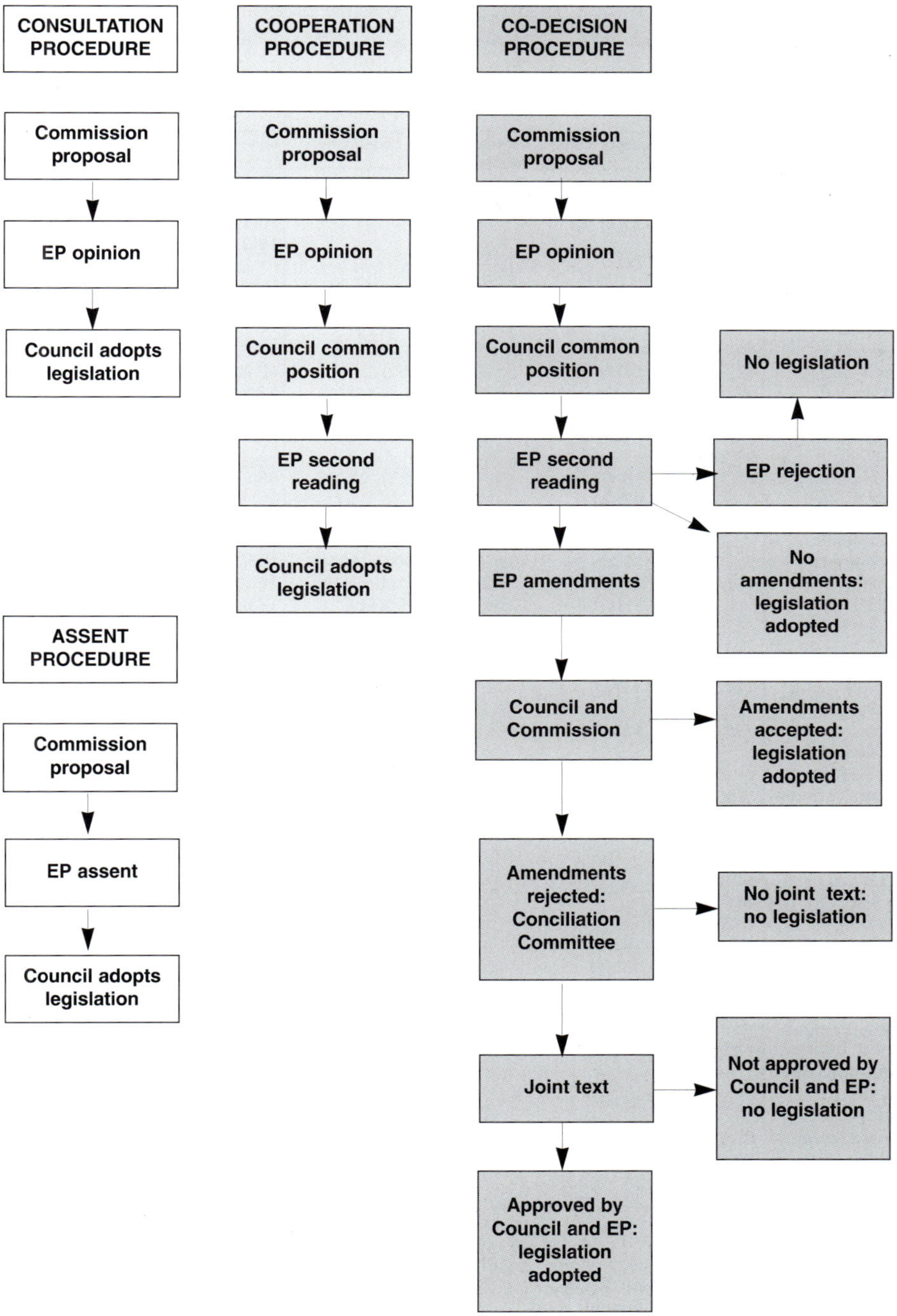

Legal Bases for Community Decision-Making

The table below describes most legal bases for internal market legislation, the procedures they follow and the Council voting required since the entry into force of the Amsterdam Treaty. For example, article 175(3) forms the basis of some legislation in the environment sphere. It requires co-decision and a qualified majority in the Council. NB - two possible procedures exist on the basis of the following articles: 57(2), 80(2), 100(2), 107(5), 111(1), 111(4), 139(2), 149(4) & 300(2ii).

Treaty articles & descriptions	**Legislative procedure:**				**Council voting:**	
	co-decision	**consultation**	**assent/ cooperation***	**no consultation**	**unanimity**	**qualified majority**
principles (1-16)	**12**	**13** ***11(2)***	-	-	**13**	**12** ***11(2)***
citizenship (17-22)	**18(2)**	19(1), 22	-	-	19(1), 22 **18(2)**	-
goods (23-31)	-	-	-	26	-	26
agriculture (32-38)	-	37(3)	-	-	-	37(3)
people, services & capital (39-69)	40, 44, 55 **42**, **46(2)** **47(2)**	**47**, **52(1)** ***67(1&3)***	-	45, 49 57(2) 59, 60(1&2) ***64(2)***	57(2) **42**, **47** ***67(1)***	40, 44, 45, 49, 55 57(2), 59, 60(1&2) **42**, **46(2)**, **47(2)** **52(1)**, ***64(2)***, ***67(3)***
transport (70-90)	**71(1)** **80(2)**	71(2)	-	75(3), 80(2)	71(2)	75(3), 80(2) **71(1)**, **80(2)**
competition, tax & laws (81-97)	95(1)	83, 89 93, 94		88(2), 92, 96	88(2), 93, 94	83, 89, 92, 95(1) 96
economic & monetary policy (98-124)	-	104(4) 107(6) 110(3) 111(1&4) 121(3&4) 122(2)	99(5)* 102(2)* 103(2)* 105(6) 106(2)* 107(5)	99(2), 100(1) 100(2), 104(6) 111(1-4),114(3) 119(2&3) 120(3), 122(1) 123(4&5)	100(1&2) 105(6), 107(5) 111(1&4) 123(4&5)	99(2&5), 100(2) 102(2), 103(2) 104(4&6), 106(2) 107(5&6), 110(3) 111(1-4), 114(3) 119(2&3), 120(3) 121(3&4), 122(1&2)
employment (125-130)	***129***	***128(2)***	-	***128(4)***	-	***128(2&4)***, ***129***
commercial & customs (131-135)	***135***	**133(5)**	-	132(1), 133(4)	**133(5)**	132(1), 133(4) ***135***
social, culture, health & consumer protection (136-153)	149(4), 151 152(4c) 153(4) **137(1&2)** **148**, **150(4)** ***141*** ***152(4a&b)***	**137(3)**	-	139(2), 144 149(4), 151(5) 152(4) **139(2)**	144, 151,151(5) **137(3)**, **139(2)**	139(2), 149(4) 152(4&4c), 153(4) **137(1&2)**, **148** **150(4)** ***141***, ***152(4a&b)***
industry, TENs cohesion and R&D (154-173)	156(i) **156**, **162** **166**, **172**	157(3), 159 166(4) **172(1)**	161	-	157(3), 159 161	156(i), 166(4) **156**, **162**, **166**, **172** **172(1)**
environment (174-176)	175(3) **175(1)**	175(2)	-	-	175(2)	175(3) **175(1)**
development & OCTs (177-188)	**179**	-	-	187	187	**179**
institutional & financial provisions (189-280)	***255(2)*** ***280(4)***	225(2) 245(ii) 247(3), 269 270, 279	190(4)	210, 213(1) 215, 221, 222 225(4), 245(iii) 247(8), 258(ii& iv), 263, 272(3) 273(ii), **207(2)**	190(4), 213(1) 215, 221, 222 225(2&4),245(ii &iii), 247(3) 258(ii),263,269 270, 279, **207(2)**	210, 247(8), 272(3), 273(ii) **258(iv)** ***255(2)***, ***280(4)***
general & final provisions (281-314)	***285(1)*** ***286(2)***	283, 300(2 &2ii), 308 **299(2)**	300(3)	290, 296(2) 301 **309(2&3)**	296(2), 290 300(2ii&3), 308	283, 300(2&2ii),301 **299(2)**, **309(2&3)** ***285(1)***, ***286(2)***

Source: European Commission

Key - the table gives Treaty article numbers, with paragraphs and subparagraphs in parentheses; eg, 152(4a&b) represents article 152, paragraph 4, subparagraphs a and b. Roman numerals indicate article indents; eg, 258(ii&iv) represents article 258, second and fourth indents. Bold represents changes to decision-making and bold italics represent completely new article numbers introduced by the Amsterdam Treaty. For the sake of clarity, Treaty Protocols have been omitted.

Outline of Legislative Acts

Below follows an outline of the Community's legal and non-binding instruments to facilitate a clear understanding of the impact of each entry featured in the **Business Guide**.

Regulation

Origin	Proposed by the Commission.
Scope	Specifically addressed to the governments of Member States: a Regulation creates binding legislation which automatically enters into force in all Member States on a given date, usually several days after official publication.
Published	First as a COM document, then as a proposal in the Official Journal C series, then, when adopted, in Official Journal L series.

Directive

Origin	Proposed by the Commission.
Scope	Defines the results to be achieved in a particular area while leaving it to national authorities to decide the form and means for achieving the desired aim. Implementation of Directives requires "national transposition", (ie, national laws must be introduced in order to implement the EU Directive, normally within two to three years after final adoption). Each of the 282 proposals of the White Paper on Completing the Internal Market were in the form of Directives.
Published	First as a COM document, then as a proposal in the Official Journal C series, then, when adopted, in Official Journal L series.

Decision

Origin	Issued by the Council or the Commission.
Scope	Decisions have a specific range of application and can be directed at individual or several Member States, companies, or private individuals. Decisions are binding upon those to whom they are addressed. Generally, they are used as instruments for the administrative implementation of EU law.
Published	In the Official Journal C or L series.

Recommendation and Opinion

Origin	Issued by Commission, Council, Parliament, Economic and Social Committee, and Committee of the Regions
Scope	They give non-binding Community views on a number of topics, normally to encourage desirable, but perhaps un-enforceable, good practices throughout the EU. Addressed to Member States and economic operators.
Published	First as a COM document, then in the Official Journal C series.

Resolution

Origin	Issued by the Council and/or the Parliament.
Scope	Resolutions are intended to establish the fundamental principles on which Community action shall be based and to determine the period within which this action shall be taken. Resolutions are only declarations of intention which express mainly the 'political wish' of the Council.
Published	As a COM document.

Green & White Paper

Origin	Prepared and issued solely by the Commission.
Scope	Green Papers focus on a particular area of interest for which the Community has not yet produced legislation, for example the Green Paper on postal services. Primarily, a Green Paper is designed to be a consultative document, addressed to interested parties, individuals, companies, and organizations all of which are then invited to give their input to any possible future legislation. A time-limit is given, by when the interested parties are required

to submit their comments to the Commission. Usually, although not always, a Green Paper will lead to a Communication, which may lead to an actual proposal for legislation.

Similar to Green Papers, White Papers are used as vehicles for the development of policy in areas that have not yet come under existing legislation. The major difference between the two papers is that White Papers focus on broader areas that cover more than one industry, such as the Delors White Paper on Growth, Competitiveness and Employment. These are drawn as a consequence of analysis of important policy to the Union as a whole. Specific proposals for legislation may follow on from a White Paper.

Published As a COM document.

Communication

Origin Prepared by the Commission.

Scope Communications are usually produced as a result of comments received after the release of a Green Paper. A Communication is thus the logical next step after a Green Paper, and may even go so far as to give the outline of a Commission proposal for legislation on the issue. Although not the rule, Communications are generally followed-up by an actual proposal or set of proposals in the area in question. The Commission has also issued Communications on the interpretation of Court cases and on several other subjects.

Published As a COM document, then in Official Journal C series.

Notice

Origin Issued solely by the Commission.

Scope Notices are published to indicate and interpret Community policy. There is no legal obligation on the Commission to publish Notices, as their purpose is purely informational. While they provide guidelines as to how the Commission may interpret relevant legislation, they are of persuasive authority only before national courts. In particular they are used in the area of competition law.

Published In Official Journal C series.

Studies

Origin Studies are usually prepared by a third party at the request of the Commission.

Scope They are designed to be an overview of a particular area of activity within the EU. Although not specifically intended to be another form of preparation for future legislation at the European level, an actual Commission proposal may well be the outcome. The study aims to present a Community-wide picture of the issue in question. For example, a Commission study on the gambling industry presented the state of the gambling industry in the context of each Member State and how the advent of the Internal Market would affect it. On this occasion the Commission did not deem it necessary to issue a proposal for legislation in this area.

Published No formal publication required.

Chapter I
Competition Policy

THE EU COMMITTEE
OF THE AMERICAN CHAMBER OF COMMERCE IN BELGIUM

1. The Reform of the Implementation of Competition Law

Background

Articles 81 and 82 of the EC Treaty set out the competition law provisions governing relations between private entities. They are the general rules governing restrictive practices and abuses of dominant positions respectively. In force since 1962 (Regulation EC/17/62), they have become cornerstones of a highly centralized anti-trust policy which the Commission believes has successfully established a 'competition culture' in the EU.

EU anti-trust law contains a general prohibition on agreements which restrict competition (Art. 81 (1) EC), while also providing powers to exempt agreements that contribute to 'improving the production or distribution of goods or to promoting technical or economic progress' (Art. 81 (3) EC). Although the prohibition is directly applicable in national courts, the Commission was given the exclusive competence to grant exemptions. As it has traditionally done this by applying a very wide interpretation of Article 81 (1), agreements frequently fall under the scope of this article and, consequently, require an exemption to be valid. According to the Commission, this has resulted in an overload of such notifications for exemptions, and has largely diverted its attention away from the important task of detecting and punishing the price-fixing and market-sharing practices of cartels.

It has had to concentrate its limited resources on the issuing of so-called 'comfort letters' which confirm that an agreement is in line with EU rules. 'Serious' cases remain more difficult to detect, as these are rarely notified. To alleviate this unsatisfactory workload, the Commission has resorted to the granting of 'block exemptions' for certain agreement categories and to the so-called '*de minimis*' handling of agreements of minor importance.

The Commission is proposing to reform this system, with the aim of reducing its workload and refocusing its resources, but also of attempting to bring competition law closer to the citizens by decentralizing its implementation.

After the publication in April 1999 of a White Paper on the 'modernization' of the implementation of Articles 81 and 82 of the EC Treaty (OJ C 132 May 12, 1999), the Commission issued in September 2000 a draft Council Regulation implementing Articles 81 and 82 (OJ C 365 December 19, 2000) that will replace Regulation EC/17/62.

The Commission's proposed reform can be summarized in three parts:

- elimination of the prior notification system for all agreements other than those falling under the Merger Regulation;
- decentralization of the implementation of Article 81 (3) EC, and consequently all EC competition law, to national courts and national competition authorities; and
- increase of the Commission's powers of investigation and sanction to improve its efficiency in combating cartels.

First, the Commission argues that a prior notification system is no longer necessary, and that companies can easily undertake a self-assessment of their agreements and decide without formal assistance by the Commission whether these agreements are in compliance with EC competition law. Its main reasons are twofold: firstly, such a system is not an effective tool in protecting competition because truly anticompetitive cartels are very rarely notified; and secondly, the corpus of EC competition rules is now well-established and companies no longer need the Commission to tell them what is legal and what is not. However, at the same time the Commission is changing some of the main rules of competition law, particularly through the issuance of entirely revised block exemptions and brand new guidelines concerning both vertical and horizontal agreements in 2000.

Secondly, the Commission proposes to allow national courts and competition authorities to apply Article 81 (3) EC for the first time, ie, to assess whether an agreement qualifies for exemption in individual cases. Member States would also be empowered to withdraw block exemptions with effect in their national territory where an agreement which complies with a block exemption nonetheless unduly restricts competition. This creates a very serious risk of inconsistent application of EC competition law, all the more so as determining whether an agreement may be exempted under Article 81 (3) EC requires complex economic analyses which not all national authorities and courts are accustomed or properly equipped to handle. The Commission has been trying to address this concern by proposing some safeguards in the draft Regulation and in some as-yet unpublished draft notices, but many questions remain as to their effectiveness.

Finally, the Commission is also requesting to have its powers of investigation and sanction significantly increased by the new Regulation. In particular, the Commission wishes to have the power to search premises other than company offices, including the homes of company personnel; the right to impose joint and several liability on members of an association in case the association has violated competition law but becomes insolvent before paying the fine, regardless of actual participation by a given member in the alleged infringement; and the possibility to fine companies if an employee refuses to answer questions. The Commission is also looking to obtain the power to impose structural remedies, such as divestments, upon a sector of the economy if such structural remedies are necessary to bring infringements to an end.

Business Perspective

The proposed reform will impact all companies doing business in more than one European country, and particularly those wishing to enter into major joint ventures or to put in place distribution networks throughout Europe. They will no longer have the benefit of a prior clearance from the Commission, but rather will have to rely on their own assessment of the compatibility of their proposed agreements with EC competition law. These agreements will be subject to the possibility of multiple challenges in front of various national bodies, with a real risk of conflicting decisions, some of which may negatively and retroactively impact a joint venture already up and running. Moreover, the rights of defense of companies suspected of wrongdoing and their guarantees of due process may be jeopardized by some of the Commission's new powers, if proper safeguards are not implemented.

2. Review of the Technology Transfer Block Exemption Regulation

Background

In March 2001, the European Commission launched a review of the Block Exemption Regulation (BER), Regulation EC/240/96, which sets out the competition rules governing technology transfer agreements. Although the Regulation is not due to expire until March 31, 2006, it nevertheless mandates the Commission to undertake regular assessments and to draw up a report on the operation of the Regulation with a view to assessing whether any changes are desirable. In order to prepare its report, the Commission has circulated a questionnaire to industry and consumers associations, individual companies and law firms with the intention of gathering evidence as to how effective the Regulation is in practice and how it may be improved.

The Regulation covers pure patent and know-how licensing agreements as well as mixed patent and know-how licensing agreements which entitle the licensee to exploit the licensed technology for the purposes of manufacture, use and commercialization. It contains very detailed rules on the types of restraints that may or may not be included in a license agreement in order to benefit from the block exemption.

The questionnaire asks numerous questions designed to help the Commission understand why companies enter into licensing agreements, in which circumstances license-specific investments are necessary, the significance and structure of royalty fees, and whether licensing activities have significantly changed over the last 10 years. In addition to this pure fact-finding exercise, the questionnaire raises many important policy issues such as:

- whether the Commission's policy approach to technology licensing should be brought in line with the approach in the new block exemptions for horizontal restraints and vertical restraints (ie, block exemption available for a broader range of agreements provided a given market share threshold is not exceeded);
- whether the Commission should take account of the effects of an agreement in both the market for technology and the market for the products produced on the basis of the licensed technology; and
- whether the scope of the Regulation should remain limited to patents and know-how or whether it should be extended to include other types of intellectual and industrial property rights.

Business Perspective

How these issues are resolved will be potentially of great significance to companies involved in licensing.

Many in the business community believe that any review should ensure that the Regulation is more user friendly whilst providing legal certainty to licensors and licensees in terms of the types of restraints that are deemed acceptable/anti-competitive. The introduction of a market share threshold above which the block exemption would not be available (as per the new horizontal and vertical block exemptions) will be opposed given the particular difficulties associated with defining the relevant market in the technology licensing sector.

3. Merger Regulation

Background

The 1989 Merger Regulation (ECMR) (Reg. 4064/89, OJ L 395 December 30, 1989) was set up with the aim of controlling the build-up of dominant firms through mergers and acquisitions or joint ventures. The ECMR is only applicable to concentrations with a 'Community dimension'. A Community dimension is mainly determined through the aggregate turnover of the undertakings involved. Once within the ECMR, the key substantive criterion is that of 'dominant position' which takes into account such factors as actual or potential competition, the market position of the firms involved, the opportunities open to third parties, and barriers to entry. The ECMR provides for compulsory prior notification by the firms concerned and a strict timetable for Commission decision-making. It enables companies to deal with one notification procedure at European level instead of several at national level.

Various attempts have been made over the years to improve the main problem areas regarding the ECMR (eg, Green Paper COM (96) 19; OJ C 350, November 21, 1996). These mainly concern the division between concentrations having a Community and a national dimension, the classification of joint ventures falling under and outside the ECMR, cooperation with national competition authorities, the methodology used to assess the competition aspects and the constant necessity to update the rules and regulations in light of the growing international dimension of mergers in globalizing economies.

The continuing rise in the number of merger notifications in 1999 underlines the importance of merger regulations and falls in line with the impact of the single market, the advent of the single currency and general globalization trends. In its Competition Policy Report (June 2000), the Commission Directorate General for Competition registered a total of 292 (235 in 1998) merger notifications within the EU, representing a growth rate of 24% on the 1998 figures and an overall increase of 70% since 1997. There has also been a substantial increase in the number of final decisions, reaching their highest rate ever in 1999 (270).

Recent Developments

The first major development concerning EU merger control in 1999 was the increased co-ordination and information exchange with US merger control authorities. This development has been motivated by the increasingly global effects of mergers, often involving transnational product markets.

Secondly, 1999 also saw an increase in the number of cases where the Commission investigated collective (or oligopolistic) dominance concerns. In its investigation into whether markets are prone to oligopolistic dominance, the Commission will rely heavily on market characteristics such as market transparency, homogeneity of the product, market maturity, rate of innovation, cost structures and multi-market contacts.

The third key development of 1999 was that, for the first time, the Commission imposed fines on a number of occasions where notification was found to be misleading. This development is in response to the Commission's view that with mergers becoming increasingly complex, in order to meet the deadlines imposed under the ECMR it must have the full and dependable cooperation of the notifying parties and, indeed, of other market participants. The Commission is contemplating whether it should request the Council to increase the maximum level of fines.

Legislative Developments

In a report to the Council on the subject of qualifying thresholds, published in June 2000, the Commission continued to fine-tune the applicability of the ECMR. The essential background to this is that from the ECMR's inception in September 1990 a principle guiding its applicability has been to provide a 'one-stop-shop'. Large concentrations, the impact of which could be presumed to extend beyond any single national market, would be subject to the Commission's exclusive control. In this way, the high regulatory costs of reporting to a multitude of national authorities, and the risk of unequal treatment between them, could be avoided.

The version of Article 1 of the ECMR which entered into force in September 1990 contained a single set of thresholds for determining the applicability of the ECMR:

- € 5 billion combined worldwide turnover for all undertakings concerned; and
- € 250 million Community-wide turnover for each of two of the undertakings concerned, provided that these two do not achieve more than two-thirds of this turnover in the same Member State.

As it was found that a significant number of cases requiring multiple Member State filings failed to meet these turnover requirements, in 1998 a secondary set of lower thresholds was introduced:

- € 2.5 billion worldwide combined turnover;

- in each of at least three Member States, a combined turnover of at least € 100 million and in at least two of these three Member States a turnover of at least € 25 million for each of the two undertakings concerned; and
- a Community-wide turnover of € 100 million for each of at least two of the undertakings, providing that each of the undertakings concerned does not achieve more than two-thirds of its Community-wide turnover in the same Member State.

The legislative instrument that introduced these secondary thresholds also required the Commission to report on their operation to the Council by July 1, 2000. Subsequently, in its June 2000 report the Commission acknowledges that the current thresholds do not capture an important number of cases with a significant cross-border impact (COM (2000) 399 June 26, 2000). It asks the Council for powers to make further investigations into what can be done to alleviate this problem and also to conduct a thorough review of other substantive and procedural rules relating to concentration control. Based on its current data, however, it recommends against lowering the thresholds and, significantly, suggests that future extensions may involve a lowering, from three to two, of the number of Member States in which significant turnover is required. Conscious of the increase in caseload that greater inclusivity will bring, it suggests that concomitant expenditure rises might be defrayed by a filing fee, perhaps to the amount of € 30,000.

On July 29, 2000 the Commission issued a 'Notice' on a simplified procedure for treatment of certain concentrations (OJ C 217 July 29, 2000). The administrative burden on notifying parties will be lightened, but Member States and third parties will have the same rights to intervene as under the ordinary procedure. This simplified procedure will apply to the following three categories of concentration which, in the Commission's experience, normally do not raise competition concerns:

- acquisition of joint control where the joint venture has, within the EEA, a turnover of less than € 100 million and assets of less than € 100 million;
- where none of the parties is engaged in the same product and geographical market, or in an upstream or downstream product market in which any other party to the concentration is engaged; and
- where there are overlapping product and geographic markets, or an upstream or downstream market, but the parties' combined market share is not 15% or more for horizontal and 25% or more for vertical relationships.

The Commission has also issued a Draft Notice on ancillary restraints. Providing that these restraints are directly related to and necessary for a merger, in conformity with the 'one-stop-shop' principle the Commission will deal with them within the merger control procedure. The Draft Notice seeks to update a 1990 Notice on the subject and covers the same categories of restraints, namely non-competition clauses, restraints in license agreements, and purchase and supply obligations. It is however considered to be more restrictive than its predecessor.

The final legislative development is a Draft Notice on commitments that undertakings may give to remove doubts about a concentration. This Draft Notice codifies the Commission's working practices as it has developed them over the years. It examines the main categories of commitments, namely divestiture, termination of exclusive agreements, access to infrastructure or key technology. There is guidance on all stages, from the assessment of commitments through to the acceptance and implementation of commitments.

Business Perspective

The outstanding trend in merger regulation in Europe is that, increasingly, mergers and acquisitions, and joint ventures, will come under the 'one-stop-shop' rule of the ECMR. With an increasing number of Member States adopting their own pre-merger filing requirements, the value of most such 'one-stops' is increasingly appreciated by the business community. Merger cases also give rise to more interactive cooperation with the US. The draft notices on simplified procedure, ancillary restraints, and commitments represent an increased degree of clarity about how important aspects of mergers will be treated. However, correspondingly, the Commission is signaling that it will show less tolerance towards businesses that fail to comply with the merger control requirements under European law.

4. State Aids

Background

The control of state aids in the EU constitutes one of the four main objectives of the EC Treaty's competition rules. Alongside Articles 81 EC (agreements between undertakings - cartels), 82 EC (abuses by dominant undertakings - monopolies), 86 EC (control of state monopolies), Articles 87-89 of the EC Treaty *(ex Articles 92-94)* provide for the control of another major distortion of competition within the EU: the unfair favoring by EU Member States of certain undertaking(s) *vis-à vis* their competitors elsewhere in the EU.

The Rules

EC state aid rules can be found, apart from Articles 87-89 of the EC Treaty, in numerous Regulations, Guidelines, Communications and Letters from the Commission to Member States. The state aid rules can be very broadly distinguished into procedural rules (with EC Regulation EC/659/99 playing a predominant role), horizontal rules (like guidelines on regional aid, on aid for restructuring/rescuing, on aid to SMEs, etc,) and sectoral rules (coal and steel, transport, shipbuilding, agriculture, fisheries, etc,).

The Policy Objectives

State aids cover all forms of public subsidies to undertakings which can frustrate free competition by preventing an efficient allocation of resources. In that respect EU competition policy is different from that found, for example, in the US. This is because besides controlling the enterprise market, competition policy seeks to remove barriers between national markets in order to pro-actively promote European integration. This aim is often most evident in the highly sensitive area of state aid.

State aids are the object of considerable tension, not only between EU competition policy and both EU and national industrial or regional policy, but also between EU Member States and third countries. Although Articles 87-89 EC provide the Commission with regulatory competencies, specific problems have arisen in the past regarding the procedure for the implementation of competition policy in the state aid field. For example, problems regularly arise when Member States fail to notify state aids, when they fail to provide the Commission with sufficient and punctual information, when they do not recover illegally paid aid and finally when they fail to abide by Commission decisions.

The EU policy on state aids and its application have often a clear political dimension which, not rarely, goes beyond economic or competition policy objectives.

Recent Initiatives

Against this background the Commission is trying to modernize the state aid rules and introduce more transparency into the system.

In terms of modernization, the Commission decided in 1998 to introduce certain block exemptions for state aid to reduce the number of state aids notified per year so that it can concentrate resources on closer monitoring of the most important cases. In 2000 the Commission adopted three such block exemptions on the basis of the enabling Regulation which provided the Commission with the legal basis to exempt certain categories of state aid from notification requirements, such as aid for SMEs, research and development, environmental aid, training aid, etc. These three block exemptions were:

- Commission Regulation EC/70/01 on exemption for aid to SMEs (OJ L 10, January 13, 2001);
- Commission Regulation EC/68/2001 on exemption for training aid (OJ L 10, January 13, 2001); and
- Commission Regulation EC/69/2001 on exemption for *de minimis* aid (OJ L 10, January 13, 2001).

Regarding transparency, the Commission has continued to publish annual surveys on state aid. Surveys cover mainly the manufacturing and certain other sectors and update the existing data on the volume of aids granted. The surveys ultimately reflect the effectiveness or not of the application by the Commission of the EC state aid rules and policy.

In addition, on July 26, 2000 the Commission adopted an amendment to the so-called Transparency Directive (80/723/EEC; OJ L 193 July 29, 2000), which requires undertakings providing services in the general economic interest (for which they are compensated) as well as normal commercial activities to keep separate accounts for such commercial activities.

The efforts to increase transparency and reduce the volume of state aid have been recently boosted by the introduction of the state aid registry and the scoreboard for state aid. These projects aim at making useful state aid information more widely available to operators and competitors, and more importantly at enabling the monitoring of the performance of each individual Member State in terms of grants and recovery of aid.

The procedural Regulation (EC/659/99) that established detailed rules for the application of Article 87-88 EC has now been in force for two years. Although the procedural rights of competitors/complainants under the Regulation could be more substantive it is expected that it will increase transparency. Also legal certainty in the state aid field will facilitate the reinforcement of state aid discipline in the area of illegal aid recovery.

Business Perspective

Despite the number of notifications in 2000 remaining unchanged compared to 1999 and the adoption of a number of important instruments for the application of state aid rules, the Commission is still struggling against a backlog of old cases. The Commission remains, however, focused on its main objectives in the sector, namely to reduce the amounts of aid granted, modernize the state aid rules even further and introduce more transparency into the system.

Under Commissioner Monti the application of the state aid rules has become stricter and the policy directions are clear: less aid, more transparency and more efficient handling of state aid cases.

The Commission has reiterated its intention to concentrate its forces on major cases, expecting that the enactment of the block exemption Regulations will reduce further the burden of the small but time-consuming cases that it is currently dealing with.

Industry has steadily expressed concerns about the impact of illegal subsidies on the competitive structure of the markets, and the proper functioning of the common market. Moreover, it is generally supportive of the Commission initiatives and supports its objectives. It would like to see the Commission being more pro-active in fighting illegal subsidies which distort competition. In addition business considers that the role of third parties (competitors of recipients of aid, other interested entities) is particularly important: third parties can assist the Commission in the enforcement of state aid rules by participating substantively in any investigation. This role should therefore be safeguarded and reinforced.

Chapter II
Consumer Affairs

THE EU COMMITTEE
OF THE AMERICAN CHAMBER OF COMMERCE IN BELGIUM

1. Product Liability

Background

Directive 85/374/EEC on product liability (OJ L 210 August, 7 1985) was adopted in 1985 with the view to ensuring a high level of consumer protection and securing the free movement of goods within the common market. The Directive imposes 'strict' and 'joint and several' liability on producers for damages caused to consumers' health or property by their defective products. Strict liability exists when liability occurs without there being any fault on the part of the producer for a defective product and joint and several liability being when two or more people are liable for the same damage and liable for the full amount of that damage. In the former instance the plaintiff must prove the damage, defect and causal relationship between the defect and damage. The same applies in the latter instance although the person required to pay the full amount may have contribution claims against other liable persons under national law.

As the Product Liability Directive only covered processed products the European Commission proposed an amendment in 1997 in order to extend the regime to cover defective goods, primary agricultural products and game produced in or imported into the single market. The proposal to extend the scope of the Directive was triggered by the BSE crisis, which had undermined consumer confidence in food (see page 27). The amended Directive 1999/39/EC was formally adopted in 1999 (OJ L 141 June 4, 1999).

Given the importance that any legislative changes regarding product liability may have for both consumers and producers, the Commission published a Green Paper on product liability for defective products in July 1999 (COM (99) 396 July 28, 1999). The Green Paper's aims were to assess the effectiveness of the application of the 1985 Directive and establish through a consultation process whether a review of the current EU product liability regime was necessary. The contentious points under consideration included:

Burden of proof - under the Product Liability Directive, the plaintiff is obliged to prove that he or she has suffered damage which was caused by a defect in the product. The Commission believes that proving causation is often technically complicated and expensive for the consumer and therefore suggests simplifying the proof through numerous options, including:

- inferring a causal relationship between the damage and the defect once the plaintiff has proved the existence of either;
- obliging the producer to provide all necessary documentation so that the plaintiff can avail himself of the facts needed to prove his case; and
- requiring the producer to pay the costs of expert opinion under certain circumstances.

Development risk - the Commission is further considering the abolishment of the so-called 'development risk defense'. Without this defense, companies could be deemed liable for a product's defect even if the state of scientific and technical knowledge at the time when the product was put in circulation was not such as to enable the existence of the defect to be detected.

Financial limits - the 1985 Directive states that the producer does not have to compensate the victim for damage to property worth less than € 500. Furthermore, Member States have the option of fixing an upper financial limit of € 70 million on liability in the case of damage to persons caused by identical items. The Green Paper looks at the possibility of removing these financial limits.

Producer liability - the Commission is proposing to extend the period of producer liability from ten years to 20 years after the product first goes into circulation.

Insurance requirement - Directive 85/374/EEC does not require producers to have any kind of financial cover, and in particular it does not impose any requirement to take out liability insurance for an amount that is adequate to cover any damage caused by a defective product. The Green Paper asks whether producers should be required to have insurance cover for risks linked to production or, alternatively, to encourage voluntary arrangements between producers and the insurance market.

The Green Paper further demanded input on issues such as problems of access to justice, supplier liability and categories of damage covered by product liability.

In its Opinion of March 30, 2000 on the Green Paper, the European Parliament stated that it would like to see any revision of the current Product Liability Directive based on clearly established factual evidence. This should involve the consultation of all interested parties, including academics and civil society, as well as the application of scientific methods.

The results of the Green Paper consultations, released in a report by the Commission (COM (2000) 893 January 31, 2001) focused particularly on the information and observations received. The conclusion reached is that any changes made at this time to the current product liability system would be premature, primarily because there is not enough information available to fully assess the effectiveness of previous product liability Directives. Firstly, Directive 85/374/EEC was belatedly transposed into national law and in many cases was transposed in parallel to national contractual/non-contractual law making it difficult to clearly assess the impact of the Directive. Secondly, what sparse data there is available does not reveal that there are any particular problems with the application of the Directive. The report proposes that a framework optimizing the costs of product liability procedures should make it possible to retain a balance between the interests of consumers and producers. Furthermore, it proposes that an expert group should be established, and two studies funded, in order to supplement data currently available and to enable the Commission to assess the product liability system more fully. On other issues covered in the Green Paper, general product safety and consumer redress for example, the Commission has recommended contingency measures.

Business Perspective

In 1985, when Directive 85/374/EEC on liability for defective products was adopted, various provisions of the Directive had already been subject to controversy, for example, between consumers and representatives of the manufacturing and insurance industries. During the recent debate on the revision of this Directive, the divergence of views and positions re-emerged.

From industry's point of view, any fundamental changes of the product liability regime presuppose a sound assessment of its legal, economic and social implications as well as consultation with all interested parties. This view is also shared by the Parliament which, in its Resolution on the Green Paper on defective products, has called upon the Commission to collect evidence justifying the review of the Directive. The Parliament's report, therefore, which makes provision for gathering more information in this field is most welcome.

In case of further reviews of the product liability system, however, business maintains its view that product liability law requires a fine balance of interests between consumers and industry. It feels that the current Directive recognizes this and establishes this balance. Any changes in this balance could be expected to result in significant increases in the number of claims with a resulting increase in the costs of litigation, insurance premiums and ultimately of products. A sound liability system must allow genuine claims to be compensated quickly and efficiently; it must not encourage poor and speculative claims. Business is now looking forward to learning the results of the Commission's further research into the current product liability system and will continue its active part in the ongoing dialogue on this important issue.

2. Food Safety - General Principles of Food Law & Establishment of a European Food Authority

Background

In its 1999 White Paper on food safety (COM (99) 719 January 12, 2000), the European Commission concluded that a comprehensive and integrated approach to food safety was required. The Commission plans to restore consumer confidence in food safety through a high level of consumer protection, in particular by:

- implementing over 80 legislative measures, within a precise timetable, by the end of 2002; and
- establishing a European Food Authority by 2002.

On November 8, 2000 the Commission published its proposal for a Regulation laying down the general principles and requirements of food law, establishing the European Food Authority and laying down procedures in matters of food safety (COM (2000) 716 November 8, 2000).

As regards general legal principles, the proposal includes a wide definition of the term food. It establishes the objectives of food law and also argues the need to take account of the precautionary principle (see page 81), the protection of consumers' interests and the traceability of food and feed. It also lays down detailed food safety requirements. It states that only safe food may be placed on the market and that food shall be considered unsafe if it is potentially dangerous to health, contaminated or unfit for human consumption. Similarly, it stresses that no feed shall be placed on the market or given to any food-producing animal, unless it satisfies the feed safety requirements.

The core task of the European Food Authority (EFA) will be to provide the Community with first-class, independent, scientific opinions. The EFA will also be responsible for the day-to-day operation of the Rapid Alert System (see page 30) and will play a key role in the management of crisis situations, under the Commission's responsibility. It will also be charged with giving clear and publicly accessible information on all matters that fall within its mandate and will be entitled to issue communications on its own initiative. The competence of the EFA will be very broad, covering all matters affecting food safety, nutrition and any matter relating to genetically modified plants and seeds, even where the latter are not intended for human or animal consumption.

The EFA will ostensibly be fully independent and accountable. Its management board will consist of 16 representatives, four appointed by the Commission, four by the Council, four by the European Parliament and four representatives of industry and consumers (also appointed by the Commission). There is no indication in the proposal, however, of how representatives will be nominated to sit on the board.

Finally, the Authority will be assisted by an Advisory Forum composed of 15 representatives from competent bodies in the Member States and by independent scientific panels.

The European Parliament is expected to give its first reading on the Regulation (co-decision) in the next few months.

Business Perspective

The proposed Regulation is of fundamental importance because the principles it lays down will underpin all EU food legislation for the foreseeable future. Currently, the proposal is defective in that the stated objectives of food law do not include maintenance of a single market in food products, nor do they ensure the competitiveness of the EU food industry in world markets. In addition, the proposal does not lay down a clearly defined process of risk analysis or clear labeling principles. It also seems to indicate that the Community is not entirely committed to international free trade in food products.

It is currently uncertain how the EFA management board will operate in practice. It will be vital for it to represent a balance of views and interests and to be independent of political influence (it seems likely that the Commission will exercise a great deal of influence over the EFA). It will also be important to ensure that the EFA is able to prioritize its work if it is not to become overloaded. Similarly, it must ensure that food safety is its sole focus, since the most pressing task is to restore consumer confidence in this area.

3. Public Health Policy

Background

Following the Maastricht Treaty, the European Community was given a new competence in the field of public health. Article 3 of the Treaty establishes the broad aim of making 'a contribution to the attainment of a high level of health protection'. Following the Amsterdam Treaty, the revised Article 152 EC sets out how the Community should pursue this aim. Both articles open up the prospect of developing a consistent Community approach to public health which would integrate various pre-existing strands of action into an overall coherent strategy.

Article 152 EC calls for a high level of human health protection to be ensured in all Community policies and activities. Community action - which shall complement national policies - shall be directed towards improving public health, preventing human illness or diseases and identifying sources of danger to human health.

Article 152 EC also includes specific provisions which allows the Community to take actions. However, Member States remain responsible for the organization and delivery of health services and medical care.

The Community may adopt under the co-decision procedure the following measures:

- setting high standards of quality and safety for organs and substances of human origin, blood and blood derivatives, without preventing Member States from maintaining or introducing more stringent protective measures;
- veterinary and phytosanitary legislation, which have as their direct objective the protection of public health;
- incentives designed to protect and improve public health (not harmonization measures); and
- non-binding Council recommendations for the purpose of public health protection.

The first Framework Program for Public Health, adopted after the Maastricht Treaty, set out the first eight non-harmonization measures. These included six action programs focused on specific diseases: cancer; AIDS and other communicable diseases; pollution-related diseases; rare diseases; drug dependence; and prevention of injuries. It also included two horizontal programs (health monitoring and health promotion, information and education). Also, a network for the epidemiological surveillance and control of communicable diseases was set up in 1999.

Before drawing up the new Community Action Program the Commission undertook a wide-ranging consultation process and on May 16, 2000 issued a Communication on the health strategy of the European Community including a proposal for a Decision for a new Public Health Program (COM (2000) 285 May 16, 2000). This program, once adopted, will run from 2001 to 2006 with a proposed budget of € 330 million.

The new proposals take a more strategic health policy approach. They focus on three priorities:

Improving health information and knowledge - a comprehensive health information system will be put in place to provide policy makers, health professionals and the general public with up-to-date and reliable information on key health-related topics. The system will make full use of the internet, including links to national web sites, and be based on agreed Community-wide indicators for health status.

Responding rapidly to major health threats (including a rapid reaction capability) - this will enable the Community to respond effectively and in a co-ordinated way to potentially serious threats to public health which cannot be tackled by Member States in isolation. It will entail improving communications between the national authorities involved, linking with the various Community alert systems, and providing the Community with the ability to respond to health threats from communicable diseases. At the same time it is intended to strengthen against the threats from non-communicable diseases, illicit drug use and the prevention of injuries and accidents.

Actions will also underpin the development and implementation of policies in such areas as safety and quality of blood, organs and substances of human origin.

Addressing health determinants - this aims to help improve the health status of the population and reduce premature deaths in the EU caused by cancer, cardiovascular disease and mental illness by tackling the underlying causes of ill health. The focus will be on lifestyle factors such as smoking, alcohol, nutrition and physical activity, stress and drug abuse as well as major socio-economic and environmental factors. By fostering effective health promotion and disease prevention and sharing best practice among Member States, it is expected that quality of life can be improved and the pressure on health care services reduced.

In the context of enlargement (see page 151), the Communication states that the program is intended to provide valuable support to applicant countries for tackling their health problems.

In addition, the network for the epidemiological surveillance and control of communicable diseases will form the basis for prevention and control strategies on communicable diseases within the Community. Its objective is to provide early warning and response, as well as epidemiological surveillance of the system and it will work in cooperation with the World Health Organization (WHO) and the US. A Communication on the future strategy of the network will be published in the near future.

Following a request from the European Parliament, a European Health Forum will be set up to give the public health community a role in the development of health policy.

While reviewing the Commission's proposals, the Parliament called for the establishment of a European Health Co-ordination and Monitoring Center (EHCMC) to help the Community to attain the Treaty goal of a high level of health protection. The EHCMC would provide a well-structured and comprehensive system for collecting, monitoring, analyzing, evaluating and imparting health information and knowledge to competent authorities, health professionals and the public. The Parliament is expected to ask for a larger budget of € 400 million to pursue the objectives outlined in the program. Should this be the case, it remains to be seen how Member States will view this in the light of their own health competences and budget considerations.

Business Perspective

The need for integrated, transparent and proactive public health leadership at all levels in the EU and within industry is gaining more and more recognition. The new policy orientation in public health correctly places the emphasis on health gain, on the need to select a limited number of priorities and on a flexible framework providing for a rapid Community-wide response to health challenges. With the limited EU competence in the field of public health and a limited budget, it is difficult to see how an EHCMC could be instituted and effective.

Business supports the creation of a freely accessible, comprehensive, up-to-date, reliable data system on key health-related topics across Europe. This should provide an opportunity to ensure that health policy formulation and decisions are based on sound data and scientific evidence. It should also make the functioning of national health care systems more transparent and comparable. As Member States will share good practice in terms of their disease prevention and health promotion strategies and because their health policy decisions will be based on the evidence of effective prevention, screening and treatment programs, scarce resources could be allocated to achieve the best outcomes in order to improve the health of Europe's citizens.

Industry welcomes the establishment of a European Public Health Forum to provide a framework for dialogue with all stakeholders, including industry. Such a forum offers the business community an opportunity for early interaction rather than reaction on the health aspect of Community policies, and to ensure that its contribution to a sound public health policy is taken into account. There is a clear link between health and economic well-being. Business both provides employment and generates wealth for governments to spend on their health and social welfare systems. Therefore more emphasis deserves to be placed on industry's contribution to the health and well-being of Europe's citizens.

4. General Product Safety

Background

The General Product Safety Directive (GPSD) (Directive 92/59/EEC; OJ L 228 August 11, 1992) is based on Article 95 EC and was adopted in 1992, before the entry into force of the Maastricht Treaty. The Directive, part of the program aimed at establishing the internal market by December 31, 1992, regulates and aims to ensure the safety of consumer products placed on the market. The products covered are those intended for consumers or likely to be used by consumers and those supplied in the course of a commercial activity. Even though Article 16 of the Directive required a review in 1998, the Commission decided to postpone the release of a proposal in order to acquire more experience, ensure better preparation and, in particular, complete a study on the implementation of the GPSD.

The study on the legal and practical application of the GPSD, including identification of problem areas and conclusions on the need for amendments, was completed in October 1999 by the Center for Consumer Law of the University of Louvain-la-Neuve, Belgium. The Commission also formed a consumer safety working party composed of representatives from the Member States, standardization bodies and consumer organizations. Industry was not originally included and only became involved in the consultations after formally requesting the right to participate.

The results from the above-mentioned study and the consultation show that the overall approach of the Directive is fundamentally sound. Nevertheless, it was determined that there were some weaknesses in the provisions of the Directive, which have limited the achievement of its objectives and, in addition, some consumer protection needs are not sufficiently addressed.

Consequently, on March 29, 2000, the Commission brought forward a proposal (COM (2000) 139 March 29, 2000), which aspires to improve the rules governing product safety in Europe. The proposal seeks to introduce new and simpler rules with the aim of ensuring that only safe products are put on the market. It includes the following:

Clarification of application and scope of the Directive - the draft Directive seeks to make a clearer link between multi-sectoral and sector specific legislation, which has been one of the main criticisms leveled at the original Directive. As for the scope of the Directive, the draft extends it to services and includes products which have 'migrated' from the professional sector to the consumer market, as has been the case, for example, with laser pens. Products used or made available by service providers such as beauty centers, hotels or gas and electricity suppliers are also explicitly included.

Market surveillance - a further aim is to achieve more active and effective market surveillance by strengthening national surveillance authorities, and promoting stronger sanctions at national level.

Improvement of rapid alert system (RAPEX) - under the improved rapid alert system it will be necessary to immediately inform the Commission if a given product poses a serious risk and of any measures or voluntary actions to be taken by a Member State. The Commission will then alert other Member States to the problem. The possibility of linking the RAPEX system to third countries in the future is also envisaged. Furthermore, the draft Directive proposes a simplification of the emergency procedures for banning the marketing of certain products, withdrawing products from shops or recalling products that have already been bought. If necessary, emergency measures in the case of 'a serious risk requiring rapid action' can be taken at EU level. The Commission will be able to ban a product for a period of up to one year (the current Directive only allows for a ban of up to three months). A permanent ban can also be imposed on an individual product or product batch. A regulatory consumer product safety committee will be established to assist the Commission in the adoption of these measures. The export to third countries of products, prohibited, recalled or withdrawn from the market by such emergency measures will also be prohibited.

Producer and distributor obligations - the revision adds the obligation for producers or distributors to inform and collaborate with the authorities when they conclude that a supplied product is dangerous. In particular this involves tracing and recalling dangerous products. Currently, unlike in the US, no such obligation exists in the EU and the Commission believes that this may lead to a situation in which the relevant authorities remain unaware of potentially unsafe products.

Transparency - to increase transparency, the proposal also introduces new obligations to exchange information on producers and distributors. It establishes the principle that all information on dangerous products should be notified to public authorities and be exchanged freely between national enforcement authorities. Consumers are also entitled to know which products are dangerous and what measures have been taken as a consequence. A European Product Safety Network will be established to facilitate this.

Standardization - the proposal allows the Commission to introduce mandates to the European standardization bodies in order to produce standards for the purpose of this Directive. Products in compliance with those standards, whose references are published in the Official Journal of the EC, will be presumed to be in conformity with the safety requirements of the Directive.

In its first reading, the Parliament proposed 30 amendments to the draft Directive, of which the Council was able to accept 21 amendments. For the second reading the Committee on the Environment, Public Health and Consumer Policy reintroduced a reference in the body of the Directive to the precautionary principle. It has also adopted ten other amendments dealing with issues such as the safety of services, greater consistency in the approach to market monitoring and monitoring programs, tightening of the provisions relating to the European product safety network and a proposal that allows for proof of conformity with the general safety requirements by means of external certification.

For the plenary session (second reading) in May 2001 the rapporteur of the Parliament's Committee on Environment and Consumer Protection had retabled the amendments adopted in the first reading and reintroduced the initial draft of the proposal. The Committee did not like the fact that the Council's common position had not given consideration to several important amendments adopted during the first reading and had introduced new provisions, which, MEPs believe, watered down the ban on the export of dangerous products by allowing descisions to be taken on a 'case-by-case' basis. However the plenary session did not obtain the necessary qualified majority and most of the tabled amendments were rejected. An amendment was adopted inviting the Commission to put forward proposals on the safety of services by January 1, 2003 and another one demanding that the competent authorities be guided by the precautionary principle. The Directive will go back to Council for final adoption.

Business Perspective

The proposal by the Commission represents a significant extension of the scope of the Directive and will have a significant impact on business. A broader range of products, including those which migrate from the professional sector to the consumer, will be included. It is likely to be difficult, in this context, for companies to determine if their products could one day be used in a wider consumer context. In addition, there will be greater responsibilities imposed upon producers to provide information to national authorities and also, now, to consumers. Although transparency is an important aspect of these proposals, confidentiality should be guaranteed where necessary. It remains to be seen how the proposal will affect industries that are already subject to sector specific Community legislation and if the balance of interests between consumers and business, formerly achieved within the Directive, has been maintained with the new text.

5. Direct Selling

Background

Direct selling is the marketing of goods and services directly to consumers in a person-to-person manner, in places other than permanent retail locations. Direct selling typically takes place in the home or at the office. It is a form of non-store retailing but is distinct from direct marketing or distance selling. According to a PriceWaterhouseCoopers report of November 1999, it is a 'vibrant and fast-growing' industry, with a total turnover in the EU of € 12 billion.

In recognition of the potential for growth in this industry and to protect consumers against dishonest business practices in connection with contracts negotiated away from business premises, the Direct Selling Directive (85/577/EEC; OJ L 372 December 31, 1985) was adopted on December 20, 1985. The consumer was seen as needing special protection in respect of such contracts because, as a rule, it is the trader who initiates the contract negotiations.

The consumer was given the important right of being able to cancel a contract concluded in this manner within seven days of being informed by the trader (in writing) of this right. The trader is obliged to inform consumers of the consumer's right to a 'cooling-off' period. The Directive does not apply to contracts involving payments below € 60, and various specific types of direct selling contracts, such as those for insurance fall outside the scope of this legislation.

The Commission intends to update the Directive in order to harmonize it with more recently adopted texts and due to the evolution of direct marketing techniques. The former reason applies in particular to the Distance Selling Directive (97/7/EC; OJ L 144 June 4, 1997). This Directive also deals with contracts, which differ from ordinary sales transactions conducted at business premises, but includes additional sophisticated provisions relating to information requirements, performance, payment methods and the right of withdrawal. Second, direct selling encompasses both classical direct selling businesses (so-called single-level marketing (SLM) and, more recently, network marketing or multi-level marketing (MLM), whereby sellers are paid commission based on a percentage of the sales achieved by new sales people whom they have introduced to the company. The much publicized, but usually banned, pyramid and snowball systems, where participants must make a payment to take part in the scheme, can also be construed as MLM techniques, although no legitimate direct selling business employs them these days.

In 1999 the Commission commissioned a study conducted by the *Institut für Europäisches Wirtschafts und Verbraucherrecht* (VIEW - Institute for European Economics and Consumer Rights) on the feasibility of adopting a common approach to direct and distance selling contracts, and whether it is necessary to adopt EU rules on pyramid/snowball systems.

In November 1999, VIEW published its final report. It recommends that Directive 85/577/EEC be harmonized with the Distance Selling Directive in so far as the provisions regulating information requirements, performance, payment and rights of withdrawal are concerned. This would result in an extension of the cooling-off period to ten days. It recommends that a new directive should contain a prohibition on pyramid selling and snowball systems, and that new rules be introduced to provide more detailed rules on MLM. Finally, the report suggests that a body such as the European Standardization Committee (CEN) should develop a Europe-wide marketing standard to increase confidence in the activities of companies involved in MLM.

In March 2000, the Commission held a public hearing on the report and other possible changes to Directive 85/577/EEC to allow stakeholder participation. The revision of the directive is currently delayed because of the priority given to advancing a new horizontal framework proposal on 'new forms of market regulation and administrative cooperation' (fair trading initiative) that will be published as a Green Paper. Direct selling may be one of the sectors considered under this approach.

Business Perspective

Business is generally supportive of the proposal in the VIEW Report that certain provisions of Directive 85/577/EEC be harmonized with the Distance Selling Directive, as this will ensure greater coherence. However, there have been objections to the cooling-off period being extended to ten days, particularly on the grounds that it would place direct selling at a competitive disadvantage when compared to conventional retailing. Furthermore, the report's inclusion of insurance and securities contracts within the scope of the proposed new Directive fails to recognize that the provision of financial services is already highly regulated. Industry strongly supports the proposed introduction of a prohibition on illegal pyramid selling but believes that the VIEW report's proposed definition is too broad and may, as a consequence, unintentionally impact other industry sectors and make many direct sellers illegitimate. Depending on the outcome of the fair trading process which is still very unclear at present and on the measures adopted to regulate direct selling practices, the Commission may still proceed with the revision of the current directive at a later stage.

6. Biotechnology & Food Labeling

Background

Modern biotechnology promises enormous potential benefits to society in the areas of health, nutrition and the environment through the provision of high quality goods produced in an environmentally sustainable way. However, the introduction of modern agricultural biotechnology in Europe has not been accompanied by a proper regulatory framework. This situation has not aided consumer confidence in modern biotechnology and has led to legal uncertainty for biotechnology and food companies operating in the EU. It is imperative that these challenging issues be addressed in a responsible and co-ordinated manner which is consistent with the EU's domestic and international obligations.

Directive 90/220/EEC required a case-by-case assessment of risks to human health, animal health and the environment prior to the release and/or placing on the market of genetically modified organisms (GMOs). This Directive was subject to a thorough review and amended by Directive 2001/18/EC, adopted on March 12, 2001 (OJ L 106, April 17, 2001). The revision of Directive 90/220/EEC was deemed necessary in order to improve transparency and the efficiency of the authorization procedure, as well as to ensure independent scientific assessment, harmonize the various risk assessment procedures, ensure surveillance of risks after crops are released, and introduce rules on labeling and traceability. New provisions cover the gradual elimination of antibiotic marker genes, the introduction of public registers for GMOs released during the trial period or for placing on the market, and time-limited consent of ten years. In addition, labeling would be required at all stages of product development specifying that, 'this product contains genetically-modified organisms'. A minimum threshold would be established to avoid unnecessary labeling of adventitious traces of authorized GMOs, where an 'adventitious presence' means the unavoidable presence of impurities in products, resulting from the natural environment or the manner of production. Finally, the Commission is requested to propose implementing legislation on the Cartagena Biosafety Protocol by July 2001 (an international agreement on the trade of living modified organisms (LMOs) derived from modern biotechnology).

Regulation EC/258/97 (OJ L 43 February 14, 1997) on novel foods and novel food ingredients sets out rules for the authorization and labeling of GMO-derived food products. Consumers must be informed whether the product contains, or is derived from, a GMO not substantially equivalent to an existing foodstuff. However, the Regulation does not define substantial equivalence, nor does it provide any labeling details. Regulation EC/1139/98 (OJ L 159 June 3, 1998) on compulsory labeling of certain GMO derived foodstuffs defines equivalence on the basis of the absence of protein or DNA resulting from genetic modification. It calls for a 'negative' list of equivalent ingredients in which DNA and protein from GMOs is considered no longer to be present and which would no longer require labeling. To date, this list has not been published. The labeling provisions contained in Regulation EC/258/97 were amplified, in January 2000, by Regulation EC/49/2000 (OJ L 6 January 11, 2000) to provide a 1% labeling threshold for the adventitious presence of material of GMO origin (during cultivation, harvest, transport or processing). Products containing less than 1% of GM material do not have to be labeled. Regulation EC/50/2000 (OJ L 6 January 11, 2000) provides specific labeling requirements for foodstuffs or food ingredients containing additives and flavorings derived from GMOs.

In July 2000, the Commission put forward a new GMO strategy aimed at regaining public trust in the GMO approval procedure. It covered different aspects, including:

- incorporation of the revised Directive 90/220/EC requirements (ie, Directive 2001/18/EC) into individual authorizations, prior to final transposition by Member States;
- comprehensive labeling provisions covering GMOs or GMO products;
- an initiative on a traceability system for GMOs;
- a regulation clarifying the authorization procedure for novel foods;
- a regulation on novel feed; and
- a directive detailing seed labeling requirements of GM plant varieties and other purity requirements concerning the adventitious presence of GM seeds in conventional seed lots.

Following the publication, in November 2000, of an options paper on traceability and labeling of GMOs and products derived from GMOs, and subsequent discussions with Member States, the Commission is now in the process of drafting new provisions on traceability and labeling of GMOs and derived food and feed products. In addition, the Commission is in the process of drafting a new Regulation on genetically modified food and feed. It is, at this stage, not clear whether the measures would be proposed separately or as part of one package. It appears that the Commission is considering introducing process-based labeling requirements, rather than content-based labeling requirements (based on the presence of modified DNA or protein). As regards traceability, it appears that traceability of individual GMOs within a product would have to be provided for on the basis of authorized transformation events (the process by which the structural make-up of a plant variety is adapted with the help of biotechnology). Traceability for products derived from GMOs, on the other hand, would not require identification of the GMOs from which they are derived.

Business Perspective

The current regulatory framework for modern biotechnology must be improved and the adoption of Directive 2001/18/EC has been an important development in this regard. However, the authorization process of new GM products is still blocked subject to the adoption of additional measures regulating the labeling and traceability of GM food- and feedingstuffs, as referred to above. Given the early stage in the decision-making process of these proposals, it is too early to anticipate their impact on consumers and business. At this stage, it is important to ensure that regulatory structures and intent are clear, independently operated and have in-built integrity which will provide the public with confidence. Such an approach will ultimately be key to the future success of agricultural biotechnology in the EU. It will help restore consumer confidence and, thus, ensure continued trade in domestic and international seed, feed and food products.

7. Fair Trade within the Single Market

Background

At European level, a body of legislation exists that touches on the commercial relationships between business and consumers. Directives such as 93/13/EEC on unfair terms in consumer contracts or Directive 84/450/EEC on comparative and misleading advertising are just two examples.

While the Commission recognizes that 13 out of 15 Member States already have some form of duty to trade fairly, the concern is that the scope and its application varies widely. A European initiative is seen as a mechanism for overcoming national diversity (particularly with regard to advertising, marketing practices and post-sales consumer protection).

The EU is now giving serious consideration to developing a piece of framework legislation on fair trade practices. A Green Paper is expected in the coming months with a follow-up proposal being presented by the end of the year. Although it was originally planned to issue the paper before the EU Consumer Ministers' meeting in Lund on April 26, 2001, this was postponed due to concerns that the very strict proposed rules on advertising and marketing could adversely affect the single market.

Early work has been led by the Health and Consumer Protection Directorate General, DG SANCO. Commission action is being driven by the following issues:

- concerns that differences between national provisions could impede the development of cross-border shopping, particularly on-line;
- interest in a 'new approach' framework that would supplement legislation and allow greater scope for co-regulation and self-regulation both at European and national level; and
- awareness of the need for enhanced cooperation between enforcement practitioners in the consumer area.

While many questions about the shape of the proposal still exist, a European fair trade framework would clearly have very wide implications. The framework could cover claims, promotions, advertising to children and perhaps environmental and fair trade labeling too. It could also have consequences for business selling and information practices. It would certainly impact the development and legal status of self-regulatory codes and codes negotiated between stakeholders. What role for co-regulation and self-regulation? A common European framework enshrining a general duty to trade fairly or one on misleading and deceptive practices would potentially offer scope to support and supplement:

- existing legislation, such as the Directive on unfair contract terms, and would potentially require the amendment of most other current EU consumer protection legislation;
- DG SANCO's proposals - these also provide the possibility for development of European codes and voluntary agreements to be developed on the basis of negotiation between stakeholders; and
- in relation to national self-regulatory codes, differences between national codes could be minimized through the establishment of a European co-ordinating committee made up of Member State experts.

It is not clear what legal status existing self-regulation possesses, nor how national and European enforcement structures and sanctions would operate in practice. For European agreements negotiated between stakeholders there is also no clear roadmap of who would be the partners in any agreement or how their representation could be assured. A number of Commission Services already share these concerns.

Business Perspective

A broad coalition of trade associations is following this issue closely. For the moment the aim is to ensure industry involvement, to encourage a co-ordinated approach within the Commission on such horizontal issues and to promote a balanced approach to trade and marketing practices. Business concerns remain that further dialogue is required on this issue. In particular, there is a heavy overlap between the fair trade initiative described above and existing Commission initiatives on commercial communications. We also believe that greater consideration should be given to current self-regulatory models where they work. The impact on business of the new initiatives is at present poorly reasoned, and remains unclear.

8. Advertising & Children

Background

There is a growing movement in Europe to place restrictions on a company's ability to advertise products or services to children. This trend has been set by pressure groups in some Member States, notably in Sweden, where legislation goes beyond existing EU rules. Sweden would like the Commission to propose EU-wide restrictive legislation and has received support from certain consumer and parents' organizations and from the Commission's Health and Consumer Protection Directorate General (DG SANCO). Significantly, advertising to children is one of several current advertising issues where calls for restrictive measures have lately been intensified.

On the one hand, it appears unlikely that the Commission will make a specific proposal on advertising to children in the near future. On the other, in the wider context of legislation regarding advertising, in particular relating to television and the internet, the impact on children's issues will be high. The main piece of legislation in this respect is the 1989 Television Without Frontiers (TWF) Directive (89/552/EEC; OJ L 298 October 17, 1989) which contains specific provisions to protect children from any content that can be physically or morally harmful (Article 22). The Directive requires the Commission to produce an evaluation report on its application no later than June 30, 2002. The current calendar indicates that the report will be presented in spring 2002 together with a proposal to revise the Directive. The revision will take on the results of the following studies, reports and seminars, all of which focus either on measures to facilitate parental control of broadcasts watched by children or on the protection of minors from harmful advertising:

- October 2000 - Parliament report in response to the Commission study on parental control of TV broadcasting carried out as required under Directive 97/36/EC (OJ L 202 July 30, 1997) amending the TWF Directive. Parliament emphasizes that all TV operators should agree to a code of self-regulation in respect of the protection of minors, including advertising, but does not call for legislation in this field.
- January 2001 - Commission Third Report on the implementation of the TWF Directive.
- February 12-13, 2001 - seminar on children and young people in the new media. This seminar was held by Sweden during its Presidency of the EU. Sweden made television advertising aimed at children a priority area for its Presidency; this area of advertising is banned in Sweden.
- February 2001 - publication of Commission evaluation report on media and the protection of minors, further to Recommendation 98/560/EC on the protection of minors and human dignity in audiovisual and information services industry, which concludes that self-regulation is a successful means to approach the issue.
- April 2001 - publication of the Commission study on the impact of advertising and teleshopping on minors, prepared by INRA (International Research Associates), together with law firm Bird&Bird for legal issues. The study states that the TWF Directive provides "an adequate and flexible framework for Member State rules in this area".
- July 2001 - deadline for results of Commission study on new advertising techniques.

In early 2001, Education and Culture Commissioner, Viviane Reding, confirmed her firm stance against any further restriction, pointing out that the Commission and the majority of Member States were opposed to an outright ban. She has stressed that she is impressed by the quantity of detailed rules already in place, and expects advertisers to put greater emphasis on self-regulation.

Business Perspective

In the past year, business has been actively involved in a debate to oppose an EU-wide ban on advertising to children as well as to object to restrictions at national level. Business has commissioned reports from academics and these have helped to discredit the view that a ban protects children and parents from unscrupulous advertisers. It has also advocated that the current combination of legislation and self-regulatory mechanisms provides an appropriate, sufficient and proportionate protection, especially as these rules apply to different media including the internet. Where at EU level the opinion seems clearly against restrictions, a growing number of Member States have taken up the issue and are considering more restrictive rules. It is premature to discount an EU ban because the revision of the TWF Directive in 2002 will allow Sweden to be more active on the issue, once it is no longer constrained by the responsibilities and workload of the Presidency. Significantly, Belgium, who holds the EU Presidency as from July 1, 2001, seems determined to continue Sweden's battle to obtain an EU-wide ban. In addition, Denmark, who will hold the Presidency in the second half of 2002, and Greece, who will take over for the first half of 2003, are also likely to support restrictions on advertising to children.

Chapter III
Environment

THE EU COMMITTEE
OF THE AMERICAN CHAMBER OF COMMERCE IN BELGIUM

1. Climate Change

Background

It is now widely accepted that human activities directly contribute to increasing atmospheric concentrations of greenhouses gases (GHGs) such as carbon dioxide (CO_2), nitrous oxide (NO_2) and methane (CH_4). These continuing increases are a cause for concern as rising levels of the atmospheric concentrations of such gases could result in warmer surface temperatures through an increase in the amount of infra-red heat which is radiated back toward the earth's surface instead of being released into space. GHGs can be natural or man made. They include water vapor, carbon dioxide (CO_2), methane (CH_4), ozone (O_3), nitrous oxide (NO_2), chlorofluorocarbons (CFCs), fluorocarbons (HCFCs), hydrofluorocarbons (HFCs), perfluorocarbons (PFCs) and sulphur hexafluoride (SF_6). Human activity is believed to have caused an increase of 25% in the concentrations of greenhouse gases over the last 150 years, mainly due to the combustion of fossil fuels and changes in land-use. Of the GHGs, CO_2 is perhaps the most important because it alone is responsible for contributing about 65% of the combined radiative effects of the GHGs.

There are still uncertainties as to whether an increase in greenhouse gases due to human activities yields a measurable impact on global climate, given the existence of many negative as well as positive feedbacks in the earth's climate system, and in view of strong natural climate variability. However, despite these uncertainties, it is now largely recognized that action to reduce greenhouse gases is both necessary and desirable.

Between 1992 and 1997, the EU further developed a series of climate change measures, including:

- a monitoring mechanism for CO_2 emissions (Decision 93/389/EC) which requires Member States to devise, publish and implement national programs to limit anthropogenic GHGs;
- a strategy to reduce CO_2 emissions from cars;
- the proposed introduction of a tax based on carbon and energy content of fuels; and
- three key programs addressing the challenge of climate change from a sustainable development perspective, namely:

  SAVE (measures to conserve energy and improve energy efficiency);

  THERMIE (development and introduction of new energy-saving technologies); and

  ALTENER (development of renewable energy).

Since 1997, the EU's strategy to combat global climate change has focused on meeting the emission reduction commitments agreed to at the third Conference of Parties (COP-3) in December 1997, where the parties to the United Nations Framework Convention on Climate Change (UNFCCC) adopted the Kyoto Protocol. In order to meet its post-Kyoto obligations, the Commission considers it essential that progress is made in two key areas, namely the development of EU-wide CO_2/energy taxation on energy products and secondly the facilitation of a reduction in emissions derived from the transport sector. Furthermore, the Kyoto Protocol also introduced, for the first time, the possibility of using flexible mechanisms such as emissions trading to achieve desired global emission reductions.

On March 8, 2000 the Commission released a Communication setting out the policies and measures it intends to pursue in order to reduce GHG emissions (COM (2000) 88 March 8, 2000). The strategy will create a European Climate Change Program (ECCP), with an EU-wide emissions trading scheme as a 'major pillar'. The Commission separately published a Green Paper sketching out potential elements of the emissions trading scheme (COM (2000) 87 March 8, 2000). The ECCP strategy aims to reinforce agreed policies, including voluntary agreements by manufacturers to reduce vehicle emissions and develop energy markets which incorporate environmental considerations. A further initiative that emerged is a Communication from the Commission on an Action Plan to improve energy efficiency in the European Community (COM (2000) 247 April 26, 2000). Improved energy efficiency will contribute to the EU's efforts to meet Kyoto Protocol targets (see below). Expected initiatives include a paper on integrating sustainable development into enterprise policy.

Among new measures proposed, the Commission foresees transport pricing and economic instruments in the aviation sector, a fiscal framework for reducing CO_2 from cars, improvements in energy efficiency standards and CO_2 'capture' in underground reservoirs. Regarding the important issue of emissions trading, the Commission suggests creating an EU-wide GHG emissions trading scheme from 2005, to provide experience before global rules are introduced, probably from 2008.

The Kyoto Protocol

At the third Conference of Parties (COP-3) in December 1997, the parties to the UNFCCC adopted, largely under the impulse of the EU, the Kyoto Protocol. This protocol to the UNFCCC further widens the scope and depth of commitments to combating climate change by establishing a legally binding requirement from the EU countries to obtain, during 2008-2012, a total reduction of emissions for six GHGs of 8% in comparison to 1990 levels. These six GHGs are: carbon dioxide, methane, nitrous oxide and three CFC substitutes (HFCs, PFCs and SF_6). This 8% commitment was later distributed among EU Member States under an internal burden-sharing agreement, which takes account of the differences in GHG emission reduction potential of the various countries as a function of their economic, environmental and social constraints. The Commission also produced a Communication in June 1998, spelling out the EU's overall strategy vis-à-vis its post-Kyoto commitments (COM (98) 353 June 3, 1998).

The Kyoto Protocol for the first time also provides for the possible use of 'flexible mechanisms' in order to reach agreed commitments. Such mechanisms include: international emissions trading (IET), which allows industrialized countries to fulfill their commitments by purchasing from countries that emit less GHG, the unused part of their emission quota; joint implementation (JI) with non-OECD countries; and a financial instrument called the 'clean development mechanism' (CDM), which will make it possible to convey private sector funds towards developing countries in order to allow them to finance projects for reducing pollutant emissions. In addition, the Kyoto Protocol honored the Berlin Mandate by not involving developing countries in any binding emission reduction commitments.

In November 1998, a fourth Conference of Parties (COP-4) was held in Buenos Aires. At this meeting, delegates adopted a plan of action which provided for further work on a number of issues, including financial mechanisms, transfer of technologies (to assist developing countries) and rules governing the Kyoto mechanisms on emissions trading, joint implementation and the clean development mechanism. Although this meeting set no time frame for implementing the Kyoto Protocol, it did specify that all these issues must be acted upon in time for the COP-6 in November 2000.

In its 1999 Communication 'preparing for implementation of the Kyoto Protocol' (COM (99) 230 May 19, 1999), the Commission suggests a number of measures, both at national and at Community level to enable a speedy fulfilment of the Kyoto commitments. The proposed measures include:

- the adoption of the proposal for a directive on an energy product tax and the development by Member States of appropriate fiscal incentives (which requires the unanimity of the Council);
- the conclusion of environmental agreements aimed at emissions reductions within specific industrial sectors (initial talks are underway with a number of industry sectors);
- reliable and pro-active monitoring and verification systems (Decision 93/389/EEC on monitoring mechanisms of Community CO_2 and other greenhouse gas emissions);
- the possible establishment of an emission trading system within the Community, after a broad consultation with stakeholders (see below);
- investment and technology transfers to developing countries and economies in transition; and
- use of overseas aid and public funds to finance climate-related projects in developing countries.

Despite these proposals it now seems increasingly unlikely that the EU will be able to fulfill its Kyoto obligations. In order to reach its target, the EU realistically needed to introduce a series of tough new policy measures by the end of 1999 at the latest. However there has been no such progress, especially in areas such as renewable energy and CO_2/energy taxation. Consequently, Environment Commissioner Margot Wallström admitted on February 10, 2000 that it is highly uncertain that the EU will meet its Kyoto emission targets. Indeed she conceded that emissions in general were increasing rather than decreasing, especially in the transport sector. This point is reinforced by reference to observed greenhouse gas emission data which clearly demonstrate that since 1994, greenhouse gas emissions in general, and CO_2 emissions in particular, are again increasing (see graph on page 41). If left unchecked (see the 'baseline scenario' of the graph), this trend means that the requirement of Article 3(2) of the Kyoto Protocol to show 'demonstrable progress' by 2005 and the EU commitment of -8% for greenhouse gases, will not be met.

Reversing this trend will necessitate a reinforcement of policy efforts. With this in mind, the Member States have made emission projections for the coming years which incorporate planned measures (see graph). However, these measures still need to be adopted and enforced and this will undoubtedly require strong political will, both from the Member States themselves and from the Community. Moreover, a timelag of several years may exist between the political decision concerning a specific measure and the actual emission reduction.

In March 2000, the Commission responded to the EU's lack of progress in meeting its Kyoto obligations by issuing a strategic Communication on policies and measures to reduce GHG emissions (COM (2000) 88 March 8, 2000) and an associated Green Paper on emissions trading (COM (2000) 87 March 8, 2000).

In November 2000, the sixth Conference of Parties took place in The Hague. The conference failed to reach an agreement on the broad range of issues, which was put before it. The failure to reach an agreement centred on specific issues, ie, Kyoto mechanisms, supplementary and North-South issues. This is symptomatic of the larger problems that have blocked the ratification and entry into force of the Kyoto Protocol since 1997. The COP-6 discussions are expected to resume on July 18, 2001.

Soon after the US elections in November 2000, the new US Bush administration announced that the US would not ratify the Kyoto Protocol because of its adverse impacts on the US economy and the lack of participation by developing countries. The EU responded that it would ratify the Kyoto Protocol by end of 2002 with or without the US. climate change will remain high on the EU political agenda in the coming years.

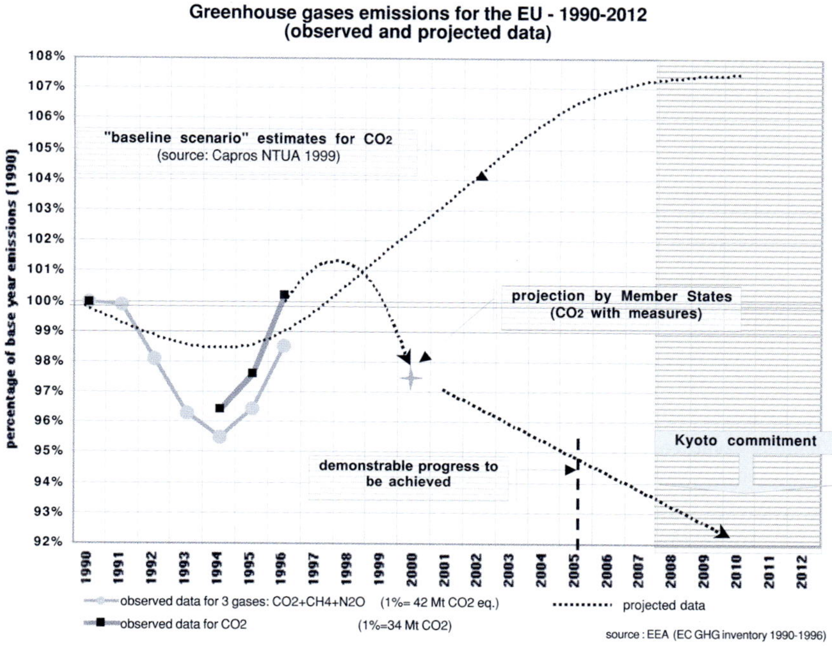

N.B.: As greenhouse gas emissions are linked to economic activity, the projections for emissions in coming years are very sensitive to economic growth. Also, technological progress could develop differently than foreseen, adding to the intrinsic uncertainty with regard to future emissions.

Business Perspective

Since the early 1990s, business has recognized the importance of the issue of climate change and its potential economic impact. Up until recently, the most visible aspect of the climate change debate at EU level has been energy/carbon taxation. Business has consistently opposed the introduction of such instruments, arguing that they were likely to further handicap the EU's industrial competitiveness in relation to the rest of the world, while probably delivering a very limited reduction of CO_2 emissions relative to EU commitments. In light of the Kyoto Protocol, a series of non-tax measures are being highlighted that may also have a strong business impact. Industry's key messages focus on the following elements:

- innovation and technological developments offer the best solutions to the climate change problem;
- energy-intensive industries should not face a cap on growth as a consequence of the Kyoto Protocol implementation;
- developing countries must take an active part in GHG emissions control; and
- the taxation option should be abandoned.

The education of EU citizens at large as the main tool to combat climate change, has yet to be addressed.

2. Environmental Liability

Background

The Commission's White Paper concerning environmental liability (COM (2000) 66 February 9, 2000) proposes the establishment of an environmental liability regime with the following objectives: implementation of key environmental principles (polluter pays, prevention and precaution) as enshrined in the EC Treaty; the need to ensure decontamination and restoration of the environment; better integration of the environment into other policy areas and improved functioning of the internal market. In order to achieve these objectives, different options for Community action have been assessed:

- Community accession to the Council of Europe's Lugano Convention (a convention produced by the Council of Europe in 1993, on civil liability for damage resulting from activities dangerous to the environment);
- a regime solely covering transboundary damage;
- a Community recommendation to guide Member State action;
- a sectoral regime focusing on biotechnology; and
- a Community framework directive.

The Commission favors the fourth option, however it should be noted that it confines the regime to the following elements:

- non-retroactivity - the EC regime should only work prospectively and Member States should be left to deal with pollution from the past. Only damage which becomes known after entry into force of the regime would be covered, unless the act or omission that resulted in the damage has taken place before the entry into force;
- damage - as the regime concerns environmental liability, environmental damage should be covered. Two different types of damage are brought together under the heading 'environmental damage' namely, damage to biodiversity and damage in the form of contamination of sites. It also includes traditional damage (to people and goods);
- strict liability - with commonly accepted defenses such as an act of God, contribution to the damage or consent by the plaintiff and intervention by a third party;
- operator liability - the person(s) who exercise control over an activity by which the damage is caused (namely the operator) should be the liable person under the regime;
- ensuring effective decontamination and restoration of the environment - clean-up standards and objectives to decide whether clean-up of pollution is warranted, to what extent it must be cleaned or restored and to ensure quick clean-up procedures when there is a threat to people and the environment;
- alleviation of burden of proof - the White Paper suggests that the regime could also contain one or other form of alleviation of the traditional burden of proof, to be more precisely defined at a later stage; and
- access to justice - this envisages a two-tier system whereby Member States would be under a duty to ensure restoration of biodiversity damage and decontamination in the first place (the first tier), by using the compensation or damages paid by the polluter. However, public interest groups would gain the right to act on a subsidiary basis, ie, only if the state fails to act at all or does not act properly (second tier). This approach would apply to administrative and judicial review and to claims against the polluter.

The Commission is drafting a proposal for a Directive on environmental liability that is scheduled to be ready by July 2001, it is more likely, however, that it will be ready for publication in September of the same year. No major departures from the White Paper are expected.

Business Perspective

Business within the EU would be strongly affected by the Commission's proposal. Most businesses believe that a liability scheme at EU level is not warranted based on the studies made for the Commission. Indeed, the US, in the context of the Superfund reform, is moving away from a federal system to state-governed liability systems (the Superfund is a colloquial term for the Comprehensive Environmental Response Compensation and Liability Act (CERCLA) which sets out the federal rules on environmental liability). Input from industry will be very important if a political decision is taken to adopt a liability scheme. Although no longer the preferred option of the Commission, the Lugano Convention suffers from many of the same uncertainties as the US Superfund system, such as joint and several liability, unlimited damage and retroactive application. Lugano goes further than the US Superfund system by providing for access to justice for individuals and NGOs. Industry takes the position that access to justice should be limited to allowing citizens or NGOs to sue in order to require government agencies to act in defense of the environment. Unlimited direct access to justice carries the risk that carefully crafted remediation plans, agreed between industry and government officials, would be overturned by claims from citizens or NGOs.

The White Paper does not provide sufficient justification for EU action. By including personal injury and property damage, the provisions proposed in the White Paper will require changes to the existing 'traditional' national liability regimes. This is not in accordance with the principles of subsidiarity and proportionality enshrined in the Treaties. In addition, the combination of strict liability, lack of adequate defenses (eg, permit or state of the art defense) and a reversal of the burden of proof would put industry in a very difficult position *vis-à-vis* unfounded claims.

3. The Chemicals Review

Background

A major revision of EU chemicals legislation is currently underway, which will significantly reshape the regulatory landscape and increase industry's responsibilities regarding human health and environmental protection during the production and use of chemicals. This review will have considerable impact throughout the chemical production chain and indeed on the trade in chemicals and downstream products both within and outside the EU.

The revision was initiated by the European Council at the Chester Summit in April 1998, giving the European Commission the mandate to develop a new, integrated and coherent chemicals policy adequately reflecting the precautionary principle and the principle of sustainability and specifying the obligations placed on the parties involved. It was based on the discovery that thirty years of EU chemicals policy allowed industry to operate within a common European market but failed to ensure that only safe chemicals were being produced and marketed in the EU.

After almost three years of consultation and internal debate, in February 2001, the Commission published its long awaited White Paper, entitled Strategy for a Future Chemicals Policy (COM (2001) 88 February 27, 2001). This document will lead to new legislation being proposed by the Commission in order to amend existing EU chemicals legislation. The Commission's first proposals are expected by end 2001/beginning 2002.

The Commission's initial objective was to put forward proposals that would streamline and simplify the four major EU legislative instruments currently in place:

- Directive 67/548/EEC on Dangerous Substances;
- Directive 88/379/EEC on Dangerous Preparations;
- Regulation 793/93/EC on Existing Substances; and
- Directive 76/769/EEC on the Marketing and Use of Certain Dangerous Chemicals.

However, the White Paper concentrates on proposals that will attempt to resolve the lack of data on 'existing substances' (those that were marketed prior to September 1981 and listed on the European Inventory of Existing Commercial Chemical Substances (EINECS)).

Under the current system, controlled by the amended Dangerous Substances Directive (67/548/EEC), any manufacturer wishing to market a new substance is required to notify the national competent authorities prior to its marketing in the EU. The notification consists of a technical dossier with extensive information on the production, use, properties and adverse effects of the substance, and a proposal for its classification and labeling. On the other hand 'existing substances' can be marketed without pre-market approval system, subject to their compliance with the classification, packaging and labeling provisions of the Dangerous Substances Directive.

The Commission's White Paper proposes the installation of a new (single) system for the registration, evaluation and authorization of both new and existing chemical substances (REACH) marketed in the EU above 1 ton. It evaluates that about 30,000 existing substances (of the 100,000 EINECS listed substances) will require registration and organizes the phase-in of existing substances in the REACH system over a period of 15 years, starting with those marketed in higher volume. An extended European Chemicals Bureau will maintain a central database of the data that shall be registered on these chemicals, including identity information, physico-chemical and toxicological properties, intended uses, quantities and a preliminary risk assessment. These chemicals will also be subject to spot checks by national control authorities.

Those substances marketed in quantities above 100 tons in the EU and substances that present particular traits or properties, including those suspected to be persistent and liable to bioaccumulation, will require evaluation at the EU or national level. Finally, substances classified as carcinogenic, mutagenic or toxic to reproduction, persistent organic pollutants and other substances will have to go through the more stringent authorization process of the REACH system. The approval will be use-specific, with the authorization being granted only if the specific use presents a negligible risk or, in the absence of safer substitute, if the risk is acceptable.

Another key element of the White Paper is that it extends the responsibility for the safety of chemicals to downstream users of chemicals. More specifically, the proposed system would require downstream users to carry out additional testing to complete the available data and risk assessments where their uses differ from those originally envisaged by the manufacturer or importer.

Despite industry criticism, the Commission hopes that the policy outlined in the White Paper will become legislation. However, many uncertainties remain concerning the implementation of the REACH system in legislation and on the other aspects of the Chemicals Review that have been subject to little if any coverage in the White Paper. Hence, much remains to be done before the future EU chemicals legislation takes its final shape.

Business Perspective

The potential business impact of the EU Chemicals Review is huge, as demonstrated above. It will certainly affect the chemicals industry, *stricto sensu*, and also downstream users of chemicals.

While the stated political objectives of the reform are generally supported, many consider that the Commission's proposed approach for the implementation of these objectives is not properly balanced and will lead to substantial societal and economic drawbacks that are neither justified, nor necessary, to achieve the desired objective. Indeed, the Commission's White Paper stresses the health and environment aspects of the reform, over the two other pillars of sustainable development, and the social and economic dimensions.

Business believes that this is essentially a global issue and an appropriate international solution should therefore be found via consultation between the EU and its trading partners. This is preferable to resolving the issue in isolation. Therefore, in the future, the Commission should give fuller account to the international dimension of this issue and further study possible synergies with existing governmental and industry-generated programs for the collection of data on existing chemicals.

4. Sustainable Development Strategy

Background

In December 1999 at the Helsinki European Council, the Commission was requested to prepare a document outlining a proposal for a long-term strategy consolidating policies for ecologically, socially and economically sustainable development before the start of the Gothenburg European Council in June 2001.

The EU and other signatories of the 1992 United Nations (UN) Rio Declaration committed themselves at the 19th Special Session of the UN General Assembly in 1997 to develop a sustainable development strategy in time for the 2002 World Summit on Sustainable Development. The Commission Communication, entitled A Sustainable Europe for a Better World: A European Union Strategy for Sustainable Development ((COM) 264 May 15, 2001) forms part of the EU strategy. The proposal builds on an inter-service consultation paper published at the end of March 2001 and on responses to that paper put forward by stakeholders. It contains a number of measures designed to improve coherency of EU policy making with a view to introducing widespread sustainable development.

The most commonly used definition of sustainable development is taken from the Brundtland report (World Commission on Environment and Development – the 'Brundtland Commission' - 1987) and states that the concept is 'development that meets the needs of the present without compromising the ability of future generations to meet their own needs'. This broad definition covers almost any issue with a significant economic, environmental or social element. Sustainable development has the potential to offer a more prosperous society with healthy economic growth in a clean and safe environment. With significant reorganization of public and private investment practices towards environmentally friendly technologies, it is believed that the hitherto detrimental effects that resource consumption has on the environment can be reversed. Achieving sustainable development in practice requires that economic growth supports social progress and respects the environment that social policy strengthens economic performance and that environmental policy is cost-effective.

The Commission states the following in its consultation paper: 'policy should focus on steady long-term management and ambitious verifiable objectives which allow business...to plan better and adjust gradually, thereby greatly reducing the costs of change'. It places importance on price adjustment on goods and services to take into account the added costs of damage caused by pollution and waste. The success of this strategy also depends on altering consumer behavior which can only be brought about by improving awareness through information provision and education.

In its Communication, the Commission proposes that the strategy should focus on a small number of issues which present the biggest threats to the future health of European and global societies. These are as follows:

Greenhouse gas emissions – these are known to cause global warming, which in turn is likely to cause drastic and potentially irreversible damage to the environment and global weather systems, thus having negative implications for health and nature as well as infrastructure and property.

Threats to public health – new antibiotic-resistant strains of diseases, long-term effects of dangerous chemicals and doubts about food safety are of increasing concern.

Poverty and social exclusion – these have direct adverse effects on individuals, such as ill health and unemployment.

An ageing population – an older population could cause a slowdown in economic growth.

Loss of biodiversity – this has increased significantly in recent years. For example, fish stocks have been diminishing and some are close to collapse, and agricultural soil has become less fertile.

Transport congestion – the number of road vehicles Europe-wide is on the increase, and urban areas are the worst affected. These areas are also affected by concentrations of poverty, inner-city decay and social exclusion.

The Commission suggests that the following action should be taken:

- each policy sector should be comprehensively assessed for its economic, social and environmental impacts within the EU and worldwide. All policies should have sustainable development as a major factor, particularly reviews of Common policy;
- the Common Agricultural Policy review in 2002 should focus on encouraging the organic sector to expand and environmentally-friendly agricultural methods to develop;

- the Common Transport Policy should attempt to deal with reducing congestion and traffic pollution;
- cohesion policies should improve their targeting of less developed regions and those with the most severe structural problems; and
- finally the Commission intends to submit an action plan for improved regulation to the Laeken European Council in December 2001. This will contain proposals for measures to ensure all key legislative proposals include an evaluation of latent economic, environmental and social benefits, the effects of action or inaction within and outside the EU.

The sustainable development strategy should become a driving-force in future years for institutional reform and changes in corporate and consumer behavior. In 2002 the Commission plans to publish another Communication further detailing its intentions on how the EU should tackle global sustainable development, in preparation for the World Summit on Sustainable Development (Rio+10) in Johannesburg.

Business Perspective

Business welcomes the Commission's initiative to start a broad and comprehensive debate on sustainable development, and is currently engaged in contributing constructively to the ongoing discussion. US companies are keen on sharing their experiences in this field and helping the European institutions in the process outlined in the strategy adopted. Business is committed, through dialogue with the institutions, to analyzing the best ways of achieving a sustainable balance between the economic, environmental and social elements of business activities.

5. Towards Sustainability – The Sixth EAP

Environmental Action Programs (EAPs) outline the Commission's proposals for initiatives relating to environmental improvement. They take a wide-ranging approach to the challenges of cleaning up the environment and give strategic direction to Community environmental policy.

The European Union's Fifth Environmental Action Program (1993-2000) 'Towards Sustainability' constituted the Community's first commitment to sustainable development. The Sixth EAP, which was published in January 2001, (COM (2001) 31 January 24, 2001) confirms sustainable development as the EU's key objective, proposing to achieve a decoupling of resource use from economic growth through improved resource efficiency.

A Commission report which examines the Fifth EAP (COM (1999) 543 November 24, 1999) stresses that the EU has so far adopted legislation covering most environmental problems. EU policies have achieved results, namely the reduction in trans-boundary air pollution and improved water quality. However, environmental trends remain worrying in many cases and the state of the environment overall remains a cause for concern. Areas identified as requiring particular attention include waste management, the problem of summer smog, chemicals in the environment, climate change and bio-diversity losses.

One reason for these negative trends is that Member States often do not implement EU environmental legislation in full. Although major efforts have been made by the Member States, gaps remain in the transposition of EU policy into their respective national laws. The Commission has repeatedly stated its ongoing commitment to ensuring implementation and enforcement of legislation. It continues to bring cases against Member States in those areas where implementation is not progressing satisfactorily. Non-implementation often reflects the state of the environment, public support and political commitment present in each of the Member States.

The Sixth EAP sets out the new policy framework to be translated into legislation. It takes over the three main principles adopted in the Fifth EAP: the precautionary principle, shared responsibility and the 'polluter pays principle'. It also adds another two basic principles which are the substitution principle (which states that wherever economically and technically feasible, countries should replace the use of hazardous substances by less hazardous ones) and the reversal of the burden of proof principle (producers have to prove that hazardous substances they use do not present unnecessary or unacceptable risks for the environment and human health). Rather than proposing very specific action steps, it sets out a strategic approach for environmental policy definition for the coming decade (2001-2010). Experience from the Fifth EAP has shown that setting a lot of specific targets, without reasonable databased reassurance that these targets can be realistically met is not effective. The Program aims to address, and take numerous pre-defined actions in four major environmental issues, namely: climate change, health and environment, nature and biodiversity, and natural resource (and waste) management (see below).

The Sixth EAP offers a strategic approach focusing on:

- the need for Member States to better implement existing environmental legislation;
- integration of environmental considerations in other policy areas (transport, energy, agriculture);
- cooperation with business and consumers to achieve more environmentally friendly forms of production and consumption (integrated product policy (see page 50), environmental liability (see page 42) fiscal measures, better information for citizens); and
- development of a more environmentally conscious attitude towards land use.

Climate Change
The goal is to stabilize atmospheric concentrations of greenhouse gases at a level not causing unnatural climate variations. The first step is an 8% reduction by 2008-2012 (Kyoto protocol requirement), the next step is a 20-40% reduction by 2020. Through structural changes especially in the transport and energy sectors, stronger efforts in energy-efficiency and energy-saving, the establishment of an EU-wide emissions trading scheme, further research and technological development and awareness-raising with citizens.

Nature and Biodiversity
The objective here is to protect and restore the functioning of natural systems, prevent the further loss of bio-diversity in the EU and globally and to protect soil against erosion and pollution. Actions designed to achieve these include:

- full establishment of the Natura 2000 network (a network of sites protected at the Community level);
- sectoral bio-diversity action plans (including GMO risk management tools);
- protection of landscapes through agricultural and regional policies;
- protection of the marine environment;
- prevention of industrial and mining accidents; and
- a new thematic strategy for protecting soils.

Environment and Health
This is Commissioner Wallström's personal priority. She stresses that a holistic approach is needed to address interlinkages between different environment health risks particularly for vulnerable groups in our society, like children and older people. The Commission plans to concentrate on:

- managing risks from chemicals/pesticides (eg, chemicals/pesticides management in developing and accession countries) (see Chemical law revision page 44);
- sustainable use and high quality of our water;
- reduction of noise pollution to acceptable levels;
- development of a thematic strategy for air quality to monitor the effectiveness of existing standards and identify gaps and priorities for further action; and
- ionising radiation (Euratom Treaty, OSPAR Convention for the marine environment of the north Atlantic).

Sustainable Use of Natural Resources and Waste (Management)
Action will include:

- decoupling of waste generation from economic growth (as part of Integrated Product Policy (IPP) (see page 50);
- a reduction of waste going to final disposal by 20% by 2010 (against 2000 levels), and by 50% by 2050; and
- an increase in eco-efficiency (will promote the competitiveness of European industry).

To achieve progress in those four priority areas, a broad mix of instruments must be developed and applied including market-based instruments (economic and fiscal instruments and voluntary agreements), horizontal supporting instruments (research, information, education), and financial support mechanisms such as the LIFE program (funding program for innovative and technical action in the field of environmental protection).

The Commission plans more dialogues with EU stakeholders (business, NGOs), with candidate countries and with international policy-makers. Decisions will be guided by sound science, economic assessments and effects monitored on the basis of indicators, working closely with the European Environment Agency and Eurostat.

Business Perspective
Business sees the Sixth EAP as offering an opportunity to move towards a more coherent European environmental policy, that is better implemented to ensure a higher environmental effectiveness. However, rather than concentrating solely on environmental aspects, the Sixth EAP should aim to contribute to sustainable development and be integrated into the sustainable development strategy. This way, proposed actions will lead to environmentally effective and economically efficient measures. The environmental effects of proposed actions that cannot be met due to social or economical constraints will obviously be very limited. Also, all decisions should be taken based on sound science, following comprehensive stakeholder consultations.

6. Integrated Product Policy (IPP)

Background

In an attempt to achieve sustainable development (see page 46), EU environment ministers and the Commission are developing a new environmental policy concentrating on the impacts of products over their entire life-cycle. Products are essential to our quality of life, but should use less resources, have lower impact and risks to the environment and waste should be prevented at the design stage. The so-called integrated product policy (IPP) approach is intended to avoid shifting potential environmental impact from one stage of a product cycle to another. It aims at continuous improvement in the performance of products and services within a life-cycle context.

Starting 1993 a number of Member States (including the Nordic countries and the Netherlands) initiated policy proposals specifically targeting products and their life-cycle impacts. In March 1998 a report was published on the issue of IPP, following a two-year study. The report identified five 'building blocks':

- managing wastes;
- stimulating the design of more environmentally-sound products;
- creating markets for environmentally-sound products;
- improving (environmental) information flow up and down the product chain; and
- allocating responsibility.

This study formed the basis for discussions at a workshop on IPP held by DG Environment in December 1998. Overall, participants were supportive of a Commission initiative based on voluntary and market-based instruments without, however, excluding the use of legal instruments and suggested the funding of research and pilot projects, to help the development of product-oriented management systems and produce an economic and cost benefit assessment of IPP.

During an informal Environment Council on IPP (Weimar, May 1999) Ministers stressed, in particular, that the new policy approach should not necessarily lead to more regulatory measures but rather an integration of instruments already in place. Also it identified the need for close stakeholder involvement. The Commission was called on to consider IPP in its Sixth Environmental Action Program and to ensure better and greater integration of environmental concerns into public procurement and in the wider international trading context. The Commission was asked to assess and clarify the potential for environmentally appropriate procurement and existing barriers and, if necessary, to amend the relevant Directives.

At the end of December 2000, the Commission published its Green Paper on IPP (COM (2001) 68 February 7 2001), referring to sustainable development in the introduction, but concentrating on 'greening' products, production and consumption in the rest of the document. The Commission proposes to achieve this through a mix of instruments, which should stimulate the consumer demand for greener products. The proposed approach is to reduce overall environmental impacts over the life-cycle of a product through ecodesign; informed consumer choice and product prices in line with the 'polluter pays principle'.

During the first half of 2001, consultations were being organized with EU institutions and broader stakeholder events have been set up on the overall IPP approach (March 8 and 9), and on specific tools (in May and June). Written comments are accepted until end June 2001. The Swedish presidency plans to publish Council conclusions on IPP by end June 2001.

Business Perspective

Business supports the approach of integrated product policy to improve or confirm the environmental performance of product systems. Sustainable development should remain the key objective, and that is more than 'greening' the market (ie, making it more environmentally friendly). It is clear that instruments and decision tools need to be based on sound science. The overall tone of the Green Paper is open and the stakeholder involvement has been extended significantly, but the environment-only bias (as against sustainability), the little attention paid to internal market mechanisms and consumer choice and responsibilities, are bound to impact negatively the chances of this Green Paper contributing realistically to measurable environmental progress. IPP represents an opportunity to review past policies and measures in an integrated fashion and complement them, where necessary, with additional measures. Stimulating an improved implementation of a more coherent environmental policy could help obtain the goal of environmental progress, adding to the quality of life for all, now and in the future.

7. Waste from Electrical & Electronic Equipment (WEEE)

Background

In June 2000, the European Commission presented a proposal for a Directive on Waste Electrical and Electronic Equipment (proposed WEEE Directive) (COM (2000) 347 June 13, 2000). The proposed WEEE Directive follows a previous draft proposal for a directive dealing with both take-back obligations and restrictions on the use of substances in electronics. The European Parliament presented its first opinion on the proposal on May 16, 2001. A Council common position could be reached at the June 2001 Environmental Council, but it is more likely that the EU ministers will reach an agreement in September. The Directive's final adoption is not likely before 2002, with national implementation during the following two years.

The most controversial issues between the Commission, the Parliament and the Council are the proposed WEEE Directive's: legal basis; electrical and electronic equipment's (EEE) excluded categories; recovery and recycling targets; and financing of WEEE take back from households.

Legal basis - the Commission has proposed to base the proposed WEEE Directive on Article 175 EC. Under this Article, Member States may impose more restrictive national measures that are compatible with the EC Treaty. The proposed WEEE Directive would grant wide discretion to Member States to impose more restrictive measures including: higher recovery and recycling targets; making producers pay for WEEE collection; and making producers pay for non-household WEEE take back. The Parliament's Industry Committee has proposed to base the proposed WEEE Directive on Article 95 EC. If the Directive is based on this Article Member States are under considerable restraints when promulgating more restrictive national measures as it is forbidden to legislate beyond the scope of the Article. However, the Parliament's Environmental Committee would prefer to leave the proposed Directive as based on Article 175 EC.

Scope - WEEE would include waste from EEE, components, sub-assemblies and consumables, which are part of the EEE at the time of discarding. The Commission proposes to impose take back obligation on large household appliances; small household appliances; IT and telecommunication equipment; consumer equipment; lighting equipment; electrical and electronic tools; and toys. The Commission proposes to exclude from the WEEE Directive's main obligations: medical equipment systems; monitoring and control instruments; and automatic dispensers. However, some Member States and the Parliament's Environmental Committee are inclined to delete these exceptions. The Parliament Environmental Committee also proposesd that long distance sales (internet, telemarketing) should be covered.

Separate collection - the proposed WEEE Directive would require EEE producers to mark their EEE with a separate collection mark. Member States would be required to ensure that final holders and distributors may return WEEE from private households free of charge. Producers would be required to provide for WEEE collection from professional users. Distributors when supplying EEE, would have to offer to take back free of charge the WEEE from private households. EEE producers would be required to take back collected WEEE from central collection points to authorized treatment facilities. The Commission proposes to require Member States to endeavor to achieve, by December 2005, a minimum separate collection rate of four kilograms per inhabitant. The Parliament's Environmental Committee proposes making this collection rate target compulsory by 2005 and increasing it to six kilograms per inhabitant.

Treatment - the proposed WEEE Directive would require producers to set up WEEE treatment facilities. The treatment would, as a minimum, include the removal of all fluids and selective treatment in accordance with specific requirements. The proposed WEEE Directive would allow treatment operations to be undertaken outside Member States or the EC provided that any shipment complies with the Waste Shipment Regulation. The Parliament's Environmental Committee proposes requiring that authorized treatment facilities introduce certified environmental management systems.

Recovery - EEE producers would be required to ensure that the following recovery and recycling targets are met by 2005:

- for large household appliances, 80% of recovery and 75% of recycling;
- for small household appliances, consumer equipment, electrical and electronic tools and toys, other than cathode ray tubes containing EEE, 75% of recovery and 65% of recycling;
- for IT and telecommunication equipment, 75% of recovery and 65% of recycling;
- for gas discharge lamps, 80% of recycling; and
- for cathode ray tube containing EEE, 75% of recovery and 70% of recycling.

New recovery and recycling targets would be adopted for the years beyond 2008. In general, Member States are inclined to reduce some recovery and recycling targets. However, the Parliament's Environmental Committee proposes increasing all the recovery targets.

Financing - the proposed WEEE Directive distinguishes between WEEE from private households and that from professional users.

- WEEE from private households: five years after the Directive's entry into force, EEE producers would be responsible for financing collection from designated points, treatment and disposal. With regard to products placed on the market after the Directive's effective date, EEE producers could fulfill their obligations either individually, or through collective systems involving other producers. Financing liability for historical waste is to be shared by all existing producers. The Parliament Environmental Committee favors individual financial responsibility for new WEEE, unless individual financing is not feasible or would involve disproportionately high costs.
- WEEE from professional users: producers and their customers would be free to arrange financing for collection, treatment and recovery/disposal of professional equipment. Some Member States favor compelling EEE producers to pay, unless producers and users conclude agreements stipulating other financing modalities.

Information to EEE users - the proposed WEEE Directive would require Member States to ensure that private households are informed of: return and collection systems available; their role in contributing to re-use, recycling and other forms of recovery; and the meaning of the separate collection mark.

Technical adaptation - the Commission, in collaboration with a national representatives committee, may revise the directive's WEEE treatment requirements, treatment facilities requirements and separate WEEE collection marking.

Business Perspective

As currently drafted, the proposed WEEE Directive would leave wide discretion to Member States on significant issues such as financing, and recovery and recycling targets. Thus, much of the final regulation would depend on the national implementation process. If adopted, the European Parliament Environmental Committee's proposal to impose restrictions on WEEE exports would be incompatible with World Trade Organization (WTO) law.

8. Electronic & Electrical Equipment (EEE)

Background

Following informal consultation with relevant industry, environment and consumer groups, a Working Paper on the impact on the environment of electronic and electrical equipment was launched by DG Enterprise of the European Commission on March 6, 2001.

The aim of the Paper is to examine harmonization requirements concerning the design of electrical and electronic equipment to ensure the free movement of these products within the internal market. The aim is also to improve their overall impact on the environment, and thus provide an efficient use of resources and a high level of environmental protection compatible with sustainable development.

The Commission is currently examining strategies to integrate environmental aspects into other policy areas, including enterprise policy, and the proposal represents the efforts of DG Enterprise to achieve this in practice. The electronic and electrical equipment (EEE) proposal is based on the application of the 'new approach' to legislation. The new approach is normally used in the areas of product safety whereby manufacturers must conform to the essential requirements laid down in the Directive, in order to place their products on the market. Specified standardization bodies such as the European Committee for Standardization (CEN), the European Committee for Electro-Technical Standardization (CENELEC) and the European Telecoms Standards Institute (ETSI) are responsible for translating the necessary detailed technical solutions to meet these essential requirements via harmonized standards. All stakeholders are involved in the standards process.

Producers can choose to apply these standards via two routes - providing a presumption of conformity, or making use of the technical specifications. So long as a product complies with the essential requirements defined in the Directive, via either route, and bears the appropriate label/mark, a product can be placed on the EU market. Manufacturers themselves are legally responsible for ensuring that all products placed on the market comply with the essential requirements. By means of market surveillance, Member States ensure that only conforming products are actually available on the market.

It is required that manufacturers of EEE request certain information regarding the environmental characteristics of the components or sub-assemblies which are used in their equipment in order to fulfill the essential requirements of the Directive. The aim is to understand the environmental impact of the end product. The Directive requires manufacturers of components or sub-assemblies of electrical and electronic equipment to provide all the necessary information to enable another manufacturer making use of the component or sub-assembly in electrical and electronic equipment to identify and estimate the magnitude of the environmental inputs and outputs of a product containing the component.

The consultation process is expected to continue into the autumn of 2001. During this time, the draft proposal for the EEE Directive has been placed on DG Enterprise's website and comments are invited in order to help develop the paper.

Business Perspective

Manufacturers of EEE products have traditionally welcomed the new approach and are supportive of its continued success. Such 'new approach' policies increase the coherency and effectiveness of legislation and ensure the free movement of goods within the EU.

However, industry has significant concerns about the draft EEE Directive because of the mis-match between the new approach style of thinking and the 'old approach' of traditional environmental legislation. The new approach works effectively when well-developed and specific guidelines are in place. It is questionable however whether it will work for environment considerations, which often lack measurable performance characteristics.

The EEE draft Directive presents a comprehensive, all-encompassing list of requirements that are vague and lack measurable characteristics. As yet there has been no proven environmental benefit connected to this Directive. The Directive could hinder design flexibility, and delay new product development without environmental gain.

Eco-design will be encouraged with the take-back requirements of the Waste from Electrical and Electronic Equipment (WEEE) Directive (see page 51) and the design requirements of the Restriction of the Use of Certain Hazardous Substances in Electrical and Electronic Equipment (RoHS) Directive (see page 54), which questions the need for the proposed EEE Directive.

9. Restriction of the Use of Certain Hazardous Substances in Electrical & Electronic Equipment (RoHS)

Background

In June 2000, the European Commission presented a proposal for a Directive on the Restriction of the Use of Certain Hazardous Substances in Electrical and Electronic Equipment (proposed RoHS Directive) (COM (2000) 347 June 13, 2000). The proposed RoHS Directive follows a previous draft proposal for a Directive dealing with both take-back obligations and restrictions on substances use in electronics. The Commission's final proposal was presented to the Environmental Council in October 2000. The European Parliament first reading took place on May 15, 2001. A Council common position could be reached at the June 2001 Environmental Council, but it is more likely that the EU ministers will reach an agreement in September. The Directive's final adoption is not likely before 2002, with national implementation during the following two years.

The most controversial issues between the Commission, the Parliament and the Council are the proposed RoHS Directive's legal basis; electrical and electronic equipment's (EEE) excluded categories; and substances' exceptions criteria.

Legal basis - the Commission has proposed to base the new RoHS Directive on Article 95 EC, the harmonization power. When a directive is based on Article 95 EC, Member States are under considerable restraints when promulgating more restrictive national measures. If the proposed RoHS Directive is based on Article 95 EC, Member States would not be able to restrict the Directive's exceptions, but they would be able to restrict the use of other substances in EEE. However, some Member States are inclined to try to fuse the proposed WEEE Directive and the proposed RoHS Directive into one Directive based on Article 175 EC. Basing the RoHS Directive on this Article would grant Member States wider discretion to impose bans on substances in EEE.

Scope - use of hazardous substances would be restricted in: large household appliances; small household appliances; IT and telecommunication equipment; consumer equipment; lighting equipment; electrical and electronic tools; and toys. The Commission proposes to exclude: medical equipment systems; monitoring and control instruments; and automatic dispensers. However, some Member States and the Parliament's Environmental Committee propose to include automatic dispensers; limit the specific EEE that would be excluded as falling under medical equipment systems and monitoring and control instruments and allow exceptions for spare parts placed on the market before January 1, 2006.

Bans - the proposed RoHS Directive would prohibit, from January 2008, the placing on the European market of EEE containing lead, mercury, cadmium, hexavalent chromium, polybrominated biphenyls (PBB) and polybrominated diphenyl ether (PBDE). The Parliament Environmental Committee proposes bringing the ban forward two years to January 2006. Some Member States are in favor of excluding certain substances, pending the outcome of risks assessment.

Exemptions - the proposed RoHS Directive includes an annex of exemptions from the substances banned. The list includes exemptions such as lead in electronic ceramic parts, lead as an alloying element, and cadmium oxide on the surface of selenium photocells. Under the Commission's proposed RoHS Directive, lead in solder is not exempted. The Commission, working through a comitology procedure, would be empowered to amend the exemptions annex. Member States would favor excluding from the exemption list mercury in laboratory equipment, lead as radiation protection, and cadmium, mercury and lead used in absorption spectroscopy instruments; and exempting lead used for interconnections for electronic assemblies. The Parliament's Environmental Committee proposes also exempting lead in high melting temperature type solders, lead in glass in electronic components and lead in piezoelectric devices.

Exemption criteria - in deciding whether to include or remove an exemption, the Commission would be required to consider whether the substance's use is technically or scientifically avoidable, and the environmental and/or health impacts caused by substitution are likely to outweigh the environmental benefits. The Commission would not be obliged to consider economic and product performance considerations when considering exemptions.

Exemption procedure - the proposed RoHS Directive assigns responsibility for managing the exemption revision process to Directorate General (DG) Environment's Waste Management Unit. This unit would submit a proposal to a committee of national representatives. If the national officials, voting by qualified majority, approve the Commission's proposal, the amendment would be adopted. If the national officials reject the proposal, it would be sent to the Council, which would have three months to act. If the Council fails to act, the Commission's proposal would be adopted. The Parliament Environmental Committee proposes assigning the responsibility to DG Enterprise.

Before the Commission amends the exemptions list, it would be required to consult EEE producers. However, the proposal does not specify the nature of the consultation and, furthermore, the Commission would not be obliged to take the EEE producer's opinion into consideration. The Parliament Environmental Committee rapporteur is in favor of requiring the Commission to consult also environmental and consumer groups before amending the exemptions list.

Review - the Commission would be required to review the Directive by December 2003 to take into account new scientific evidence.

Business Perspective

The proposed Directive would impose enormous burdens on EEE producers and importers. In the long run it would encourage countries around the world to ban the use of the targeted substances in electronic products. Despite this, the proposal lacks any reasonable risk assessment of the banned substances. Thus, it would not withstand any serious challenge under WTO law.

Chapter IV
Financial Services

THE EU COMMITTEE
OF THE AMERICAN CHAMBER OF COMMERCE IN BELGIUM

1. Financial Services Action Plan

Background

Although the single market for financial services has been under construction since 1973, the EU's financial markets have remained segmented. With the introduction of the euro, however, the Commission believed that there was fresh impetus to equip the EU with a modern financial apparatus in which the cost of capital and financial intermediation would be kept to a minimum. In this context, following the Cardiff European Council in June 1998, the Commission was invited to put forward a proposal and responded by publishing a Communication entitled 'Financial Services – building a framework for action' (COM (98) 625 October 28, 1998). This document identified a range of issues and called for urgent action to secure the full benefits of the single currency and an optimally functioning European financial market. The Vienna European Council of December 1999 decided that this should be translated into a more formal work program.

The result was the adoption by the Commission of a new Action Plan for implementing the framework for financial markets (COM (99) 232 May 11, 1999). This document outlined indicative priorities and time-scales for legislative and other measures to tackle three strategic objectives: ensuring a single market for wholesale financial services; open and secure retail markets; and state of the art prudential rules and supervision. The action plan also invited the Council and Parliament to adopt, by the end of 1999, a series of legislative proposals, some of which were subject to political deadlock. These included:

- collective investment undertakings (COM (94) 329; OJ C 242 August 30, 1994);
- distance selling of financial services (COM (98) 468 October 14, 1998; see page 66); and
- electronic money institutions (COM (98) 461 September 21, 1998).

Progress on these issues did not achieve the targets set, although agreement has now been reached on the e-money Directive.

In the Action Plan the Commission focused on implementing the single wholesale market in response to the market-driven modernization of EU securities and derivatives markets. Alongside the advent of the euro, and easier issuing and trading of securities across the EU, there now exists the potential to generate significant benefits in terms of liquidity, risk spreading and the emergence of viable risk capital markets. The Commission believed that these benefits could be further enhanced by EU regulatory measures, focusing on:

- the removal of outstanding barriers to raising capital on an EU-wide basis;
- a common legal framework for integrated services and derivatives markets, leading to an amendment of the Investment Services Directive and a proposal for a Directive on market manipulation;
- moving towards a single set of financial reporting standards for listed companies (meaning an amendment to the 4th and 7th Company Law Directives);
- providing legal security to underpin cross-border securities trades involving collateral;
- creating a secure and transparent environment for cross-border restructuring. This will require agreement on proposals for a European Company Statute and the Takeover Directive;
- creating a sound framework for supplementary pension funds in which asset managers can optimize the performance of their portfolios in the interest of fund holders (see page 72); and
- providing a new structure for the regulation of securities markets in the EU (the Lamfalussy Report, see page 61).

In order to develop open and secure markets, the Commission called for enhanced information, transparency and security for cross-border provision of retail financial services. It is in this context that the Commission recommended the adoption of the Distance Selling of Financial Services Directive (as well as the recommendation on mortgage credit information, a proposed Directive on insurance intermediaries, and an action plan to prevent counterfeiting and fraud in payment systems). It also listed measures to expedite speedy resolution of consumer disputes through effective extra-judicial procedures and a balanced application of local consumer protection rules.

The Action Plan also addressed the need to ensure the continued stability of EU financial markets. According to the Commission, this would require regulatory safeguards to be kept in line with new sources of financial risk (eg, solvency margins for insurance and capital adequacy; for the latter). To achieve this, the Commission foresaw a number of measures, including:

- moves to bring banking insurance and securities prudential legislation up to the highest standards, taking account of the work of existing bodies such as the Basel Committee and the Forum of European Securities Commissions;
- work on prudential supervision of financial conglomerates (a proposal for a directive); and
- arrangements to increase cross-sectoral discussion and cooperation between authorities on issues of common concern (creation of a Securities Advisory Committee).

Elimination of tax obstacles to financial market integration was another issue addressed by the Action Plan. For this reason the Commission believes that it would be technically unbalanced and politically difficult to fully realize the single market for financial services unless the parallel process of tax co-ordination currently under way delivers the expected results. The document underlines the need to adopt the proposed Directive on minimum effective taxation of cross-border income from savings (which was agreed in principle at the Feira Summit in June 2000; see page 116).

Progress in achieving the targets set in the Action Plan has been monitored by the Commission, which has issued periodic progress reports (third report see COM (2000) 692 November 28, 2000). The Financial Services Policy Group, comprising representatives of national finance ministers (which helped drive and prioritize issues in the Action Plan), has also been retained to monitor progress. The March 2000 Lisbon Summit launched the *e*Europe agenda and subsequent Action Plan (see page 127), which refers to the Financial Services Action Plan as a key pillar in the development of a modern economy.

Business Perspective

In general, business welcomes the Commission's initiative to involve the private sector in helping to identify some of the remaining barriers to the single market in financial services. There continues to be frustration at the pace of development and adoption of directives and also that effective implementation of existing directives has not already been achieved. In particular, some key issues need to be solved, such as: (i) the definition of wholesale versus retail counterparties needed to determine the appropriate approach to conducting business regulation; and (ii) a definitive statement of which country's rules should apply when transacting cross-border business.

There are a number of initiatives in the Action Plan that will have a profound impact on European financial markets, most notably, the Distance Selling Directive, upgrading the Investment Services Directive and the Pensions Directive. It is essential that industry practitioners including US companies active in the EU are involved in continuing consultation on these issues, as well as other initiatives outlined in the plan.

2. Lamfalussy Group: Regulation of European Securities Markets

Background

In July 2000 the Council of Ministers mandated a Committee of Wise Men, under the Chairmanship of Baron Alexandre Lamfalussy, to review the current regulation of securities markets in the EU and to assess how the mechanisms for regulating those markets can best respond to rapid market developments such as stock exchange alliances and technical innovation (alternative trading systems). The so-called Lamfalussy Group's Report was intended to provide impetus to the European Commission's Action Plan for Financial Services (COM (1999) 232 May 11, 1999 – see page 59) which set out a timetable of legislative measures for creating integrated wholesale and retail financial markets in the EU by 2005.

The Lamfalussy Group proposed a revision of the current EU legislative process, with the intention of making it speedier and more flexible, by introducing a new four-tier structure:

Level 1 – framework principles to be decided by normal EU legislative procedures;

Level 2 – establishment of two new committees: a European Securities Committee made up of Member State representatives and chaired by the Commission; and a European Securities Regulators Committee based largely on the existing Forum of European Securities Commissions (FESCO) – with power to amend and implement technical measures;

Level 3 - enhanced cooperation among securities regulators; and

Level 4 - strengthened enforcement of Community law by the Commission.

The Committee also suggested, where appropriate, the use of regulations (which have immediate direct effect) rather than directives (which require national implementing legislation) as a means of more quickly introducing financial rules.

As priorities under the Action Plan, the Lamfalussy Group recommended that the following legislative initiatives be brought into effect by the end of 2003:

- a single prospectus for issuers;
- modernization of admission to listing requirements;
- generalized application of the 'country of origin' (mutual recognition) principle for wholesale markets, including a clear definition of the professional investor (see page 65);
- modernization and expansion of investment rules for investment funds (see page 68) and pension funds (see page 72);
- adoption of international accounting standards; and
- a single passport for recognized stock markets.

The Stockholm European Council of March 24, 2001 broadly endorsed the recommendations of the Lamfalussy Group. However, certain Member States, concerned that the Commission would be able to use the Level 2 Securities Committee to push through rules in the face of significant Member State opposition, insisted on modifications to the proposed voting procedures.

The Commission eventually agreed to such a modification on the condition that it would not form a precedent for other policy areas. The Stockholm communiqué therefore states that for particularly sensitive implementing measures, the Commission would avoid going against predominant views which might emerge within the Council. In practice, this will probably mean that if a simple majority of Member States (or perhaps even a vocal minority) objects to a Commission proposal, it will be withdrawn or amended. Thus, these changes might make it more difficult to move implementing measures through the Securities Committee than would have been the case under the proposals advanced by the Lamfalussy Group, running counter to the stated aim of ensuring speedier and more flexible legislation.

Attention is now focussed on the European Parliament, whose cooperation is required in order to smoothly implement the proposals. Most EU securities legislation is dealt with under the co-decision procedure, giving Parliament broad powers of amendment and ultimately veto. Parliament is concerned that the delegation of implementing measures to a Securities Committee will amount to a loss of control over the legislative process. Similar concerns led the Parliament to block the creation of a Securities Committee when previously proposed in 1997. The fact that the Stockholm agreement, which strengthened the position of the Council *vis-à-vis* the Commission, has not led to similar gains for the Parliament has heightened the Parliament's sensitivity on this issue.

The Parliament is seeking a written understanding with the Commission on a mechanism for ensuring

Parliamentary oversight of delegated legislation adopted by the Securities Committee. Specifically, it wants access to documents, and a three-month period for Parliament to consider draft implementation measures submitted by the Securities Committee. The Lamfalussy Group's report proposes that the Parliament be given only one month to respond. It also wants the Commission to commit itself not to go against a Parliamentary resolution stating that a draft implementing measure adopted by the Securities Committee goes beyond the scope of implementing measures as agreed in the framework Directive. Though this falls short of the formal 'call-back mechanism' originally sought by the Parliament, it goes beyond the Wise Men's proposals, which only required the Commission to take the 'utmost account' of the Parliament's views.

Discussions between the Commission and the Parliament are ongoing, with both parties committed to finding a workable compromise. However, the distance between the two parties is such that reaching a compromise before the first pieces of 'post-Lamfalussy' legislation come before Parliament this summer is likely to be difficult. A recently published draft Directive on cross-border use of collateral, and proposals on market abuse and prospectuses, foresee the implementation of the Lamfalussy Group's four-tier regulatory structure, specifically referring to a Securities Committee. It may be that the Parliament's concerns will have to be worked-out in the context of such legislation.

In the meantime, the Commission will take the steps necessary to set up the Securities Committee and the Regulators Committee. The Securities Committee will initially operate in an advisory function before being fully incorporated into the EU framework. It is envisaged that the Regulatory Committee will continue to operate in an advisory status.

Business Perspective

The financial services industry is supportive of efforts to speed up the adoption of key legislation and to improve the mechanisms for keeping that legislation up-to-date. The key issue for business is whether the work of the Lamfalussy Group achieves the intended goal of making the EU legislative process speedier and more flexible, or whether the debate over implementation of their recommendations turns into a protracted inter-institutional dispute, which, rather than providing much needed impetus to the Financial Services Action Plan, creates blockages and distracts attention from the essential legislation it contains. Such an outcome would seriously damage the credibility of the EU's legislative process and prevent the EU from reaping the benefits of an integrated financial market.

Another important concern for business is whether the new four-tier structure is sufficiently infused at all levels with a high level of openness and transparency so that interested parties are able to take part in dialogue aimed at improving the quality of the resultant laws. The Lamfalussy Group's recommendations make important steps in that direction, but there is still concern that the proposed Regulators Committee has no mandatory obligation to consult with the broader community of interested parties, including non-EU financial services firms.

3. Collateral

Background

Collateral is used effectively to provide a guarantee against numerous liabilities and is a common feature of many financial transactions. The ability to provide collateral may make a transaction possible or may result in more favorable terms for the collateral provider. Collateral is important because it helps market participants mitigate risks. The number of collateralized arrangements within the financial services sector is increasing, particularly in cross-border payment and securities transactions. The exposures involved are significant, as hundreds of billions of euro are provided each day to collateralize transactions. Internationally, however, there is no uniform or coherent legal treatment of collateral.

Within the EU, Member States' laws and rules relating to collateral differ, in some cases significantly, with the result that the issues arising in connection with cross-border collateral are complex. The only (essentially) uniform approach is established by Article 9 (2) of the 1998 Settlement Finality Directive (98/26/EC; OJ L 166 June 11, 1998) and is limited to security provided in connection with the operations of the central banks of Member States and the European Central Bank in the performance of their central banking responsibilities.

The lack of a consistent approach to collateral generally means that collateral takers are confronted with a number of difficulties, including:

- varying specific requirements to establish a valid interest in collateral;
- conflict of legal principles where securities are provided cross-border as collateral (especially where the securities are book-entry securities); and
- differing treatment of, and interference with, collateral by different insolvency regimes, all of which may have an impact on the value of the collateral to the collateral taker. The result is legal uncertainty which contributes to inefficient use of collateral and potential systemic risks.

The Proposed Directive on Financial Collateral Arrangements

The Commission has recognized the significance of cross-border use of collateral in its Financial Services Action Plan (see page 59), where a Directive on the cross-border use of collateral has been given high priority. In March 2001, the Commission published its proposal for a Directive on financial collateral arrangements (COM (2001) 168 March 27, 2001).

The proposed Directive applies to collateral in the form of cash and securities. The definition of collateral taker and provider, the principal beneficiaries under the proposed Directive, further limits the scope of the Directive. Collateral taker and provider are defined as (1) public authorities, (2) financial institutions under prudential supervision and (3) non-natural persons with capital bases in excess of € 100 million or gross assets greater than € 1 billion. As drafted, the thresholds in the definition, which affect the scope of the proposed Directive, may be adjusted by the Securities Committee that has been recommended by the Lamfalussy Report (see page 61).

The proposed Directive addresses many of the issues of concern and sets out five objectives:

- to establish a simple regime for the creation of valid security interests, whether by pledge or transfer;
- to provide limited, but important, protection from some rules of insolvency law;
- to create legal certainty through a uniform conflict of laws treatment;
- to limit administrative burdens affecting the use of collateral; and
- to permit the re-use of collateral.

To achieve these objectives, the proposed Directive provides:

- that, for book-entry securities, the only perfection requirement or procedure to be followed should be the notification to, and recording by, the relevant intermediary maintaining the securities account. Bearer securities would need to be delivered to the collateral taker. This would eliminate the myriad of formal requirements currently specified by Member States, including filings using specified forms and registrations with certain authorities;
- limited protection of collateral arrangements from some rules of insolvency laws. In particular, the Directive will permit close-out netting, top-up collateral and substitution, which may be subject to challenge under some Member States' insolvency laws. Close-out netting replaces reciprocal obligations between the collateral taker and the provider with an obligation owed by one party to

pay the other the net difference between the estimated current values of the parties' obligations. Top-up collateral describes an arrangement where the value of collateral held is marked-to-market so that if the value of the collateral declines, the provider is obliged to top-up the collateral to make up the short-fall. Substitution enables a provider to withdraw certain securities from the collateral basket and replace them with other securities of equivalent value;

- for a broader application of the principle of Article 9 (2) of the Settlement Finality Directive to cover financial collateral arrangements generally, where the collateral consists of book-entry securities or cash. The principle, which is known as the 'place of the relevant intermediary approach' (PRIMA), establishes that the law which governs is the law of the country where the intermediary (ie, the securities account) is located;
- restrictions on formal requirements for the perfection or enforcement of collateral arrangements. The Directive will exempt collateral arrangements from the effects of automatic stays and from provisions in insolvency laws which permit or require the unwinding of transactions entered into during a specified period prior to the date of actual insolvency; and
- for the use or re-use of collateral, enabling collateral takers to use collateral by (re)pledging or (re)hypothecating it to a third-party, subject to the rights of the original collateral provider. Re-use of collateral increases liquidity in the market and, by effectively increasing the value of the collateral to the collateral taker, enables the collateral taker to offer better terms to the collateral provider.

The Hague Conference Initiative

The Hague Conference on private international law (held in mid-January 2001 with a committee of legal experts) is also pursuing an initiative relating to the cross-border use of collateral, although with a much narrower goal. Unlike the proposed Directive, the Hague Conference initiative is not intended to affect Member States' insolvency regimes or rules governing the creation and perfection of interests in collateral. The Hague Conference is focused on establishing PRIMA as the conflict of laws approach in its Member States. The overlap between the Commission's Directive and the Hague Conference's convention with respect to the adoption of PRIMA is deliberate: although all current Member States of the EU are also members of the Hague Conference, this is not true of the countries applying for EU membership. The timing of both the proposed Directive and convention is uncertain. The Commission anticipates that the proposed Directive should be adopted by 2003 with implementation to be completed by Member States by the end of 2004. The Hague Conference is committed to dealing with PRIMA on a fasttrack basis. It is hoped that the final text of a convention can be adopted by the beginning of next year, after which Member States would need to take the steps necessary to become party to the convention.

Business Perspective

Adoption of the proposed Directive will represent a significant step in achieving a single European market in financial services, as envisaged in the Financial Services Action Plan (see page 59). By creating a framework for the (limited) uniform treatment of cross-border collateral within the EU, the Directive will contribute to more efficient financial markets and reduce systemic risks.

4. E-Commerce & Financial Services

Background

The fast growth in the electronic provision of financial services, whether business-to-business (B2B) or business-to-consumer (B2C), in banking, investment, insurance and payment systems is rapidly changing the face of the financial industry, with the emergence of new online players and the 'e-remaking' of established companies.

The E-commerce Directive (2000/31/EC; OJ L 178 July 17, 2000) laid down for all sectors, including financial services (with a few limited exceptions), the principle that e-services could be provided across borders under the laws of the country of the provider (the 'country of origin' principle, also known as 'mutual recognition'), thus allowing for the integration of the 15 national online markets into a single one. The Directive however allowed three types of derogation:

- a number of other directives on, in particular, insurance and the advertising of mutual funds do not provide for mutual recognition;
- mandatory provisions protecting consumers in national contractual laws still apply; and
- Member States are allowed to enact derogations to protect investors and consumers for reasons of 'general interest'.

To determine how the country of origin principle should be applied to the financial sector, the Commission published a Communication (COM (2001) 66 February 7, 2001) outlining a three-step strategy:

- to review all online financial services-related derogations;
- on the basis of this review, bring about a 'high degree of convergence' in national laws (including through harmonization); and
- to ensure the application of country of origin rules takes place.

The Communication also seeks to address the need for greater "e-confidence" (consumer confidence in the internet as a secure and trustworthy shopping environment). The EU institutions heralded the December 2000 adoption of the 'Brussels Regulation' (amending the Brussels Convention of 1968), giving consumers the right to sue and be sued in their national courts rather than in the courts of the country where their online services provider is established, as a strong e-confidence factor. Many industry groups however see the Regulation as a powerful disincentive for online traders who may face judicial proceedings all over the EU. Current initiatives to promote alternative dispute resolution (COM (2001) 161 April 4, 2001) (non-judicial settlement of B2C disputes through, for example, arbitration or mediation) also aim to allay consumer fears and are addressed in the Communication. Finally, the Communication announced legislative proposals to ensure that consumers obtain refunds of card payments in cases of non-authorized transactions and non-delivery of goods ordered. Such legislation would also give a role to credit card companies in resolving disputes between consumers and merchants.

At the time of writing, the Council and European Parliament had not reacted to the Commission's proposed strategy, but the first debates held suggest the Parliament will come out fairly strongly in favor of the Communication's country of origin principle. The Council is divided, with a few Member States, and in particular France, acknowledging they had not fully understood how the E-commerce Directive would apply to financial services.

Furthermore, the Parliament and Council's approach to the proposed Directive on the distance marketing of consumer financial services (COM (1998) 468 October 14, 1998) (see page 66) sheds a useful light on their possible positions. In its first reading, the Parliament supported maximum harmonization, while the Council has struggled to overcome internal French-led efforts to stipulate that national law is broadly applicable within the scope of the Directive, and is set to agree at best to minimum harmonization without mutual recognition.

Business Perspective

A broad application of the key principle of mutual recognition would greatly contribute to the establishment of the single financial services market, while numerous and extensive derogations would risk killing industry hopes of operating across borders without having to comply with 15 differing sets of rules. Eventually, the issue will also determine how much competition there is throughout the EU, or whether online banking, investment services and insurance markets remain dominated by traditional national players.

5. Distance Selling of Financial Services

Background

Directive 97/7/EC (OJ L 144 June 4, 1997) on distance selling does not apply to financial services. However, following the trend set by this Directive, and in order to address this issue, the Commission drafted a Green Paper on financial services and consumers' expectations (COM (96) 209 May 22, 1996), which showed that poor and inadequate information is being offered to consumers buying cross-border financial services (eg, misleading presentation of data and absence of information in the language of the consumer). The Green Paper was followed up with a Communication (COM (97) 309 June 26, 1997).

The Commission finally proposed a Directive on distance marketing of consumer financial services in late 1998 (COM (98) 468 October 14, 1998). The draft Directive lays down a common basis for which distance marketing of financial services contracts are proposed, requested, negotiated and concluded. Its main aim is to ensure that consumers do not experience restrictions when seeking financial services (banking, insurance, investments). The principle behind the proposal is that consumers must be in a position to:

- receive and examine the terms and conditions of the contract in advance, before deciding to be bound by it (time limit for deciding); and
- withdraw when they have concluded a contract without having been acquainted with the contractual terms and conditions, or when the supplier has unfairly induced them to conclude a contract, during the reflection/cooling off period.

The proposal granted consumers a cooling-off period of 14 days between the time information is supplied relating to the contract and the time the consumer is contractually committed. The recommended withdrawal period was also set at 14 days. This period would be capable of extension to 30 days for those contracts involving mortgage loans, life assurance and personal pensions. The right of withdrawal, however, has not been applied to non-life insurance contracts of very short duration (eg, one month), foreign exchange services or reception, transmission or execution of financial products such as money market instruments, transferable securities, UCITS and other collective investment schemes, financial futures and options, exchange and interest rate instruments.

In order to maintain a balance between safeguarding consumer rights and ensuring a single market in financial services, the Commission also recommended that the proposal includes a maximum harmonization standard. In practice, and in order to avoid distortion in the single market, this would forbid Member States to introduce or maintain stricter consumer protection requirements than those set out in the Directive.

On May 5, 1999 the European Parliament approved the proposal with amendments at first reading. The Commission accepted most of the Parliament's amendments, *inter alia*: consumers would be entitled to receive a comprehensive set of information prior to its conclusion (enabling them to compare offerings) and the introduction of a consumers' general right of withdrawal without penalty or justification. Member States would be free to define a cooling-off period of between 14 and 30 days.

Since publication of the amended proposal (COM (1999) 385 July 23, 1999) the Council has struggled to agree on a common position. The essence of the division is the maximum harmonization approach, which is backed by the Commission, the Parliament and, with regard to Member States, by the UK, France, Luxembourg and the Netherlands.

In March 2000 the Commission submitted a Report emphasizing the need to break down the barriers to consumers' cross-border complaints, and providing information on the current situation on access by consumers to legal redress. The Commission noted that nearly all consumer complaints can benefit from national complaints channels. In some cases, there are voluntary arrangements which supplement the official systems. Nevertheless, consumers are often reluctant to use such channels because of lack of adequate information and advice. For both national complaints and cross-border complaints, the quality and effectiveness of mandatory and voluntary systems varies substantially on the basis of the typical problems inherent in consumer access to legal redress (distance, cost, legal formalities, etc.). In this sense, it is worth noting the launch on February 2001 of the Commission's Financial Services Complaints Network (FIN-Net), a specific Community-wide redress network for disputes involving financial services.

The Council instructed the Commission to prepare an inventory of existing national provisions. These findings have been used as a basis for discussions within the Council. However, divergences continue to exist on:

- the information to be provided to consumers;
- the right for consumers to withdraw after signing contracts; and
- the relevant jurisdiction in case of dispute (rule of the consumer's country of residence versus rule of the country where the service provider is established).

The Council has stressed the need to ensure consistency with other legislative and non-legislative acts, in particular the E-commerce Directive (see page 65), the two UCITS draft Directives (see page 70) and the Commission's Communication on e-commerce and financial services (see page 65).

Business Perspective

The financial services industry remains convinced that there is a need for special provisions for financial services negotiated at a distance. It is also concerned about the potential systematic application of host country rules, which could result from the Directive.

The provision of a lengthy withdrawal period has created concerns in the financial services sector. Although withdrawal from a short-term loan may be managed relatively easily by the lender through short-term liquidity management, withdrawal from a high-value loan could cause serious difficulties. Mortgage loans fall into this category and there are fears that a right of withdrawal could expose the lender to unpredictable and unrecoverable costs. As a result, financial institutions could in the long run be forced to restrict the range of services, to the disadvantage of consumers.

Investment Services
6. Upgrading the Investment Services Directive (ISD)

Background

The Investment Services Directive (Dir. 93/22/EEC; OJ L 141 June 11, 1993) forms the cornerstone of the single market in securities trading. It provides a European passport to investment firms allowing them to offer their services cross-border, subject to common core fitness and properness and conduct of business rule requirements and to the capital requirements set down in separate capital adequacy legislation. It also sets minimum standards, notably on transparency and trade reporting, for 'regulated markets' (exchanges) and allows them to place their trading screens across the EU. The ISD was supposed to be fully implemented by 1996.

The main advantage of the ISD for investment firms is the ability to access remote exchanges and to trade cross-border subject only to home country authorization. Experience of the ISD has, however, been mixed, and not helped by late transposition in several Member States. Some exchanges still do not accept remote members in apparent contradiction of the Directive. The Directive furthermore appears to allow some measures to continue which seem at odds with the principles of a single market, such as the concentration rule that permits the requirement that trading must be conducted on a regulated market. The most serious problem faced by industry however is that the principle of mutual recognition of home country regulation is persistently undermined by the application by some Member States of supervisory or regulatory provisions on a host country basis. This results in firms being subject to double, duplicative regulation.

Industry attention has therefore focused on Article 11 of the ISD, whose ambiguity has encouraged Member States systematically to apply duplicative conduct of business rules. Article 11 states that conduct of business rules should be applied by the regulator in the Member State 'in which a service is provided'. Article 11 also requires such rules to take into account the 'professional nature' of the counterparty. But despite these requirements, many Member States continue to apply rules both to firms operating out of their territory and to business conducted with clients in their territory, in both cases often with no differentiation for wholesale business.

The Commission is well aware of these problems and, following the Cardiff European Council conclusions calling for action on economic reform in the area of capital markets, has set up a Forum Group of market practitioners to discuss them. It also held extensive discussions with national regulators and with the Financial Services Policy Group (representatives of EU Finance Ministers) in the context of agreeing and implementing the subsequent Financial Services Action Plan (FSAP) endorsed by heads of state and government. The FSAP also indicated that a Green Paper on upgrading the ISD would be published by mid-2000.

In the event, the Communication on Article 11 (COM (2000) 722 November 14, 2000) and the treatment of sophisticated investors was delayed until November 2000, first by the perceived need to wait for agreement in FESCO (Forum of European Securities Commissions) on a common definition of a professional investor and second by disagreements between the Commission and Member States on the home/host issue. In the event, the FESCO definition of March 2000 set quite a narrow definition of professional investor under which only authorized firms would automatically be treated as professional. It did not really comment on the key question of whether home or host rules apply.

The Commission Communication does, however, address the home/host issue and supports the view that the answer should be 'home' for professional investors. The Commission, however, uses the rigid and narrow FESCO definition of professional investors. Interestingly, a European Parliament report by Piia-Noora Kauppi, MEP, has urged the Commission to go further on both the definition of professional investors and the extension of the home country principle, in line with industry views.

The second promised ISD Communication was also issued in November 2000 (COM (2000) 729 November 15, 2000). It proved more wide-ranging than some had expected and sought views by the end of March 2001 on a number of areas for legislative amendment. It focused on:

- an effective passport for investment firms: the usefulness of the single passport has been impaired, as noted above, by widespread application of host country requirements. Subsequently there is a call for amendments to ensure home country control for all wholesale business;
- appropriate regulation for new forms of service provision: technology has spurred the emergence of Alternative Trading Systems (ATSs) which compete with existing investment firms and exchanges. New suitably calibrated and common safeguards need to be applied to such systems, which would then be more clearly passported;

- effective competition between exchanges and trading platforms: potential barriers to competition such as the concentration rule should be abolished. Improved ISD core provisions for 'regulated markets', particularly on transparency and disclosure, are called for to underpin high EU standards, possibly in self-standing legislation; and
- the growing cross-border dimension of clearing and settlement: increasing consolidation concentrates systemic risk and requires closer supervisory cooperation. Removal of the remaining technical and legal impediments to linkages between systems is called for.

A consultation on proposed ISD amendments is now expected in the summer of 2001, with a separate Communication on clearing and settlement to come later in the year following discussion of this issue in the 'Giovannini Group', an advisory group of financial market practitioners.

Business Perspective

The FESCO paper has been the subject of considerable industry activity on the grounds that other sophisticated investors such as large corporates should not be treated as retail investors. In February 2001, FESCO issued for consultation proposed common conduct of business rules, applying its earlier professional/retail split. Again, this did not address the question of whose rules apply in a cross-border context. Industry is concerned both that this latest FESCO proposal applies unnecessary levels of regulation to professional investors – even as narrowly defined – and that it does not help in a cross-border context. It is critical for business that the home versus host conflict be resolved and that there be legal and regulatory certainty that cross-border service provision is subject to home country rules – at least for wholesale business. This is particularly important given that the E-commerce Directive (see page 65) applies the home country principle to purely online business. Given the failure of the Communication on Article 11 to deliver this, because of ambiguities in the original ISD text, legislation looks necessary. Wider revision of the ISD, however, needs careful consideration and should only be agreed if it can be shown to facilitate cross-border activity. It is, for example, important that new rules on ATSs do not hamper innovation and competition nor restrict access to clients. It is essential therefore that the securities industry be fully engaged in the process of ISD reform and engage the Commission in debate on the follow-up to its two Communications.

7. Collective Investments

Background

Undertakings for the collective investment in transferable securities (UCITS) are unit trusts/mutual funds and investment trusts. UCITS have as their aim the collective investment in transferable securities (essentially, securities listed on official stock exchanges or similar regulated markets) with capital raised publicly. Directive 85/611/EEC (OJ L 375 December 31, 1985) on the co-ordination of laws, regulations and administrative provisions relating to UCITS was the first of the single license measures in the financial services sector, designed to enable certain UCITS (open-ended unit trusts) to market their units throughout the EU on the basis of home state authorization. The objective of the Directive is to harmonize national laws concerning UCITS regulations so as to establish a level playing field at Community level and ensure the effective and uniform protection of unit-holders.

Under the terms of the Directive, each Member State is responsible for upholding certain obligations concerning: (i) the structure of unit trusts, management and investment companies and depositories; (ii) investment policies of UCITS relating to the particular instruments a UCITS may hold in relation to its total assets (eg, a combined total of 10% of assets may be invested in unlisted transferable securities or debt instruments); and (iii) information to be supplied to unit-holders (publication of a prospectus, including requirements for the publication in an official language where a UCITS intends to market its units, and periodical reports including pricing information).

The 1985 Directive limits investment to transferable securities traded on stock exchanges and regulated markets and confines managers to manage collective but not individual portfolios. UCITS may invest no more than between 5% and 10% of their assets in securities from one issuer. This limit is raised to 35% in the case of state bonds. Member States are required to notify the Commission of any bonds which fall under this category. Up to 5% of the UCITS may be invested in open-ended transactions, such as derivatives. In 1988 the UCITS Directive was amended to raise the investment limit for transferable securities from one issuer to 25% in the case of mortgage credit bonds (88/220/EEC; OJ L 100 April 19, 1988).

In February 1993, the Commission proposed further amendments to the UCITS Directive in order to widen its scope, allowing UCITS to invest in banking deposits, funds of other UCITS and money market instruments; and to liberalize the use of depositories. The proposal was amended by the Commission in July 1994 to take account of the Parliament's opinion, including allowing for 'master-feeder-funds' (a feeder-fund which invests exclusively in the units issued by a single UCITS - the master-fund).

However, the proposal became deadlocked in the Council of Ministers. Discussions reached a standstill on the following three issues: the inclusion of money market instruments under the scope of the Directive; the inclusion of master-feeder funds; and the provision that a UCITS' depository may be situated in another Member State. The Commission officially withdrew its original proposal in August 1999.

In July 1998 the Commission made another attempt to broaden the scope of the 1985 UCITS Directive by submitting two new proposals. The first focuses essentially on the 'product' (the types of investment instruments) and seeks to remove barriers to the cross-border marketing of UCITS (COM (98) 449 July 17, 1998). The second focuses on the 'service provider' (the management company) and will introduce an EU passport for management companies, on the basis of new harmonized regulation, as well as widening the range of permitted activities of such companies. It will also seek a simplified harmonization of prospectuses for UCITS (COM (98) 451 July 17, 1998).

The first proposal would foresee that collective investment undertakings investing in financial instruments, such as money market instruments, units of other UCITS, bank deposits and standardized options and futures contracts, could be marketed throughout the EU. In addition, it updates the original Directive to take account of new portfolio management techniques. It also attempts to clarify certain interpretative uncertainties relating to a number of provisions of the UCITS Directive by introducing:

- a definition of 'transferable securities' (referring essentially to shares and securitized debt instruments). It clarifies that 'money market instruments' are types of 'transferable securities';
- minimum risk control measures - in particular, the proposal will regulate the use of financial derivatives, and securities lending transactions in which UCITS acts as a lender; and
- clarification that subsidiaries of investment companies must normally be incorporated in a Member State.

The second proposal should reinforce the single market in UCITS by ensuring that all management companies operating UCITS would receive a 'single passport' enabling them to open branches in other Member States and to operate anywhere in the EU. It also revises current restrictions which prevent management companies from engaging in activities other than the management of assets of common funds/unit trusts and investment companies (collective portfolio management). This means that they would be allowed to manage assets from individual and institutional investors, like pension funds (see page 72).

The Parliament concluded its first reading on the UCITS proposals in February 2000. In particular, it called for the wider use of over-the-counter (OTC) derivatives as an investment tool. With regard to the second proposal, the Parliament proposed a minimum initial capital for UCITS similar to that in the Investment Services Directive (see page 68).

On the basis of the Parliament's first reading, the Commission published the revised proposals on UCITS on June 5, 2000 taking into account the Parliament's amendments (COM (2000) 329 and COM (2000) 331 May 30, 2000). Most significant is the Commission's concession on OTC derivatives. Revising its previous position, the Commission principally accepts the use of OTC derivatives as an investment tool, subject to a number of rather extensive restrictions and information requirements. The Commission has also followed the Parliament's views on increasing capital requirements for UCITS.

Finance ministers reached political agreement on the first proposal on October 17, 2000 and the second proposal on March 12, 2001. On the first proposal, the Council has removed ambiguities of the Commission's revised proposals, in particular with reference to money market instruments. The Council also followed the Parliament's approach to derivatives. With reference to the second proposal, Member States agreed to substantially increase the regulatory capital requirements for UCITS. This is to take into account the prospect of discretionary fund management and the use of derivatives as an investment tool.

Council adopted a formal common position on June 5, 2001. Second reading in the European Parliament will follow later in 2001.

Business Perspective

Business supports the Commission's objective of broadening the scope of Directive 85/611/EEC to include UCITS specializing in financial instruments (eg, money market instruments, cash funds and real estate funds) currently not covered by the scope of the Directive. The introduction of discretionary fund management under the UCITS Directive is another positive development. This, nonetheless, needs to be balanced against the high regulatory capital charges which have been proposed which could be particularly damaging for smaller fund managers. More broadly, updated UCITS legislation should facilitate the already rapid growth of UCITS in the EU market and enhance the efficiency of European capital markets.

8. Pan-European Pensions

Background

The provision of pan-European pensions within the EU has long been an area of focus for employers, their service providers and the Commission. Multinational employers wish to harmonize their employment policies, reduce the costs of implementing them and aid mobility of their employees among their operations in Member States. These companies have successfully provided pan-European solutions to core aspects of their business such as procurement, technology and treasury and they are frustrated with the obstacles hampering them to implement similar solutions which provide flexible pensions for their staff.

The pension service providers to these employers - be they asset managers, consultants, actuaries or custodians - naturally wish to meet the requirements of their clients and develop a growing and profitable business commensurate with the breadth and sophistication of the EU.

Most importantly, the Commission recognizes that pension provision is the only major sector of the financial services industry that does not benefit from an EU Directive, unlike banks, insurers and mutual funds. It has long wished to provide the necessary framework for pension provision to both improve the productivity of employers within the EU and enhance the mobility of EU citizens, a core tenet of the Commission. The Commission recognizes that current pension arrangements in the community are unsustainable in the long term, given EU demographics and dependence on tax-financed first pillar (ie, state) pensions in many Member States. These arrangements impose high, and rising, costs on employers and citizens alike. They could lead to businesses relocating to Member States with more flexible regimes in order to lower costs unless action is taken at Commission level to address these issues. Pan-European pensions and the goal of free mobility of labor are central to these issues.

The current proposal from the Commission (COM (2000) 507 October 11, 2000) follows the draft report on the proposal for a Directive on the activities of institutions for occupational retirement provision, better known as the Karas report after its rapporteur, which, with regard to occupational or second pillar (ie, private) pension provision, focuses on four key areas:

- the protection of beneficiaries and the securities of their pensions (through member communication and effective regulation);
- the facilitation of the provision of cross-border pensions;
- the achievement of cost transparency of occupational schemes, particularly with regard to coverage of biometric risks (eg, death, invalidity and longevity);
- the acceptance of the 'prudent man' investment principle (and concomitant repeal of quantitative investment restrictions, albeit after a 10 year grace period); and
- the establishment of a 'level playing field' for the service providers to occupational pension funds.

The Karas report received broad support from the Parliament's Economic and Monetary Affairs Committee in March 2001 as well as among industry professionals, despite continued misgivings about the continued focus on biometric risks. The report explicitly recognized that the proposal for a Directive, particularly the provisions stipulating mutual recognition of prudential standards, only represented a first step. On its own it would be insufficient to free up pan-European pension provision. To achieve this resolution, the report calls for Member States to reach agreement on uniform tax principles to enable portability of pensions, mobility within the EU and non-discrimination between service providers and citizens. It argues that current 'discriminatory practices' breach the principles of the EC Treaty, concluding that such fiscal agreement 'would clear the way for development of a functioning internal market in supplementary pensions, without additional legislation being required at European level.'

This call was followed in April 2001 by Tax Commissioner Frits Bolkestein's ground-breaking Communication on the elimination of tax obstacles to the cross-border provision of occupational pensions (COM (2001) 214 April 19, 2001), which in turn supported Karas's call for the removal of tax obstacles to cross-border pensions and led to the full support of the Commission in the form of a Communication. This revived urgency and action from the Commission is part of its new strategy, determined at the March 2001 Stockholm Summit, which aims at facilitating the emergence of pan-European labor markets by 2005. It signals an important departure from the Commission's prior strategy aimed at a Directive eliminating the barriers for cross-border membership of pension funds.

Commissioner Bolkestein's Communication details the Commission's interpretation of how the EC treaty rules on the free movement of labor, capital and services apply with regard to cross-border pensions. It concludes that Member States are required to eliminate discrimination against occupational schemes established in other Member States, particularly with regard to tax treatment of contributions and benefits. It states explicitly that recourse to the ECJ will be sought if Member States maintain discriminatory provisions. This measure is designed to remove the fiscal obstacles to cross-border pensions and, together with the proposed Pension Fund Directive, allow a fully functioning single market for occupational pensions.

The Communication proposes to safeguard Member State tax revenues through automatic exchange of information between Member States on supplementary pensions. It also aims to cut through the differing tax treatments among Member States of pension contributions, investments and benefits by applying the EET system - Exempt contributions, Exempt investment income and capital gains of the pension institution and Taxed benefits. This EET approach is already in place in 10 Member States (while Denmark, Sweden and Italy use the ETT system - Exempt contributions, Taxed investment income and capital gains of the pension institution and Taxed benefits - and Germany and Luxembourg have the TEE system – Taxing the contributions and Exempting the pension institution and the benefits).

Finally, the Communication suggests a Pan–European Pension Institution (or PEPI) as an effective vehicle to establish tax-neutral cross-border pension funds. The PEPI closely resembles the structure proposed in September 2000 by the European Federation for Retirement Provision (EFRP), namely the European Institution for Occupational Retirement Provision (or EIORP). The PEPI/EIORP structure incorporates a single fund in one location but with the fund divided into individual sections, each corresponding to and complying with the national tax regimes where the individual scheme member is employed. If the member moved country with the same employer, contributions would be paid into the relevant new section, with benefits being paid at retirement from each national section in accordance with national rules. The Commission argues that this structure is flexible, widely applicable and could be implemented without new tax legislation. It has invited Member States to explore how such vehicles can be made operational.

Business Perspective

Commissioner Bolkestein's ambitious and innovative Communication has the potential to realize finally the pan-European pension fund that has long been sought by multinational employers in Europe. This realization would help such employers better deploy their most important resource: their human capital. It would enable them to meet their business priorities, which are increasingly being organized and addressed without regard to the hindrance of national borders. The cost savings and flexibility inherent in the Commissioner's proposals can make companies in Europe more efficient and competitive and, as a consequence, help protect employment in the EU. As a longer-term effect, it will add impetus to the first pillar pension reforms being implemented or complemented by many Member States, with beneficial consequences for European capital markets as Member States embrace funded provision for the retirement needs of their citizens.

Chapter V
Horizontal Issues & Institutional Affairs

THE EU COMMITTEE
OF THE AMERICAN CHAMBER OF COMMERCE IN BELGIUM

Horizontal Issues
1. Risk & its Analysis

Background

Risk assessment is already well established with respect to chemicals legislation and practice. There are, however, wider areas of policy where the process for analyzing what constitutes a risk has not evolved at an equal pace. This causes concern as public perceptions regarding health and consumer issues are changing and the end user is demanding ever more information about the products sold. Examples, such as the BSE crisis and the dioxin case in Belgium, have shown the negative Europe-wide implications caused by the failure of a Member State to respond to a potential health threat. However, it is equally important to avoid publishing uncertain information about unproven potential risks, which might have repercussions across the EU.

The Commission, as the initiator of legislation at EU level, has necessarily become involved in finding an acceptable compromise. Whilst accepting *inter alia* that this problem can be reduced by basing policy decisions on sound science, Commission Services (the Health and Consumer Protection Directorate General is taking the lead on the initiative, together with the Enterprise, Environment and Agriculture Directorates General) are also involved in targeted risk assessment and technical review of risk assessments in wider areas such as food and health policy. The Commission is in the process of investigating how different sectors review risk and how risk assessment can be made more coherent and transparent. It is clear that heightened consumer awareness together with the apparent need for action at EU level means that the analysis of risk warrants attention.

On October 26-27, 2000 the Community's Scientific Steering Committee's Working Group produced a report on harmonization of risk assessment procedures in the scientific committees.

Risk assessment is a science-based process for the comprehensive evaluation of research data and other information regarding the likelihood that adverse health or environmental effects will result from exposure to an identified hazard, and typically comprises four steps:

- hazard identification of the adverse effects which a substance or preparation can cause;
- hazard characterization - typically a dose-response assessment to estimate the relationship between exposure and the incidence and severity of effects;
- exposure assessment - to identify the source and likely exposure to the hazard; and
- risk characterization - an estimate of the incidence and severity of any adverse effects likely to result from actual or predicted exposure.

The report on the Harmonization of Risk Assessment Procedures consists of two parts. Part one (166 pages) comprises a main report, a list of references and membership of the Working Party and its working groups. Part 2 (265 pages) comprises 8 appendices: Glossary of terms; Report on exposure assessment; Report on quantitative risk assessment of chemicals in relation to human heath; Report on quantitative microbiological risk assessment for food and other contaminated products; Report on quantitative microbiological risk assessment for infectious diseases; Report on presentation of risk assessment findings; Legal framework for risk assessment activities for new and existing chemicals; and Mandate of the Scientific Advisory Committees.

The Scientific Steering Committee (SSC) looked at the potential benefits of the progressive harmonization of human and environmental risk assessment procedures and produced a number of provisional recommendations, which will be implemented in a timely manner.

Furthermore the SSC established an Inter-Committee Task Force which is composed of one member from each Scientific Committee plus several members of the SSC. The Task Force will be charged to promote the harmonization of risk assessment procedures across the EC Scientific Committees, while taking account of other international and national developments. The SSC agreed that the remit of the Inter-Committee Task Force should include the following, as early activities:

- suggestion for adoption of a common glossary of terms. Specifically, suggestions should be made for a common language to describe different degrees of risk and to take account of the uncertainties in risk characterization;
- scientific watch on, and review of, the advances in risk assessment methodologies. In particular, the SSC stressed the need to make explicit, and contrast, the related activities in the different Scientific Committees; and

- explore the potential for harmonization of risk assessment between different categories of risk, ie, chemical, biological and physical.

At the meeting of the SSC in May 2001, the Inter-Committee Task Force will provide a progress report on Task Force activities concerning the Common format for opinions and the glossary of terms.

Risk assessment is but one step, however, in the much wider process of risk analysis. This is a process for identifying, classifying and prioritizing hazards to reflect their nature and magnitude, organizing appropriate risk assessments and communicating risk information to decision-makers. It consists of three elements:

- risk assessment;
- risk management - the process of identifying, evaluating selecting and implementing actions to reduce risk to human health and the environment; and
- risk communication - an activity which goes on throughout the whole process between stakeholders.

To be effective, however, risk analysis must be practiced in conjunction with the proper application of a number of appropriate principles. These are now being discussed and developed in a wide-ranging debate between regulators, industry and others concerned. Of particular importance are:

- sound science - an essential basis without which there can be no proper analysis and decision;
- transparency - of data, debate and decision, involving all stakeholders throughout the process and the need to listen as well as to communicate;
- functional separation of risk assessment and risk management - to maintain credibility and avoid the politicization of science;
- proportionality - a principle to be applied to the amount and scope of scientific data required and the action to be taken; and
- iteration - recognizing that as information and opinions move forward, the understanding of risk (and the action that needs to be taken to address that risk) will evolve and change.

The theory of risk analysis is, of course, only of value when applied in practice. An important application of the process emerged in the Commission White Paper on Food Safety (COM (99) 719 January 12, 2000). The paper pledges *inter alia* the creation of a European Food Authority (see page 27). The proposed authority will not have any powers of enforcement, but will assess risks and make recommendations to the Commission based on the assessment. The Commission should then act upon the recommendations when considering legislation, embargoes or other measures.

At the same time the Committee on General Principles in the Codex Alimentarius (organization tasked with advising governments on measures to protect the health of consumers) is revising its working principles for risk analysis. The principles are intended for application in the Codex framework as well as by governments where applicable. The objective of the Working Principles is to ensure that Codex standards and related texts intended to protect the health of consumers are based on risk analysis.

Due to discussion at the last meeting in April 2001 concerning the section dealing with precaution in the proposed draft principles of risk analysis and the proposal to convene a working group to deal with this issue, the Committee agreed to return the Draft for further comments and consideration. It will be discussed at the next session in April 2002.

Business Perspective

Business advocates a comprehensive approach to the analysis of risk, with clear distinctions drawn between the steps of risk assessment, risk management, and risk communication. It believes that there is a pre-step in the process that should take place even before the risk assessment stage and that this should be based on stakeholder involvement, openness and transparency. This approach is discussed in more detail in the EU Committee brochure 'Promoting Coherency' (available at the EU Committee's web site - http://www.eucommittee.be) and in its September 1999 Position Paper on the same subject. Industry welcomes the fact that this approach seems to have been followed by the Commission in its recent White Paper on Food Safety (see page 27). Business will follow the outcome of the discussion in the Codex Alimentarius and the application of risk analysis within the framework of the European Food Authority.

2. Public Procurement

Background

The public procurement market represents more than € 1000 billion annually (about 14% of EU GDP, or half that of Germany), and is therefore an area of vital importance to the EU. The Union's policy on public procurement aims to:

- create the necessary conditions of competition for the non-discriminatory award of public contracts;
- allow the rational allocation of public money through selection of the best tender;
- provide suppliers with access to a single market with significant business opportunities; and
- reinforce competition.

New global rules for procurement were agreed under the WTO Uruguay Round and incorporated into the Government Procurement Agreement (GPA) in 1994. These were subsequently incorporated into EU law through Directive 97/52/EC amending Directives 92/50/EEC (public service contracts), 93/36/EEC (supply contracts) and 93/37/EEC (work contracts) (OJ L 328 November 28, 1997). Directive 93/38/EEC relating to utilities including water, energy, transport and telecoms sectors (OJ L 101 April 1, 1998) was also amended.

In 1996, the Commission initiated a wide-ranging debate on the EU public procurement rules through its publication of a Green Paper on the issue. On the basis of the comments received from interested parties by the Green Paper, the Commission drew up a Communication in 1998, which outlined the key areas which needed addressing (COM (98) 143 March 11, 1998). The main themes identified in the Communication were the simplification of the existing legal framework and adaptation to the electronic age, better national implementation of public procurement legislation, and improved access to public procurement information.

Another aim in the Communication was to establish uniform rules for all types of concessions, as it had hitherto been unclear which EC rules applied in this field. Concessions, which are being increasingly used across the Member States, are specific types of public/private partnerships in which public authorities invite the private sector to perform public services. The key criterion for distinguishing between a concession and other forms of public/private partnership is the exploitation risk: in concessions, a public authority entrusts a third party with the overall or partial management of works or services which are normally the authority's responsibility and for which the third party in essence assumes the operating risk for economic activities (eg, for the operation of motorways or the supply of water). On the basis of the results obtained from a consultation process in 1999, the Commission adopted an interpretative Communication on concessions on April 12, 2000. The Communication contains a definition of concessions and sets out guidelines on how EU rules and principles are to apply in this area. Importantly, it confirms that EU rules on non-discrimination, equal treatment, transparency, mutual recognition and transparency apply to these types of partnership.

As a follow-up to the Communication, the Commission finally adopted a legislative package on May 10, 2000, aiming at capturing the necessary change and designed to simplify and modernize EU public procurement laws (COM (2000) 275 May 10, 2000). Under the proposals, the recently liberalized telecoms sector will no longer be covered by EU public procurement rules. Further sectors (eg, electricity, water) may also be excluded from the scope of public procurement legislation once they, too, have been fully liberalized.

Simplification of the legal framework is a key characteristic of the legislative package aimed at making the Directives more easily understandable for both purchasers and tenderers. The legal framework currently consists of six Directives. The Commission aims to clarify the existing rules for example by consolidating three of these Directives, on public supplies (93/36/EC), works (93/37/EC) and services (92/50/EEC), into a single coherent Directive. The new provisions and structure will be more user-friendly and will guide users though all stages of an award procedure.

Another key characteristic of the package is the empahasis on modernization and flexibility. The results of the consultation process showed a real need to modernize and enhance transparency of an out-dated award procedure. As a result, some of the provisions surrounding the award of tenders will be relaxed. The proposal introduces greater flexibility by providing for two new purchasing mechanisms:

Framework agreements - following the 1998 Communication the current proposal provides for the possibility for the contracting authority to conclude more flexible agreements for which not all conditions are fixed and on the basis of which contracts can be awarded without applying all the obligations of the Directive to each one.

Complex contracts - the Directive proposes greater flexibility for particularly complex contracts by the introduction of the negotiated procedure. A dialogue between the contracting authority and the tenderers will be permitted, which makes it possible for the contracting authority to not specify in advance what its requirements are. The discussion between the contracting authority and the tenderers concerning the contract would allow the authority to specify its needs. However, when using the negotiated procedure it is necessary that compliance with the principles of transparency and equality of treatment are not compromised.

In addition, the change in the provisions will allow public sector buyers more flexibility in defining the purpose of the contract when the public sector purchasers will be able to specify their requirements in terms of performance and not only in terms of standards.

Further adjustments are needed to keep up with the changing economic environment. Progress in information technology and the liberalization of telecommunications have opened up opportunities unavailable when public procurement rules were first drawn up 30 years ago. It also proposes to use information technologies to help the public authorities to adapt to the changing environment and to make procurement more effective. Public authorities are to make it easier for companies to gain access to procurement opportunities through the introduction of electronic procurement. The target of 25% of procurement actions to be carried out electronically by the year 2003 in the 1998 Communication is confirmed by the Commission's strategic *e*Europe initiative.

At the Lisbon Summit in March 2000, the EU heads of state and government declared the legislative package vital to economic growth, job creation and effective allocation of public resources in Europe and recommended its adoption and implementation by 2002. The political willingness for accomplishing this was shown by the endorsement of the Lisbon Summit's declaration at the Stockholm Summit in March 2001. At present the Directive is awaiting a vote in the EP plenary.

However, despite rapid adoption and implementation another major problem which persists is the insufficient implementation of public procurement rules into national law. The twice yearly 'Single Market Scoreboard' assesses the application of single market rules in terms of implementation of directives, outstanding infringement procedures and progress in applying the 1997 Single Market Action Plan (CSE (97) 1 June 4, 1997). The May 2000 scoreboard (COM (2000) 257 May 3, 2000) shows that only around 63% of directives in this area have been correctly implemented by Member States so far.

Business Perspective

Most business concerns are well addressed by the legislative package. However, the translation of these measures into legal instruments has to be monitored closely. Particular attention should be paid to the following points: stability, transparency, implementation and electronic tendering. Regarding legal stability, only small changes should be made to the present procurement regime at this stage. Any big changes would result in uncertainty, which in turn would hinder the liberalization process.

Secondly, truly competitive conditions depend on the full transparency of the tendering procedures. Transparency would be achieved by an obligation to make public all elements of the elimination process, ie, the requirements, criteria and their respective priorities (before the start of the selection process), and how bidders met them (after the award of the contract).

Thirdly, all efforts to make the process more electronic are welcomed. Electronic tendering will provide channels for major improvements in access to tenders and in understanding their requirements. The question is how widely and how soon the contracting authorities will integrate these new management technologies. It would therefore be appropriate to put in place strong incentives to speed up the transition process.

Lastly, business should pay particular attention to the discussions concerning environmental and social criteria that would have to be fulfilled for them to be eligible to tender. The public procurement Directives are not the right place to pursue the environmental and social ambitions of the EU. Inclusion of these issues could distort competition and become a tool for discriminatory purchasing.

3. The Precautionary Principle

Background

The precautionary principle is being introduced into more and more sectoral legislative proposals. There are clear indications that the Commission is trying to establish the precautionary principle as an integral part of EU environmental, food and health policy.

The Commission's Communication on the use of the precautionary principle (COM (2000) 1 February 2, 2000), was published in response to food scares (such as BSE and dioxin), GMOs, phthalates in toys, etc, which had undermined consumer confidence. The Communication does not constitute binding legislation, but aims to establish guidelines for the application of the precautionary principle and to contribute to the ongoing debate on this issue at both EU and international level. The Communication states that the precautionary principle should be considered within a structured approach to risk analysis comprising of risk assessment, risk management and risk communication, and that it is particularly 'relevant' to risk management. According to the Communication, the precautionary principle, which is essentially used by decision-makers in the management of risk, should not be confused with the element of caution that scientists apply in their assessment of scientific data. The application of the precautionary principle would cover cases 'where scientific evidence is insufficient, inconclusive, uncertain, and preliminary scientific evaluation indicates that there are reasonable grounds for concern that the potentially dangerous effects on the environment, human, animal or plant health may be inconsistent with the high level of protection chosen by the EU'. To prevent unwarranted recourse to the precautionary principle as a disguised form of protectionism, the Communication states that measures based on the precautionary principle:

- must be proportionate to the chosen level of protection;
- must not discriminate;
- should be based on a cost-benefit analysis;
- should be subject to review in the light of new scientific data; and
- may assign responsibility (or the burden of proof) for producing the scientific evidence necessary for a comprehensive risk assessment.

The precautionary principle is not defined in the EC Treaty, but it is referred to in Article 174 EC which relates to the environment. Like other general notions, such as subsidiarity and proportionality, the Communication states that it is for the decision-makers and ultimately the courts to 'flesh out' the principle. The scope of the precautionary principle also depends on trends in case law, which to some degree may be influenced by prevailing social and political values. According to the Communication, the precautionary principle should not be considered a politicization of science, nor a form of disguised protectionism, nor acceptance of zero-risk, but provide a basis for action when science is unable to give a clear answer. Decision-makers need to be aware of the degree of uncertainty attached to the results of the evaluation of the available scientific information. Determining what is an 'acceptable' level of risk for society is a political responsibility. The Communication also refers to 'horizontal guidelines', which will be a 'useful tool in the future for taking political decisions'. They will contribute to 'legitimate decisions taken when science is unable to assess completely the risk rather than decisions based on irrational fears or perceptions'.

In its December 2000 plenary session, the European Parliament adopted a Resolution on this Communication welcoming the initiative and calling for clear and precise guidelines regarding the application of the principle. Moreover, the Resolution adopted at the Nice European Council in December 2000, calls on the Commission:

- to systematically apply its guidelines on the conditions for use of the precautionary principle, making allowance for the specific features of the various areas in which they may be implemented; and
- to incorporate the precautionary principle, wherever necessary, in drawing up its legislative proposals in all its actions.

The Council calls on the Member States and the Commission to attach particular importance to the development of scientific expertise and to the necessary institutional co-ordination, and to ensure that the precautionary principle is fully recognized in the relevant international fora (eg, the WTO). Member States are also urged to ensure that the public and the various parties involved are informed as fully as possible about the state of scientific knowledge, the issues at stake and the risks to which they are exposed.

Both the European Parliament and the Council requested the Commission to adopt specific guidelines on how the precautionary principle should be used. However, it is unlikely that the Commission will make any further changes to the guidelines included in the Communication in the short term, which implies that *de facto* the latter will form the 'horizontal' basis for the application of the principle. Examples of instances where the Precautionary Principle is explicitly referred to in the legislative text include the recent adoption of Directive 2001/18/EC amending Directive 90/220/EC on the deliberate release of genetically modified organisms (GMOs) into the environment and the proposal on general principles and requirements of food law and the establishment of the European Food Authority (COM (2000) 716 November 8, 2000). In addition, the European Parliament Committee on the Environment, Public Health and Consumer Policy also wishes to see reference made to the precautionary principle in the text of the General Product Safety Directive (see page 30), which is currently going through the adoption process. The EU defended the precautionary principle at the last meeting of the Codex Alimentarius Committee (see page 78) on General Principles in April 2001. During the debate, the United States, Canada, Australia and New Zealand, joined by developing countries delegations from Latin America, strongly opposed any mention of the precautionary principle in the draft text, even in a footnote. The US is particularly concerned with the potential use of the precautionary principle at the risk management stage and the fact that politicians could overrule findings of scientists, that a particular product or process is safe. There is a fear that this would open the door to arbitrary decisions and trade barriers.

Business Perspective

According to the Communication, the Commission envisages applying the Precautionary Principle not just to environmental, but also to human, animal and plant health issues in general. Consequently, the application of the precautionary principle is of importance to a wide range of industry sectors, including the chemical, agro-food, pharmaceutical and general consumer product sectors. The Communication introduces certain general concepts, which, if not addressed, could have negative implications for industry at large. The Communication mentions, for instance, that it would be up to decision-makers in situations of scientific uncertainty to determine the acceptable level of risk, taking into consideration public concern. Since any scientific risk assessment will necessarily involve some doubt or lack of evidence, this approach would result in great uncertainty for business and would be a disincentive for innovation. Due to the diverging views on the application of the precautionary approach between the EU and the US further trade disputes are likely to occur and could result, as has been observed in the past, in trade embargoes. It is therefore important that there is a common understanding between the US and the EU on the use of precaution.

Business recommends that the Commission establish a framework for risk analysis based on risk identification, risk analysis, risk management and risk communication. Business believes that many of the issues surrounding the application of the Precautionary Principle would be more easily resolved in the context of an established risk analysis process in which structured risk assessment, communication and stakeholder participation are integral elements from the beginning of the process.

Institutional Affairs
4. White Paper on Governance

Background

In February 2000, in response to consistent questions and concerns regarding the openness and legitimacy of the European integration process, the European Commission identified the promotion of new modes of governance as a key priority aimed at making European policy-making more transparent and democratic. As a result, the Commission began the process of preparing its White Paper on Governance to achieve the following four strategic objectives:

- promoting new forms of European governance;
- stabilizing Europe and boosting its voice in the world;
- moving towards a new economic and social agenda; and
- working to provide a better quality of life for all.

When finalized this White Paper will highlight ways to improve the exercise of powers and decision-making at European level, better taking into account the principle of subsidiarity and thereby changing the way the Commission and, in principle, the EU operates.

Since December 2000, this project has been given even greater importance due to the Intergovernmental Conference (IGC) in Nice. Nice left a considerable number of questions and issues regarding institutional reform unanswered. Instead, the Member States agreed to launch a large and in-depth debate on the future of the European Union with an eye on a new IGC planned for 2004. Thus, the importance of the Commission's White Paper on Governance has grown, with many viewing it as the necessary catalyst to kick-start the whole process of institutional reform. Though beginning in the EU institutions, this debate now involves representatives from national parliaments and public opinion at large, including decision makers, industry and civil society actors.

The final White Paper is not expected until late July 2001, however the Commission released a work program on October 11, 2000 (SEC (2000) 154/7), offering a general outline of the White Paper for the following six work areas of European governance.

Broadening and enriching the public debate on European matters.
As the Union has grown and integrated more deeply, decisions made in Brussels have had a far-reaching effect on European citizens, often without their awareness and understanding. The recent backlash against the WTO in Seattle and the IGC in Nice has demonstrated the danger of making political decisions behind closed doors. Therefore, the White Paper will address the problem of the EU's perceived democratic deficit and lack of transparency by bringing together all stakeholders (industry and representatives from civil society) and decision makers (national and EU level) so that citizens do not feel marginalized and powerless in decisions that will directly affect them.

Handling the process of producing and implementing Community rules.
Due to the growing and fast-changing needs of the Single Market due to new technologies (ie, IT and telecommunications) and the growing degree of competition through globalization, the Commission wants to move to more efficient rule-making. Traditional directives and regulations are not only cumbersome but also slow in development and implementation, often coming into force too late. This has led the Commission to explore alternative regulatory models (ie, co-regulation, self-regulation, etc.) that would be more flexible and timely than traditional regulations (see page 85). These rules must not only respect the principle of subsidiarity and proportionality, there must also be mechanisms that can objectively evaluate their effectiveness.

Improving the exercise of European executive responsibilities through decentralization.
Commission President Romano Prodi argued that "by demonstrating that it is possible to improve the service provided by the institutions, it will be easier to solicit citizens' support for further integration". To do this, the Commission believes it is necessary to introduce more decentralization, both horizontally (delegating technical tasks to agencies independent of the Commission at a pan-European level) and vertically (sharing more responsibilities with national, regional, and local authorities). Decentralization will allow more involvement by European citizens, thereby changing the perception of the EU as an unaccountable top-down institution.

Promoting coherence and co-operation within a 'networked' Europe.
Due to the success of the Single Market, Member States are becoming more interdependent and, therefore, should, according to the Commission, benefit from a 'convergence' of national and/or regional policies (even in areas where the Community has limited competency). While this co-ordination lies within the competencies of the Council of Ministers, the Commission has been given the mandate to prepare the ways and means to achieve the goals.

Strengthening Europe's contribution to world governance.
Recently, there has been a growing public backlash against globalization and free trade. These public demonstrations have been most visible in Seattle against the WTO, Quebec City against the Free Trade Area of the Americas (FTAA), and in Nice against the EU. Thus, there is a need to put European governance in a wider context so that the EU has the opportunity to lead the way in showing and promoting a 'better world governance in harmony with its own internal governance'. Consequently, as part of the White Paper on Governance, the Commission presented a Communication on a European Strategy of Sustainable Development in May 2001 (COM (2001) 264 May 15, 2001; see page 46).

Strengthening the integration and strategic dimension of policies across the continent.
In the context of the approaching enlargement of the EU, the Commission is calling for a more coherent and strategic *ex ante* redefinition of EU policies so that deeper integration can continue after enlargement. The governance debate therefore involves not only Member States but also applicant states as well.

The timetable of the White Paper on governance and the governance debate is as follows:

- presentation of the White Paper on Governance to the European Parliament in July 2001 (though this may be delayed till the autumn);
- organization of discussions in the Member States and the candidate countries before the end of 2001; and
- submission of a report on the results of the debate to the Laeken European Council in December 2001 under the Belgian Presidency.

The White Paper on Governance's objective is nothing less than a fundamental re-examination and debate surrounding the future of the EU. The White Paper on governance is the Commission's first step (and main contribution) towards a broad and fundamental overhaul and reform of the EU institutional system, from the democratic process at the EU level in Brussels all the way down to the regional and local level. Through this White Paper on Governance, the Commission is setting and preparing the tone and tenor of the debate concerning the EU's long-term future – a debate that will be concluded at the 2004 IGC.

Business Perspective

As is always the case regarding institutional reform, the impact of the White Paper on business will be indirect but nevertheless significant in the long term. The forthcoming reform to be concluded in 2004 could have an impact on the very nature of the EU, as the main issues to be considered (ie, status of the Charter of Fundamental Rights, a catalogue of competencies, the role of national parliaments) all involve a debate on the necessity of the drafting of a European Constitution.

However, paradoxically, the White Paper is being prepared by the Commission 'behind closed doors'. In this sense, much more work needs to be done by the Commission to involve relevant stakeholders from industry and civil society so that the debate and process can be as transparent, open and accountable as possible. Moreover, the institution seems to be struggling to keep the Paper focused given the range of issues to be addressed.

Business will continue to promote its position in what is already viewed as one of the first and most essential contributions to the debate on the future of the EU. The debate will be launched at the Laeken EU Summit in December 2001 and conclude with the 2004 IGC.

5. Alternative Regulatory Models (ARMs)

Background

In March 2000, the Lisbon Summit endorsed the Member States request that the Commission should bring forward 'a new integrated regulatory and simplification initiative'. This instruction underpinned the concept of 'Governance' announced by Commission President Romano Prodi, and formed the philosophical underpinning of the post-Amsterdam European Union. Against the backdrop of globalization, enlargement and the IGC, the Council has launched a search for new regulatory models in Community law. The quest is, however, equally driven by the demands of the digital economy and the need for more flexible and more inclusive methods of making rules. Furthermore, any future standards adopted are not likely to be introduced purely as a result of internal market motives, but in the pursuit of other Treaty goals such as consumer protection and sustainable development.

The October 1999 Internal Market Council invited the Commission to 'report to the Council on the action it has taken' to expand the role of standardization into new business areas. In both its public hearing on the Governance Debate (March 15, 2001) and its Communication on the review of the internal market strategy (COM (2000) 257 May 3, 2000) the Commission confirmed that its response to the Council would be delivered by June 2001 in a White Paper on Governance (though its release may be delayed to July 2001). Such an initiative would include 'consideration of alternatives to regulation, soft law, better regulation and the need for better public administration...'.

Allied to the search for a new regulatory process is the search for a different kind of regulation. Traditionally, the EU has regulated through directives and regulations on the one hand, and non-binding instruments such as recommendations and resolutions on the other. The traditional Community model involves the co-existence, rather than interdependence of self-regulation and legislation. This model is under scrutiny and is perceived as unwieldy, inflexible, and too slow, especially in response to the fast changing demands of the high-tech sectors (ie, e-commerce and mobile telephony). Complicated, controversial and time-consuming, directives must give way to leaner legislation which allows wider participation in rule-making (through mandated standards). In its place will be inclusive, consensus-driven alternative regulatory models (ARMs) whereby voluntary rules carry legal effect, effective enforcement and sanctions.

A wide range of alternative regulatory instruments currently exist, with co-regulation being one of the most prominent. Movement towards co-regulation comes in response to both the rejection of voluntary self-regulation as a 'legislative panacea' and to the perceived shortcomings of directives, which are considered difficult both to adopt and implement effectively. There are over 20 identifiable models of co-regulation with differing criteria and vocabulary. However, all contain similar aspects of self-regulation existing within a legal framework, a framework of compliance and enforcement, involvement of all relevant stakeholders, and representing a real and adequate alternative to traditional regulation.

However, it is becoming clear that one form of ARM will not suit all industries and sectors. The advertising industry, for example, has regulated itself very effectively to date using the self-regulatory model, whilst other industries have had limited success and have moved towards other models. Similarly several industries favor regulation by standardization, whilst others, such as the manufacturing industry rejects such a system. It is clear that these shortcomings can only be overcome if a fuller definition of co-regulatory terminology and procedure is accepted. Moreover, for understanding and consensus to be reached, the process must provide greater transparency and participation of all interested and relevant stakeholders from industry and civil society.

Business Perspective

Business welcomes the determination to promote a more flexible and enforceable Community regulatory environment. It shares the view that the prescriptive, command-and-control approach to Community law is not an appropriate response to the globalization of world economies, the enlargement of the Union, or the digital economy and is therefore not as likely to be able to protect consumers. Business strongly supports efforts directed at better law-making and responsible self-regulation. It also believes that these alternative regulatory models should incorporate the following principles of:

- improving the transparency and openness of the Community regulatory process;
- reinforcing the accountability and representativeness of all alternative regulatory fora;
- restating the essential democratic role fulfilled by each of the institutions;
- introducing an *ex-ante* regulatory impact assessment;
- ensuring their authority is drawn from a legal framework that adheres to the principles of proportionality and subsidiarity; and
- respecting international norms.

6. The Treaty of Nice

Background

The Intergovernmental Conference (IGC) that culminated in the Nice European Council (December 7-9, 2000) was made necessary by the failure of EU leaders to reach agreement in Amsterdam in 1997 on certain key points that needed to be addressed before the EU could accept the first candidate countries from Central and Eastern Europe. However, the ten months of negotiations during 2000 highlighted some deep and persisting divisions between Member States. At several points, the Nice summit appeared to risk failure, as the smaller Member States, led by Belgium and Portugal, struggled to preserve their influence in the face of pressure from the larger countries for a re-weighting of Council votes in their favor.

Yet, despite the tense and protracted negotiations and however imperfect the final Treaty, Nice can be considered a success in that it achieved its overriding aim of forging an agreement on the minimum reforms necessary to allow enlargement to proceed. The Nice Treaty was signed on February 26, 2001, and ought to enter into force by the end of 2002. It has been made clear that whilst a new IGC will take place and will conclude in 2004, this will not be a prerequisite to enlargement.

Several MEPs have expressed reservations about the agreement reached at Nice, in particular regarding the allocation of Council votes and EP seats to candidate countries. The Parliament's formal approval of the Treaty is not a legal requirement for its ratification. However, both Belgium and Italy have, in the past, said that they would not ratify a Treaty that had been rejected by the European Parliament. Considering the efforts made to reach a compromise, and the need to ratify the new Treaty as a precursor to enlargement, the pressure on Parliament to approve the Treaty will be immense.

The following key reforms were agreed at the Nice Summit:

Reform of the Commission

From 2005, each Member State will have just one Commissioner. Once the Union reaches 27 Member States, a system of rotation will be agreed upon and a permanent cap will be set on the number of Commissioners, which will fall below 27. The final number of Commissioners will therefore not be settled for several years. Members of the Commission, including the President, will be chosen by the Council by qualified majority vote. This is an important issue: in 1994, Jacques Santer was appointed when the UK vetoed the candidacy of Belgian Prime Minister Jean-Luc Dehaene. The President will also have increased powers, including the right to demand that individual Commissioners resign. Commissioners will work under the political guidance of the President, who may also reshuffle the allocation of portfolios during the lifetime of the Commission.

Extension of Qualified Majority Voting (QMV)

Agreement was reached in Nice on the extension of QMV to 39 areas currently subject to unanimity. However, not all of these will become subject to QMV upon its entry into force. Some areas will move to QMV only at a later date, and in some cases, only following a decision by the Council, acting unanimously.

Moreover, many of the areas that are to move to QMV are relatively trivial, whilst many important yet politically sensitive areas remain subject to unanimity.

Among the most important areas that will come under QMV are:

- certain aspects of immigration and asylum policy, as of 2004 (Article 67 EC);
- trade in services and commercial aspects of intellectual property, with the exception of trade in cultural and audiovisual services, education services, and social and human health services, which remain subject to unanimity (Article 133 EC);
- certain aspects of social policy (Article 137 and 144 EC);
- distribution of the structural funds, as of 2007. The current main beneficiaries thus retain their veto for the establishment of the budget for 2007-2013 (Article 161 EC);
- appointment of the CSFP High Representative/Secretary General of the Council and of the Deputy Secretary General (Article 207 EC); and
- appointment of the President and Members of the Commission (Article 214 EC).

Re-weighting of votes in the Council
The re-weighting of Council votes was the most controversial issue of the negotiations. Germany pressed hard to see its greater population reflected through a re-weighting of Council votes in its favor, a move strongly opposed by France. The final agreement saw parity retained between the big four Member States, although Germany is widely recognized as the main beneficiary of a new population clause. Essentially, the new system requires three conditions to be fulfilled for legislation to be adopted: a minimum number of votes, a minimum population threshold, and a minimum number of Member States.

As of January 1, 2005, 169 votes out of a total of 237 will be required to pass legislation. However, a Member State can also request verification that 62% of the EU's population is represented by those voting in favor. One of the main consequences of this clause is that Germany, acting together with two of the other big three Member States, will be able to block a proposal. The requirements of the third condition will change according to whether the legislation in question is a Commission proposal or a Member State initiative. For proposals presented by the Commission, at least half of the Member States must be in favor; while for other proposals, a majority of two-thirds is required.

When the Union reaches 27 Member States, the total number of votes in Council will be 345. The qualified majority required to pass legislation will rise to 258 votes, or 73.4% of the total. 91 votes will be required to form a blocking minority.

The new weighting of votes in a Union of 27 Member States will be as follows: France, Germany, UK and Italy – 29; Spain and Poland – 27; Romania – 14; the Netherlands – 13; Greece, the Czech Republic, Belgium, Hungary and Portugal – 12; Sweden, Bulgaria and Austria – 10; Slovakia, Denmark, Finland, Ireland and Lithuania – 7; Latvia, Slovenia, Estonia, Cyprus and Luxembourg – 4; and Malta – 3.

European Parliament
The European Parliament will be allowed to grow from 626 members today to a maximum of 732. The Amsterdam Treaty had foreseen a cap of 700. The Germans will retain 99 MEPs, while most other Member States will see their representation reduced (from 87 to 72 for France, Italy and the UK). The Czech Republic and Hungary may seek to renegotiate their allocation of seats in the Parliament prior to accession: they emerged from Nice with fewer seats than current Member States with similar population sizes.

It should be noted that both the allocation of seats in the Parliament and the re-weighting of votes in the Council have been settled with the aim of enabling the accession of the twelve candidate countries currently engaged in negotiations. The delicate solution agreed upon will have to be reopened to discussion if and when Turkey, or other Balkan States such as Croatia, begin accession negotiations.

Other developments at Nice
A number of other important reforms were also agreed upon at Nice. They include:

Enhanced Cooperation – This will allow groups of eight or more Member States to push ahead with closer integration in chosen areas (see page 88).

The Charter of Fundamental Rights - The Charter of Fundamental Rights was adopted as a non-legally binding political declaration by the President of the Council, the President of the Parliament and the President of the Commission. It is addressed to the institutions and bodies of the EU, and to the Member States only when they are acting in the field of Union law. The status of the Charter is to be reviewed during the next reform negotiations.

2004 IGC - The Member States have agreed to hold another IGC in 2004 under the German Presidency. This will consider a 'more specific determination of responsibilities' between the EU and the Member States, the status of the Charter of Fundamental Rights, the simplification of the Treaties 'without changing their meaning' and the 'role national Parliaments should play in the European architecture'.

Article 7 – A final important development at Nice was the change made to Article 7 of the EU Treaty, dealing with how to penalize a Member State that fails to observe the EU's fundamental rights.

Business Perspective

The reforms undertaken at Nice will have a broad and fundamental impact on the way business interacts with the EU. The Nice Treaty is by no means perfect, but it does remove the main institutional obstacles to enlargement, which can now take place on schedule. Business supports a rapid ratification of the Nice Treaty by Member States and looks forward to participating actively in a broad and inclusive debate on the future shape of the EU in the run-up to the next IGC in 2004.

7. Enhanced Cooperation

Background

The Treaty of Nice (see page 87) has revised the clauses, introduced by the Amsterdam Treaty allowing for a number of Member States to establish a special enhanced cooperation agreement between themselves in a given policy area. The possibility is provided for in both the EU Treaty (Articles 43-45 EU: general rules; and Article 40 EU: cooperation in criminal matters) and the EC Treaty (Article 11 EC). However, such cooperation must respect the EU institutions and procedures. The provisions on closer cooperation have so far not been used, mainly due to the strict conditions placed on entering into closer cooperation agreements as well as the veto right of each Member State to oppose their establishment.

The new provisions adopted at Nice extend the possibility for closer cooperation to matters relating to the common foreign and security policy (second pillar, see page 5) with the exception of those with defence implications. The Nice Treaty also abolishes the right of veto. A Member State opposing enhanced cooperation in a given area can raise the issue at European Council level but the final decision will nevertheless be taken by majority voting. Notwithstanding this, any enhanced cooperation must involve eight or more Member States in order to proceed.

Within the first pillar (EC Treaty) the Council, acting by qualified majority and following a proposal from the Commission, may decide to set up enhanced cooperation in a given area. If the subject of the cooperation is a matter dealt with by the co-decision procedure, the European Parliament must give its assent. In the third pillar (justice and home affairs; see page 6) the proposal may come either from the Commission or from at least eight Member States (if the Commission rejects the request to make a proposal). A decision in the Council is taken by qualified majority after consultation with the Parliament. In the second pillar (common foreign and security policy) the request to begin enhanced cooperation is made by one or several Member States to the Council, which then consults the Commission and informs the Parliament. The Council decides by qualified majority.

The Nice Treaty has not modified the strict pre-conditions for enhanced cooperation (Article 43 EU). Such cooperation should serve the objectives of the EU, respect the EU institutional framework and the *acquis communautaire*, should not undermine the internal market, EU regional aid policy nor EU competition rules. It should be open to all non-participating Member States. It should only be envisaged as a last resort, 'when it has been established within the Council that the objectives of such cooperation cannot be attained within a reasonable period of time' through regular decision making rules (new Article 43a added by Nice).

Business Perspective

If enhanced cooperation were to be introduced in matters relating to EC policies, there would clearly be a direct impact on business. The mechanism has been envisaged as a way of escaping deadlocks on legislation where unanimity remains the rule. Commissioners Wallström and Schreyer have thus stated that an energy tax could be introduced within the framework of enhanced cooperation as Spain continues to veto such current proposals. Other voices have suggested similar application in the field of social policy (eg, employees' rights) or the environment (eg, environmental liability). A study commissioned by the Austrian Government in 2000 concluded that the enhanced cooperation procedure could be used in environment policy especially in process-related legislation where the effect on the internal market is likely to be quite limited compared to product-related legislation. The Belgian Presidency is willing to launch the debate at the Council level on ecotaxes and energy taxation and in this context sees enhanced cooperation as an interesting option.

A survey conducted in 2000 by the Forward Studies Unit of the European Commission has shown that EU officials and MEPs do not see enhanced cooperation as a way of increasing the effectiveness of EU decision-making and fear that it could lead to the parcelling of important policy fields. The actual use of the provision in first pillar policies will very much depend on the interpretation given to the conditions. It will result from a trade-off between the potential negative effects of enhanced cooperation on the internal market and/or competition rules and the potential positive objectives of the cooperation. One key interpretation point will be whether enhanced cooperation can apply only to comprehensive policy areas or whether they can also be used for any individual proposals, as the two Commissioners seemed to suggest in the case of energy taxation. Another important aspect will be how the 'last resort' condition will be interpreted. Given the controversies likely to arise on the interpretation of the Treaty provisions, enhanced cooperation may become more of a bargaining tool in negotiations against obstruction from opposing Member States than an effective policy tool.

Chapter VI
Intellectual Property

THE EU COMMITTEE
OF THE AMERICAN CHAMBER OF COMMERCE IN BELGIUM

1. Copyright & Related Rights

Background

With the development of the information society, fears have grown that without adequate legal protection for works in digital form, the necessary investments in the development of new products and services will be jeopardized. As a result, efforts are being made to introduce a coherent regulatory framework to address the impact that new technologies are having on copyright and related rights. With the publication of a Green Paper on copyright and related rights in the information society (COM (95) 382 July 19, 1995), the Commission sought to ensure that an appropriate level of protection of intellectual property rights (IPRs) was applied in a non-material, digital environment, in order to facilitate the development of electronic commerce. Following a questionnaire and extensive consultation with industry the Commission decided to narrow its focus to four fundamental issues concerning online products and services: reproduction rights, communication to the public, distribution and circumvention of copy protection technologies.

These conclusions also formed the basis of the EU proposals for an international treaty designed to supplement the Berne Convention for the Protection of Literary and Artistic Works, last revised in 1971. The World Intellectual Property Organization (WIPO) Copyright Treaty, negotiated by over 150 countries, was completed in December 1996. It includes provisions regarding computer programs such as copyrightable subject matter, exclusive rights of communication to the public and distribution. It provides authors with a cause of action against unauthorized circumvention of technical protection and in addition the Treaty defines certain statements (the 'Agreed Statements') to assist in its application. Although the WIPO Copyright Treaty gained the EU's approval in Council Decision 2000/278/EC (and the WIPO Performances and Phonograms Treaty; OJ L 89 April 11, 2000) there exists to date just over half the ratifications necessary for the WIPO Treaty to take effect. Once at least 30 countries have acceded to it, the treaty will be important in confirming a substantive worldwide protection for works in digital form.

In line with the WIPO Treaty, the Commission put forward a proposal for a Directive to harmonize other aspects of copyright and related rights in the information society (COM (97) 628; OJ C 108 April 7, 1998). This proposal, which applies 'without prejudice' to the *acquis communautaire*, includes a broad definition of the reproduction right. The one mandatory exception is for temporary reproductions that are 'integral' to a technological process and have no separate economic significance. This exception, however, has been criticized as being unprecedented in any copyright legislation and unclear.

Other exceptions to this proposed Directive are included in an exhaustive list from which Member States can pick and choose. Amongst them are: the option of maintaining or introducing private copying exceptions in return for right-holder compensation; exclusive rights for the right-holder to make originals or copies of their works available to the public and, with Community-only exhaustion (ie, rights exhausted anywhere in the Community), to control any form of distribution of their works. Finally, it provides legal protection for anti-copying and rights management systems.

On the difficult issue of network operator and service provider liability, a separate Directive was adopted because this was a 'horizontal' internal market matter, applicable not just to copyright but to all types of user activities on the internet. The Directive, which covers the legal aspects of electronic commerce, was adopted in May 2000 (Directive 2000/31/EC; OJ L 178 May 4, 2000).

Following the first reading of the Copyright Directive in the European Parliament in February 1999, the Commission adopted many of the amendments put forward (see COM (99) 250 May 21, 1999). Substantive changes were made relating to private copying, including a fair compensation for right-holders (in such cases where exceptions could be granted), covering analogue as well as digital media, while leaving its implementation up to the Member States.

The common position of the Council of Ministers was adopted on September 28, 2000 and in the following October the Commission Communication gave its full approval to the Council's amendments of its proposal. In essence these amendments have created a broader definition of protected technologies, have heightened protection for private copying and include protection against the neutralization of technology, obliging Member States to provide appropriate legal protection against any attempt to by-pass technical provisions. Although these amendments increase the controls of right-holders, they are counter-balanced by exceptions, which benefit the rights of the beneficiaries (ie, the consumers or users of these copyrighted works), including the idea that Member States must ensure that it is feasible in practice for the beneficiaries to make such copies.

The second reading of the proposal in the European Parliament on February 14, 2001 saw the approval of a number of the Council's amendments, although there were also proposals for new amendments which would signal a return to greater protection for rightholders' rights. These new amendments sought to restrict the scope of those exceptions and limitations to the underlying principle of the Directive, that rightholders should enjoy exclusive rights to their works. For example, concerning the reproduction of works on any medium the Parliament wanted to see a clearer stipulation in the wording of the Directive that natural persons are acting for private use and not for ends that are either 'directly or indirectly commercial' (the Council's common position referred only to 'non-commercial ends' in general). Similarly, regarding the four areas in which reproduction is allowed (teaching, scientific research, criticism or review purposes) the Parliament stipulated that the source should be indicated 'except where it proves impossible' and not simply 'wherever possible'. The Parliament would also like to see the deadline for the Directive's entry into force reduced from 24 months to 18 months so that it coincides with the E-Commerce Directive (see page 65).

On April 9, 2001, the Council accepted the Parliament's second reading amendments and, therefore, the Directive was deemed to have been adopted. Member States have 18 months to transpose the Directive into national legislation.

Business Perspective

The proposed Directive represents a first step in granting the necessary copyright protection for works in digital form. It also provides for the legal protection of ad hoc technology, which allows the right-holders to identify and track usage, and discreetly license the exploitation of their works.

In an environment where creation (including production, access, distribution, use, and similar activities) will be facilitated, differences between Member States' laws could obstruct trade in goods and services hampering the EU vision of a single market. Moreover, technical developments in the information society will create ever increasing new business opportunities. Right-holders of copyrighted works circulated in digital, non-material form, must be protected against any misappropriation of their rights and any consequent decrease in the economic value of their works.

2. Counterfeiting & Piracy

Background

A major concern for manufacturers is that their products are imitated or copied, and that all the creative efforts and the substantial investments made in research and development or marketing are undermined. Counterfeiting and piracy are also causes of social problems, such as the exploitation of children as a cheap working force, the loss of jobs in companies and industrial concerns. Piracy reduces the incentive to innovate and create whilst also causing uncertainty for consumers. Pirated goods are normally of a lower standard and quality, therefore, damaging the commercial reputation of original manufacturers. These practices are often linked to organized crime. Furthermore, the distortions of trade and free competition which derive from these illegal practices and from the different levels of protection of intellectual property in the 15 Member States constitute an obstacle to Single Market objectives in the European Union.

Figures indicate that trade in counterfeit and pirate goods represent 5-7 % of world trade. It is estimated that businesses active in the EU are losing between € 400 million and € 800 million and up to 200,000 jobs have been lost as a result. European companies with international activities lose € 2,000 million outside the EU. Whilst in the past counterfeiting concerned mainly luxury goods, this now impacts on all sectors. 1999 figures show that the luxury trademark sector only represented 1% of counterfeited items seized. Counterfeiting and piracy account for the following percentages of trade in the single market: Data processing - 39%; Audio-visual sector - 16%; Textiles – 10-16%; Music - 10%; Vehicle spare parts – 5-10%; and Sport and leisure - 5-7%.

At an international level the agreement on Trade-Related Aspect of Intellectual Property Rights (TRIPS) Agreement, concluded within the framework of the World Trade Organization (WTO) sets out standards, measures for enforcement and dispute settlement procedures for breaches of intellectual property rights in several areas: copyright; trademarks; geographic indications; industrial designs; microchips; trade secrets; and test data. The implementation of such provisions varies depending on the country.

There have been several EU-level actions aimed at protecting original goods. At first, Community initiatives focused on the protection of its external frontiers from counterfeit goods originating from outside the EU. Regulation EC/3842/86, (OJ L 357, December 18, 1986), laid down measures to prohibit the release for free circulation of counterfeited goods. This Regulation was replaced by Regulation EC/3295/94 (OJ L 341, December 22, 1994) and modified in 1999. The text prohibits not only the entry into the Community and the release for free circulation, but also the export and re-export from the Community, and the placing under suspensive procedure or in a free zone or free warehouse of goods infringing certain intellectual property rights. The value of counterfeit goods seized by EU customs officers in 2000 was over € 1.6 billion. However, the Commission is not satisfied with the functioning of this mechanism, as few firms warn the authorities of their concerns about particular products or request action.

Within the EU, anti-counterfeiting measures were specifically mentioned in the Green Paper on innovation (COM (95) 688 December 20, 1995) and in the Commission's First Action Plan for Innovation in Europe, (COM (96) 589 November 20, 1996). Moreover, the Commission's Action Plan for the Single Market (CSE (97) 1 June 4, 1997) aimed at the effectiveness of legislation combating counterfeiting and piracy. The Amsterdam European Council of June 16, 1997 agreed on an Action Plan to combat organized crime and specifically called for Community provisions to strengthen the fight against commercial counterfeiting (OJ C 251 August 15, 1997). In spite of these efforts, the measures adopted to ensure the respect of intellectual property rights within the internal market applied only to specific sectors (trademarks, patents or copyright) and had a very limited scope.

In 1998, the Commission launched an EU-wide consultation through the Green Paper combating counterfeiting and piracy in the single market (COM (1998) 569 October 15, 1998). The purpose of this initiative was the assessment of the real economic impact of counterfeiting and piracy and the evaluation of the functioning of the existing mechanisms to combat them.

The Green Paper focused on four areas of future action:

- monitoring of market trends and suspect activities by professional associations or organizations;
- use of technical devices by the holders of intellectual property rights in order to protect and authenticate their products;
- harmonization of sanctions and means of enforcing intellectual property rights, and
- cooperation between the Member States' authorities and with the Commission.

The consultation was completed by a public hearing of all interested parties held in Munich on March 2/3 1999. A report on the responses to the Green Paper was presented in June 1999.

The consultation procedure led to the conclusion that counterfeiting and piracy were major problems in most economic and indutrial sectors in the single market. Therefore, the Commission announced a package of measures to strengthen the fight against counterfeiting and piracy as a follow-up to the Green Paper (COM (2000) 789, November 17, 2000). These measures included:

Urgent measures:

- proposal for a Directive harmonising the provisions of the Member States relating to enforcement of intellectual property rights. The proposal will include the right of professional bodies to take legal action to defend their collective interests, the possibility of closing down establishments and shops hosting acts of counterfeiting and piracy and of confiscating equipment;
- training and exchange of law enforcement officials on the basis of existing and future programs, and training and technical assistance to applicant countries;
- organization of public awareness and information campaigns;
- definition of a methodology for the collection, analysis and comparison of data on counterfeiting and piracy; and
- establishment of a contact-point at Commission level to interface between the various Commission departments concerned.

Medium-term activities:

- administrative cooperation between the Commission and national authorities;
- harmonisation of minimum thresholds for national criminal sanctions;
- extension of the powers of Europol for combating counterfeiting and piracy going beyond First Pillar matters; and
- improvement of access to information for business and associations through a web site through which legal decisions published in the Member States would be accessible to operators and to the law-enforcement authorities.

Other initiatives:

- improvement of cooperation between the private sector and public authorities;
- European judicial cooperation; and
- use of the possibilities afforded by the Fifth Research and Development Framework Program to develop new technologies and new technical devices.

The Commission refers to counterfeiting and piracy on the internet as a growing cause for concern and intends to monitor closely the developments in this field, as well as to introduce, if necessary, further initiatives in this sector as part of the implementation of the action plan. A recent example of legislation in this respect is the Copyright Directive adopted in April 2001 (see page 91).

As regards other initiatives, a Council Framework Decision on combating fraud and counterfeiting of non-cash means of payments is awaiting final signature as of June 2001. This instrument aims at ensuring that fraud and counterfeiting involving all forms of non-cash means of payment are recognized as criminal offences and are subject to effective, proportionate and dissuasive sanctions in all Member States.

Business Perspective

Counterfeiting is a major problem facing all sectors of industry. Business welcomes the EU initiatives, which have provided EU customs authorities since 1995 with legal instruments to intercept at EU borders goods suspected of being counterfeited. This has undeniably led to positive results: latest figures for optical discs (audio and video), for example, show that the number of intercepted articles increased from approximately 260,000 in 1999 to nearly 6,000,000 in 2000. However, the EU authorities will have to come up with rapid and concrete responses in order to resolve counterfeiting and piracy practices stemming from the following recent trends/circumstances:

- *counterfeiting and piracy on the internet* - the emergence of sophisticated technologies, easy to use for the purpose of copying products, is another reason for which counterfeiting and piracy have grown considerably. From a business perspective, this requires the EU to ensure that appropriate legislation will be adopted at both international and EU level; and
- *enlargement* - several EU businesses particularly suffer from counterfeiting and piracy actions carried out in Central and Eastern European countries. In view of EU enlargement, expected to take place in the near future, the EU must ensure that the *acquis communautaire* in the field of counterfeiting and piracy legislation will also be fully transposed and enforced in those countries.

3. Parallel Imports & the Exhaustion of Trademarks

Background

Under current EU law (Directive 89/104/EEC) and the well-established jurisprudence of the European Court of Justice, trademark owners can prevent the importation into the EEA (European Economic Area), and subsequent distribution of their products by third parties. In sum, they can prevent parallel importation. This prerogative of brand owners is however exhausted once they have themselves placed on the market or otherwise authorized others to place their products on the market anywhere in the EEA. Once they do this, third parties can freely re-sell the very same products whose distribution was carried out or authorized by the trade mark owner. Since this exhaustion rule applies to the EEA as a whole, it is also known as 'Community exhaustion' to differentiate it from national, regional or international exhaustion regimes that may apply elsewhere in the world.

In recent years, the idea of a possible change to a regime of international exhaustion has been explored in the EU. Such a change would in practice mean that the placing of a product by the trademark owner, or with his consent, on the market anywhere in the world would exhaust his rights within the EU as well, ie, he would no longer benefit from the Community exhaustion regime. In 1998, a study on 'The Economic Consequences of the Choice of Regime of Exhaustion in the Area of Trademarks', commissioned by the EU and carried out by the National Economic Research Associates (NERA), looked at the possible economic implications of such a change. On the most burning question, ie, whether a change in regime would bring down prices, the study unequivocally concluded that the price changes would be entirely negligible (from 0-2% if at all) and of limited duration. Additionally, it appeared that countries which previously applied international exhaustion did not experience an increase in prices with the change to the more limited and stringent regime of Community exhaustion. Following the release of the study and a hearing to consult with interested parties, the Commission released, in July 2000, a communiqué in which it expressed the view that the regime of Community exhaustion should not be changed mainly as it would not benefit consumers in terms of prices, it would limit choice, could deter investment in brands and related services in Europe. The discussion continues both at the level of the Council of Ministers (where Member States are split on the issue) and at the European Parliament level. A report is scheduled for debate and adoption by the Parliament in the near future.

Additionally, the European Court of Justice is due to decide the Davidoff, Levi and Tesco cases jointly in late 2001. The main issue at stake in those proceedings is the interpretation of what 'consent' by the trademark owner means and whether, for example, implicit or indirect consent is also included in that notion. The resolution of these cases is awaited with some trepidation by trademark owners since it may have an indirect impact on the practical application and usefulness of current rules on Community exhaustion.

Business Perspective

The exhaustion of intellectual property rights is of enormous importance to the large majority of intellectual property rights related business interests across Europe. Price discrimination and abusive practices are normally dealt with via competition rules. There is no doubt that the protection against parallel imports from outside the EEA is instrumental to an even more successful fight against counterfeiting. Finally, a unilateral change of regime by the EU *vis-à-vis* its main trading partners would have trade-related consequences which are perhaps better considered in the context of bilateral negotiations.

4. Community Design

Background

In all but three (the Benelux countries) Member States of the European Union, the protection of designs is still a matter for the relevant national law and is confined to the territory of the Member State concerned. Though national laws have to a great extent been harmonized through the Design Directive (98/71/EC), the lack of a Community-wide protection system for design seriously hampers the functioning of the internal market.

With its Proposal for a Council Regulation on Community design (COM (2000) 660; OJ C 67 March 1, 2001), which also incorporates the relevant provisions on substantive design law already captured by the Design Directive, the Commission aims to create a unitary design right. A design shall be protected by Community design legislation to the extent that it is new and has individual character. Once granted, such a design right shall be valid throughout the European Union.

The proposal suggests two forms of design-protection. The first is a short-term unregistered design and is meant for those sectors that produce large numbers of designs for products having a short market life where protection without the burden of registration formalities is an advantage and the duration of protection is of lesser significance. The second form of protection relates to the longer term registered design which will apply to those sectors of industry which value the advantages of registration for the greater legal certainty it provides and which require the possibility of a longer term of protection corresponding to the foreseeable market life of the products.

A registered design right will be obtained through one application made to the Office for Harmonization in the Internal Market – Trademarks and Designs (instituted by Council Regulation EC/40/94) in accordance with a single procedure.

The proposal remains prudent on one of the most debated issues over the last years, ie, the design protection of spare components of complex products (the so-called 'repair clause'). The Commission maintains its view that spare parts cannot enjoy Community design protection until a final solution has been reached in the framework of a consultation exercise on the issue carried out by the Commission pursuant to Article 18 of the Design Directive. The Commission aims at arriving at a voluntary agreement among the parties interested on the use of spare parts for repair purposes and on their protection. The Commission is flexible to adopt a solution along the lines of what the European Parliament has proposed, ie, to grant protection for spare parts of complex products as far as they are not used for repair purposes.

The Commission's proposal, which takes into account the opinion of the European Parliament in an amended version adopted on October 20, 2000, now awaits adoption by the Council which has to agree unanimously as the legal basis for the proposal has been changed from Article 95 EC (internal market) to 308 EC. Article 308 EC allows the Community to adopt measures in cases where the Treaty does not provide for a specific competence but where Community action furthers the objectives of the Treaty.

Business Perspective

The similarities between the Community Trade Mark system and the proposed Regulation on Community designs, are striking and will certainly bring along the same benefits to industry. The use of unified protection rules will allow a Community-wide protection for designs and thus provide companies with greater legal certainty in their cross-border operations.

Hopefully, the Commission's consultation will bring an end to a long but nevertheless interesting and useful debate on the repair clause and finally bring along legal certainty at Community level.

5. Community Patent

Background

On August 1, 2000 the European Commission presented a proposal for a Council Regulation on the Community patent (COM (2000) 412 Auguat 1, 2000). The proposal aims to simplify the quite complex institutional framework regarding patents in the European Union.

In the EU, patent protection is currently provided by two systems. Companies can either apply for a national patent or for a European patent. The filing of an application for a European patent is done with the European Patent Office, which is, together with the Administrative Council, one of the constituent bodies of the European Patent Organisation (EPO). The EPO was created through the Munich Convention (European Patent Convention or EPC) which is a conventional international law instrument. Membership of the EPC is broader than the 15 EU Member States. It includes Switzerland, Liechtenstein, Monaco, Cyprus and Turkey and will soon extend to several Central and Eastern European countries.

The draft Regulation, which is an EU legislative instrument, aims at introducing a Community patent. The objective is not to replace the existing national and European patent systems but to create a new unitary industrial property right which will produce the same effect throughout the EU territory and may be granted, transferred, declared invalid or allowed to lapse only in respect of the whole of the EU. The proposed system aims to be complementary to the EPO in the sense that an application will still need to be filed with the European Patent Office and in respect of the substantive rules of the EPC. The draft Regulation will govern the effects of the Community patent once granted. The draft proposal further deviates from the EPC on some very specific points: (i) the cost of a patent; (ii) the translations and (iii) the system of appeals to the courts of law.

Key issues in the proposals include:

Filing costs - according to the Commission, the cost of a European patent is three to five times higher than that of Japanese and US patents and thus constitutes a serious impediment for inventors to apply for a patent. The draft Regulation cannot influence the fee charged by the EPO for the examination of the patent application but it does propose to have further legislation adopted that will propose to lower the annual fees to be paid once the patent is granted.

Translation costs - the proposal further suggests to eliminate the requirement for a translation of a patent into all EU official languages. According to the proposal, a Community patent, once granted in one of the procedural languages of the EPO and published in that language, with a translation of the claim in the other two languages, would be valid without any further translation. A translation could become an issue in case of litigation: the proposal provides that a suspected infringer who has been unable to consult the text of the patent in the official language of the Member State in which he is domiciled is presumed not to have knowingly infringed the patent. If the presumption is not rebutted, damages shall only be due for the period from the time when the suspected infringer is notified of a translation in the official language of his Member State.

Judicial system - discussions have mainly concentrated on the need to have a centralized Community Intellectual Property Court that will examine questions concerning the validity and infringement of the Community patent. The Commission favors a centralized court because only such a system will provide inventors with Community-level legal certainty and thus encourage them to file for a Community patent. This two-tier court (ie, with chambers of first instance and of appeal) will consist of highly specialized judges and its aim will be to deliver judgements within a time frame of two years. Some Member States may insist on having national first instance courts and only a common appeal court. Such initiative risks putting the unitary nature of the Community patent at stake, however. The speediness of the process is considered crucial given the relatively short duration of patent protection and the rapid advance of technology. This proposed judicial system leaves the appeals procedure against decisions of the EPO unaffected.

Discussions about the judicial structure will need to be co-ordinated with parallel initiatives in the European Patent Convention (see page 101).

Given the significant link between the intergovernmental initiatives in the Munich Convention and the EU proposal, it is clear that a cooperation between both fora is imperative. The EPO currently does not have the power to grant a Community patent and the EPC needs to be amended for that purpose. Furthermore there is no doubt that an optimal symbiosis between the EU patent Regulation and the system provided for by the Munich Convention can only be achieved if the European Union accedes to the Munich Convention, so that the latter's substantial provisions form part of the EU legal order.

Such accession of the European Union to the EPC, however, has raised concerns. On the one hand, the Member States are concerned that the role of the national patent offices, in the case of the Regulation being adopted, is not sufficiently clear and might even be in danger, whilst on the other, non EU members of the EPC are reluctant to see the power of the EU within the EPO increased either through an additional vote or through the expected tendency for the EU Member States to vote as a bloc.

Views on accession to the Munich Convention have been reported to differ among EU Member States. As a consequence, there is no significant progress being made to the Commission's proposal on a Community patent. Some Member States have also voiced concerns about the language regime in the draft Regulation which would not take full account of the need to respect cultural diversity within the European Union.

Business Perspective

Business endorses the Commission's proposal. The initiative is welcomed as it will allow companies to benefit from the internal market and engage in innovation while being able to obtain patent protection at economically acceptable conditions. Business believes an appropriate balance is struck by, on the one hand, restricting the number of languages used in order for the patent to be valid while, on the other hand, maintaining the requirement of a translation into the language of a suspected infringer in specific circumstances so as to guarantee full legal protection.

The business community would welcome clarification on issues such as the need to have damages that, though not punitive, should be properly compensatory or on the circumstances in which an infringer is considered to understand the language of the Community patent. Business also considers that the language which allows for compulsory licensing in cases of anti-competitive behavior is too broad and should be restricted to those exceptional cases where the case law of both the European Court of Justice and the Commission have considered that compulsory licensing was an appropriate remedy to a violation of Article 82 EC (abuse of dominance). Business also asked for a clarification on the provisions of the draft proposal which deals with the relationship between the Community patent and national utility models.

6. Patentability of Computer-Implemented Inventions

Background

Article 27(1) of the Trade-Related Aspect of Intellectual Property (TRIPs) Agreement prescribes that patents shall be available for any inventions, whether products or processes, in all fields of technology, provided that they are new, involve an inventive step and are capable of industrial application. Current European Patent Office (EPO) and national patent office practice throughout Europe corresponds with this TRIPs obligation.

However, under Article 52(2) and (3) of the European Patent Convention (EPC, an instrument of conventional international law and not EU legislation), computer programs, as such, are excluded from patentability. The same provision has been reproduced in the patent laws of the EU Member States. In practice, however, both the national patent offices and the EPO have interpreted this provision in a way that has allowed thousands of patents to be granted for technical inventions using a computer program. This apparent contradiction between the text of the law and its practical application has given rise to legal uncertainty which, in its turn, had a negative impact on investment and innovation in the software sector and ultimately on the functioning of the internal market.

It is against this background that the European Commission launched its consultation process on October 19, 2000. The Commission's objective is to strike a right balance between promoting innovation through the possibility of obtaining patents for computer-implemented inventions, on the one hand, and ensuring adequate competition in the market place, on the other hand. To that end, the Commission was keen to obtain views from all interested parties as to whether harmonization of national patent laws on the issue would be desirable and, if so, at what level such harmonization should take place. In relation to the latter point, the Commission was specifically interested in being able to assess possible differences between the legal requirements between the United States and Europe, and more particularly on the patentability of business methods.

In order to facilitate the consultation process, the Commission issued a consultation document as a basis for discussion along with an independent study entitled 'The Economic Impact of Patentability of Computer Programs' that was made on the Commission's request. The Commission invited all interested parties to comment on the impact of harmonization of (i) innovation in software and underlying techniques and knowledge; (ii) the ability of SME's to enter the market of innovative software tools and services; (iii) the creation and dissemination of free/open source software; (iv) the position of European software industry in global competition; and (v) the general development of the information society.

The Commission is expected to issue a proposed Directive for consideration by the Council of Ministers and European Parliament before summer 2001.

The key elements for a harmonized approach addressed in the Commission's consultation document and on which comments were invited are:

- granting of patents for any inventions in all fields of technology, provided that they are new, involve an inventive step and are susceptible of industrial application. This assumes that a computer-implemented invention belongs to a field of technology because its purpose generally is to control the operation of a computer;
- involving an inventive step, a computer-implemented invention must make a technical contribution to the state of the art. A computer-implemented invention which merely automates a known process using well-known automation techniques will be obvious and not be considered to involve an inventive step; and
- determining the technical contribution, the invention must be assessed as a whole. It may consist of a mix of technical and non-technical features but in determining the technical contribution only the technical features are taken into account. Where the contribution lies merely in non-technical features, the invention will not be considered as involving an inventive step. Any approach adopted should prevent monopolies for business methods arising from patents with business applications in Europe.

The consultation process revealed that business interests and most significant players in the IT industry generally support EU action to harmonize national legislation in line with current EPO practice. They believe that patents will stimulate innovation by encouraging investment. Some members of the Open Source Community consider, however, that patents for computer-implemented inventions tend to stifle fair competition, hinder innovation and put SME's at a disadvantage compared to larger companies with more experience in managing patents. The Commission is now awaiting the final report summarizing all comments made during the consultation process before deciding whether to present a draft directive on the issue. Opinions in the Council are divided although it would seem that Member States are mostly concerned about the degree of harmonization than with the principle that harmonization is needed.

Business Perspective

Business supports the Commission's initiative to address the patentability of computer-implemented inventions. Patents are recognized as a significant incentive to research and development and consequent innovation in industry worldwide. In this context, a clarification on the ability to seek patent protection for software implemented inventions is very useful. Business does not believe that EU action to incorporate existing EPO practice and case law into national legislation would result in an extension of the scope of patentable subject matter in Europe particularly with respect to business methods.

In response to concerns that patentability of software related inventions might hinder the continued growth of open source software, business considers that this is not supported by the US experience. This is illustrated by the following:

- in the information technology field, patent activity has not stifled innovation and has been an incentive and reward for innovation;
- open source software has recently developed as a business model along with the traditional proprietary software model and products generated under this new model have generated a wide interest. US experience shows, however, that both models are able to co-exist leaving companies free to select one or the other, depending upon their business strategies; and
- US experience does not support the view that the granting of patents is to the disadvantage of SME's. On the contrary, new developments and breakthroughs in the information and communication technology field have been realized by smaller companies that have benefited from patents on their computer-implemented inventions.

7. Patent Litigation in Europe

Background

At present patents have to be enforced in the individual countries where they are registered. This is so whether the patents are granted on the basis of a national application procedure or the European Patent Office (EPO) application procedure. The process for litigating patents varies widely across Europe depending on the individual national legal systems. Therefore, for example, in Germany the issues of validity and infringement of the patent are tried separately, whereas the norm elsewhere is for the two issues to be tried together. The speed of litigation in different jurisdictions is also very different. The present system in Europe has inevitably led to a multiplicity of actions in important cases, and also the phenomenon of forum shopping.

There are two quite separate initiatives under consideration at present. The first is the reform of the European Patent Convention (EPC) under which European Patents (EPs) are granted - that is a modification of the existing system. The second is under the proposed Community Patent – ie, a new system for litigating the new right when it is created.

Reform under the EPC

The proposal for revision of the EPC is not an EU initiative, because the EPO is not an EU body, and the signatories to the EPC include not only the EU states, but also others such as Switzerland. However, the initiative is closely linked to the Community Patent proposals. It arose out of initial discussions at an Intergovernmental Conference of the European Patent Organization initiated by France and held in Paris in June 1999 aimed mainly at reducing the costs of obtaining EPs and streamlining procedures at the EPO. A mandate was given to a Working Party on Litigation (WPL) chaired jointly by Germany, Luxembourg and Switzerland to look at the three alternative improvements to the enforcement system, namely Arbitration, creation of a 'Common Entity', and an 'Optional Protocol' to the EPC.

The Arbitration proposal appears to have lost momentum. It was proposed that a new international arbitration system should be established for EPs. It is generally recognized, however, that patent cases are usually not well suited to arbitration, since the arbitrators can never have jurisdiction to revoke a patent held to be invalid. Moreover, the existing possibility of arbitration (eg, under WIPO) suggests that little is to be gained by creating a new system. It appears unlikely that this proposal will be pursued.

The Common Entity proposal contemplates that national courts will have the ability to refer a question of law to a central 'common entity' (latterly named the Facultative Advisory Council) which will give a ruling on the question. However, it is contemplated that the reference will be both optional and non-binding. Whilst therefore in principle such a regime ought to help standardize the interpretation of the EPC, it is in practice unlikely to be attractive. Nonetheless, under the optional protocol proposals outlined below, it is proposed that the second instance Court could also function as the common entity.

The optional protocol proposal contemplates that there would be created an optional protocol to the EPC. States could sign this optional protocol and cede their jurisdiction over patent matters to a single European Patent Court for litigating EPs. A sub-group led by Switzerland took the third proposal for a European Patent Litigation Protocol (EPLP) to the next stage and produced (in November 1999) a draft discussion paper.

This has now reached the stage where Jan Willems (formerly of The Hague High Court in the Netherlands, and now of the EPO Appeals Board) has produced a detailed draft proposal for an EPLP; and an alternative, less detailed proposal has been produced by Jürgen Schade and Jochen Pagenberg promulgating the preferred German position. The essential difference between these proposals is that the German proposal contemplates only a second instance (appellate) Court; whereas the Willems proposal also provides for a common first instance Court.

The Willems Proposal

Willems put out an initial document in November 2000, and followed this up with a very detailed draft in late February 2001. This was accompanied by a summary which includes a series of questions posed to the individual delegations of the WPL. The highlights of the proposal are as follows:

The European Patent Judiciary (EPJ) shall comprise a central Chamber with regional chambers. There are two possible alternatives as to how these might be organized, but these regional chambers "cannot just be national Courts acting as the European Patent Court of First Instance".

Subject to a transitional period of seven years, the Court will have exclusive jurisdiction. Hence member countries are being asked to cede their patent jurisdiction for EPs to the new Court.

The European Patent Court of First Instance will sit with three judges, whilst the appellate Court will sit with five judges. (The judges for the two Courts will be drawn from the same pool, however.) At least one judge will be a technical judge who will be qualified in one of four or five technical areas: chemical, physical, mechanical, electro-technical and/or software.

The European Patent Court of Second Instance will also function as the Facultative Advisory Council - the Common Entity.

Procedurally, infringement and validity issues will be heard together.

Cases at first instance will be divided into three phases: written, instruction and oral. The proposed system appears to take parts of many different national systems. Therefore it includes the use of a rapporteur who will also sit on the trial panel, and who will be a pro-active case manager. Evidence from witnesses of fact will generally not be cross-examined, but if the parties appoint experts, they must be subject to cross-examination. Alternatively (and this is preferred by Willems) the Court will appoint the expert after consultation with the parties, but take steps to ensure that this was not a source of excessive delay in the proceedings. Limited discovery/disclosure (termed production of documents) will be permitted. So too will inspections of processes and experiments in appropriate cases. Provisional injunctions will also be available.

There will be provision for the loser to pay a reasonable amount in respect of the winner's legal costs and Court and expert fees.

Cases at second instance will be based upon objections to the first instance decision with new facts/evidence being admitted only exceptionally.

These proposals may to some extent represent a political compromise designed to encourage participation in the EPLP. However, they may also represent a sensible way forward, with a real prospect of providing a viable regime to replace the present multiplicity of systems.

It is very unlikely that every country which is part of the EP system would sign up to this protocol. However, a number of countries (UK, The Netherlands, Sweden, Switzerland, Belgium, Denmark, and Luxembourg) are known to be in favor and negotiations are continuing.

The Community Patent Proposal

The Community Patent would require a new enforcement procedure (see page 97). This would be through a newly created tribunal affiliated to the European Court of Justice. Such a Court would consider issues of both validity and infringement and its decisions would apply throughout the EC. There may be pressure for national Courts to retain first instance jurisdiction, with only a common second instance/appeal Court. However, it is difficult to see how this could work in practice, since the Community Patent is intended to be a unitary right. Nonetheless, there may be a good case for the creation of national registries or 'chambers'. This, the procedures to be adopted by the Court, and other matters such as the extent of damages recoverable, will continue to be intense topics of debate.

The Commission wishes to put forward its draft Regulation for a Community patent, including a unitary litigation system before the next wave of Member States accedes possibly in 2002. It has arrangements in hand for the accession of the Community to the EPC as part of the 'second basket' of EPC revisions. The agreements reached at the Nice Summit have provided two possible legal bases for establishing a single Community Patents Court (first and second instance) having exclusive jurisdiction over Community patent cases.

Business Perspective

The present system of enforcing patents in Europe is unsatisfactory. Not only is the creation of a Community patent of great importance, but so too is the system of its enforcement. The system must permit an EU-wide decision to be obtained in a swift, consistent and cost-effective manner.

The Community patent system, even if implemented soon, will leave in place the existing national enforcement system for European patents which will be important to industry for at least the next 20 years. Therefore, the initiative under the EPC for an optional protocol to establish a single Court is also to be supported by business. However, it is important that these initiatives are co-ordinated in a way which has not occurred to date.

Chapter VII
Social Affairs

THE EU COMMITTEE
OF THE AMERICAN CHAMBER OF COMMERCE IN BELGIUM

1. Social Policy Agenda 2000-2005

Background

At the Nice Summit in December 2000, the EU's Social Policy Agenda for 2000-2005 was endorsed by EU heads of state and government. The Agenda sets out the Union's priorities in the social sphere, outlines a long-term program of action and establishes monitoring and follow-up procedures to ensure its implementation. The overarching aim is to strengthen the role of social policy as a productive factor of the European economy. First released in June 2000 (COM (2000) 379 June 28, 2000) the Agenda is the result of a wide-ranging informal consultation and was set the impressive aim 'to build within Europe a new, modern, active, social model'.

The Agenda follows a Commission Communication on 'Strategic Objectives 2000-2005: Shaping the New Europe' (COM (2000) 154 February 9, 2000) which was designed to help the Union to adapt to globalization and the evolving information society in order to remain competitive and to achieve the objective of long-term sustainable growth. The new opportunities arising from the adoption of the euro were also cited as reasons for more co-ordinated economic and employment policy objectives. The March 24-25, 2000 Lisbon Summit on economic reform, employment and social cohesion gave substance to this theme and set a strategic goal ('the way forward') for the next decade: 'to become the most competitive and dynamic knowledge-based economy in the world capable of sustainable economic growth with more and better jobs and greater social cohesion'. To achieve this goal the heads of state and government adopted a four-pronged strategy: preparing the transition to the knowledge-based economy and society by promoting the information society and R&D; promoting structural reform for competitiveness and innovation, completing the internal market; modernizing the European Social Model by investing in people and combating social exclusion; and maintaining a macroeconomics policy mix for sustainable growth.

This strategy aims to promote full employment with more opportunities for men and women, to reduce regional disparities and to achieve annual average economic growth of 3% of GDP. The European Council assumes the guiding strategic role in this process, with the support of the European Commission, and meets each spring to monitor progress and assign tasks.

Employment and Social Affairs Commissioner Anna Diamantopoulou responded to this mandate and drew up a Social Policy Agenda for the duration of the present Commission based on current and pending initiatives and proposals. It received visible support from the French Presidency in July 2000. The Agenda was the subject of an in-depth debate involving stakeholders from across Europe at a European Parliament-hosted conference on September 21-22, 2000. Participants contributed to the development of the Agenda, particularly in terms of emphasizing that any reform should endeavor to improve 'quality in all aspects of life': quality of work; quality of social policy; and quality of industrial relations. The Parliament's own Opinion was passed in September 2000.

The Agenda seeks to achieve the new strategic goals by following a program of actions in a range of areas:

- seeking full employment and quality of work;
- anticipating and managing change and adapting to the new working environment;
- exploiting the knowledge-based economy;
- promoting mobility (of the work-force and their families);
- modernizing and improving social protection;
- promoting social inclusion;
- addressing fundamental rights and discrimination;
- enhancing dialogue and industrial relations; and
- preparing for enlargement and promoting international cooperation.

It then specifies a number of proposals already in motion or planned for the near future by the Commission. The most important of these, classified here under general headings, include:

Employment in the knowledge-based economy

- improve the dialogue between the institutions and the Social Partners (employers' and employees' representatives) and input into the annual employment package (COM (2000) 78 March 1, 2000);
- invite the Social Partners to develop new forms of dialogue, particularly in relation to lifelong learning, opportunities in the information society and improved employment relations (COM (2000) 48 February 4, 2000);
- support the local and regional dimensions of employment strategy (COM (2000) 196 April 7, 2000);

- publish a communication on the social aspects of public procurement in 2001;
- follow up consultations on temporary work in 2001;
- publish a communication and undertake a conference on corporate social responsibility in 2001 (see page 107);
- complete and codify Community legislation on working time in 2002;
- codify and simplify health and safety legislation in 2002;
- adopt a Community strategy on health and safety at work in 2002;
- propose an instrument on transferability of supplementary pensions in 2002 (see page 72); and
- remove obstacles to the mobility of researchers, students, trainees, teachers and trainers (COM (2000) 723 November 11, 2000).

Reforming and modernizing social protection

- hold consultations aimed at integrating people excluded from the labor market (COM (2000) 308 June 16, 2000);
- review the impact of the European Social Fund in addressing regional disparities (COM (2000) 894 January 12, 2001) by 2003;
- propose an equal treatment directive in areas other than employment and occupation (COM (99) 564 December 21, 1999) by 2002;
- move forward the Communication on a barrier-free Europe for people with disabilities (COM (2000) 284 May 12, 2000) by 2003; and
- consult the Social Partners on data protection.

Quality in industrial relations

- launch a reflection group (in 2000) on the future of industrial relations;
- involve the Social Partners in determining possibilities for collective bargaining; and
- hold a review of the Social Dialogue (between the Social Partners) by 2002.

Enlargement and the international dimension

- monitor implementation of the social and employment *acquis communautaire* (ie, the existing body of EU legislation) by the candidate countries;
- allow for participation of the candidate countries in Community action programs as part of the pre-accession strategy;
- submit a proposal for a recommendation to ratify the ILO Convention on child labor in 2001; and
- promote the social dimension in EU external relations with a conference in 2001.

Finally, a systematic approach for monitoring and following up on the agenda's action points is foreseen. This includes new mechanisms for monitoring the implementation of the social and employment *acquis*, including a high-level working group of Commission and Member State officials and networks of national labor inspectors in the health and safety area. At the Nice summit the Commission was invited to present annually a scoreboard on implementing the Social Policy Agenda, the first of which was submitted to the Stockholm summit, March 23-24, 2001 (COM (2001) 104, February 22, 2001). The Commission will also undertake, in co-ordination with Member States, to improve the social and employment statistics on which to base indicators and benchmarks. All these initiatives will be used to contribute to regular monitoring and updating of the Agenda both before and after the planned mid-term review in 2003.

Business Perspective

Industry welcomes the Commission's social agenda for the next five years and recognizes the need to strengthen the role of social policy in the European economy. No company operating today can truly consider itself sustainable without incorporating social - in addition to economic and environmental - objectives into its overall business plan. Industry is encouraged to see the continued commitment to achieving a dynamic knowledge-based economy and supports any initiatives that help business and its employees adapt to the new working environment. Increasing the involvement of the Social Partners in this respect is important as the fast-paced new economy may require alternative solutions outside of the regulatory framework. Job creation is and should continue to be the number one objective in the EU. However, it is important to acknowledge that this will not be achieved through the imposition of rigid rules and regulations but rather by ensuring European business can compete effectively on the global stage while guaranteeing employee protection and operating in a socially conscious manner.

2. Corporate Social Responsibility (CSR)

Background

Corporate social responsibility (CSR) is understood here as all companies' activities beyond profit making, and includes employee relations, ethical manufacturing and trading, involvement in the local community and environmental protection. Companies increasingly define their ethical principles in corporate codes of conduct, which cover economic, environmental and social performance. This concept is commonly referred to as the 'Triple Bottom Line' approach.

Civil society (consumers, NGOs, governments) recognizes the growing impact of business on society and is increasing its expectations regarding companies' behavior and contributions toward society. According to a recent survey conducted by MORI, 70% of European consumers feel that a company's commitment to social responsibility is important when buying a product or service. The growth in socially responsible investment (SRI) in recent years demonstrates the increasing interest of investors in the nature of companies' investment activities. Widespread media coverage of the World Economic Forum in Davos and, in parallel, the World Social Forum in Porto Alegre in February 2001, which both focused on sustainable development, further illustrates this concern. There have been several global initiatives, notably the June 2000 International Code of Conduct for Multinational Companies agreed upon by OECD governments.

At the political level in the European Union, CSR is currently high on the agenda of the EU institutions:

- The Lisbon Strategy 2010 - at the Lisbon Summit in March 2000, European heads of state and government made a 'special appeal' to business, setting a strategic goal for 2010: "to become the most competitive and dynamic knowledge-based economy in the world capable of sustainable economic growth with more and better jobs and greater social cohesion".
- In March 2001, EU leaders held their first annualized Spring Summit focusing on the Lisbon Strategy. For the first time, CSR features in the conclusions as a means of modernizing the European Social Model, by directly improving the quality and quantity of employment.
- A sustainable development strategy, including an environmental dimension will be adopted as part of the Lisbon Strategy at the June 2001 Summit in Gothenburg. Progress on this front will be reviewed at the next Spring Summit in 2002.
- The Commission intends to present a Green Paper on CSR in June 2001. It hopes to encourage a wide exchange of ideas with a view to promoting future initiatives in this area. In May 2001, it hosted a review of the OECD guidelines and their meaning for multinational enterprises.
- The European Parliament has also been active in the past year, especially the Party of European Socialists Group (PES). Initially the focus was almost solely on human rights issues but is increasingly viewed from a wider angle. In November 2000, the Parliament set up a hearing on codes of conduct for multinationals, on the initiative of the UK Socialist Richard Howitt, MEP, the rapporteur of a 1999 Parliament Resolution on the issue (OJ C 104 April 14, 1999). In April 2001, the Parliament also organized its first Conference on Corporate Social Responsibility and Governance.
- To cap off developments in this field in 2001, the first European Presidency Conference on Corporate Social Responsibility is to be hosted by the Belgian Presidency of the EU, in November 2001. The Conference will also be part of the consultations on the Commission's Green Paper.

Business Perspective

European companies of all sizes, public or private, are recognizing the importance of their role in society and the need to develop, execute and communicate corporate responsibility strategies. They recognize that real bottom line benefits of adopting a proactive approach to corporate social responsibility can include: strengthening the brand, enhancing corporate reputation with customers and suppliers, and attracting and retaining a committed and skilled workforce. Consequently, a number of concrete business initiatives have been taken in this field. They include:

- In the above-described political context, and responding to the 'special appeal' made at Lisbon in 2000, European business leaders have joined together to promote the European Business Campaign 2005 for Sustainable Growth and Human Progress. The campaign aims to mobilize half a million business people on CSR by 2005. The Action Plan is to be launched in June 2001 at a Conference (Partnerships and Social Responsibility in the New Economy) taking place in Copenhagen.
- To respond to the rising demand for CSR information, five European and US-based organizations launched www.WorldCSR.com, a global information portal linking up the most experienced CSR resource centers currently available. The main resource for Europe is www.csreurope.org.

3. Mobility of Workers

Background

The mobility of workers in the European Union is extremely limited. On average, only 2% of the resident population in one EU Member State is from another. Mobility on an annual basis within the EU involves about 1.5 million people, most of whom are predominantly under 30 years and highly skilled. While Europe's many languages pose a natural barrier to mobility, the very different tax regulations and social security systems create additional major hurdles for people wanting to take up employment in another Member State. Third country nationals face even greater obstacles due to the non-transferability of many of their employment rights (eg, social security entitlements) from one EU Member State to another.

In February 2001 the European Commission launched a strategy paper on building new labor markets by 2005 (COM (2001) 116 February 28, 2001) that was approved by EU heads of state and government at the Stockholm Summit in March. The document puts forward a number of policies aimed at increasing the mobility of workers as well as increasing the overall level of skills, needed to make Europe 'the most competitive knowledge-based economy by 2010'.

Technological change and globalization, the need to improve the functioning of the European labor market and skills gaps form the bases of this Community initiative. Given the disparity between existing national policies, the Commission contends that only a policy at European level can lead to the expected positive results. Business leaders will be directly involved as a high level task force has been asked to come up with an implementation plan by the end of 2001.

A number of plans and actions are foreseen:

- a proposal by 2002 for a more uniform, transparent and flexible regime for the recognition of professional qualifications;
- facilitating the mutual recognition of skills acquired at work;
- preparing an action plan by March 2002 to ensure that lifelong learning becomes a reality for all citizens;
- implementation of the Commission's strategy to remove barriers on services;
- elimination of obstacles to the cross border provision of supplementary pensions (see page 72) including a proposal to deal with the obstacles caused by the tax system is expected in 2001;
- a proposal on the transferability of pensions between Member States before the end of 2001;
- creation of a one-stop European mobility information web site to provide comprehensive and easily accessible information on key aspects of jobs, mobility and learning opportunities in Europe;
- adoption of the pending proposals on the modernization of social security systems for migrant workers that are presently held up in the Council of Ministers and the European Parliament; and
- defining the criteria and the conditions under which third country nationals would be allowed to settle and work in any of the Member States. In principle, they should be accorded the same treatment as Community nationals. The Commission intends to try to get around the blockage in the Council on two proposed Directives on the detachment of third country nationals within the EU "so that additional guarantees of free movement can be obtained in 2002".

Business Perspective

The lack of harmonization of national regulations and of initiatives that facilitate access to employment poses a significant burden on companies operating across the EU. The divergent national social security systems and taxation systems, the lack of recognition of professional qualifications and the disparate treatment of extra-legal benefits like occupational pensions, make movement between subsidiaries throughout the EU a costly and, administratively, cumbersome exercise. It is more and more difficult for companies to offer an attractive package to employees whom they wish to relocate.

For many companies these constraints are compounded by the discrimination faced by third country nationals, particularly due to the non-transferability of their social security rights from one Member State to another.

While elimination of the obstacles to cross-border pensions provision is an important element for increased mobility, the associated tax issues should be tackled promptly.

4. Worker Information & Consultation

Background

The adaptability of employees to structural changes in the job market is a key element of the employment strategy adopted by the Luxembourg European Council in November 1997, the so-called 'Luxembourg Process'. This is intended to increase the flexibility of Europe's labor markets and ultimately reduce the high level of unemployment in the EU. The Commission maintains that this objective can be met most effectively if proper worker information and consultation takes place, allowing employees to "face and anticipate change as it confronts them".

Worker information and consultation has been an issue of some significance for the European Community since the 1970s. A 1975 Directive on the approximation of laws concerning collective redundancies (consolidated as Directive 98/59/EC; OJ L 225 August 12, 1998) and a 1977 Directive concerning employees' rights in the event of transfers of undertakings (last amended by Directive 98/50/EC; OJ L 201 July 17, 1998) laid down the basic principles for worker information and consultation.

In 2000/2001, three separate EU initiatives broached the issue of workers' rights to information and consultation: the ongoing negotiations for a European Company Statute (ECS); a 1998 proposal for a Directive on national worker information and consultation; and a possible review of the European Works Council (EWC) Directive.

European Company Statute

For more than 25 years, the Council has been unable to reach a common position on which approach should be taken over worker participation provisions in the proposals for a European Company Statute (ECS). These consist of a proposal for a Regulation establishing a statute for the future European company and a proposal for a Directive concerning employee participation in a European company, last revised in 1991 (COM (91) 174; OJ C 138 May 29, 1991). The essence of this problem has been that Member States with established and more extensive worker participation at board level (eg, Germany) fear that some companies might use the ECS to circumvent stricter, existing national rules in this area. Instead, these countries would prefer to see similar provisions imposed on companies intending to adopt the ECS.

There have been many attempts to break this deadlock. In November 1995, for example, the European Commission issued a Communication (COM (95) 547 November 14, 1995) which was intended to provide a basis for harmonizing Member State systems for worker information, consultation and participation. The Communication outlined three possible options: maintenance of a piecemeal approach with continued negotiations within the Council; a global approach by attempting to establish, at the EU level, a general framework for worker information and consultation; or immediate action on the ECS-related proposals.

As no immediate solution emerged based on the Communication, a high-level expert working group on worker involvement was established and chaired by former Industry Commissioner Etienne Davignon. In the Davignon report, published in May 1997, the Group rejected the theory that general harmonization of the rules relating to worker participation was possible. The Group put forward the pragmatic recommendation that the worker participation model be negotiated between employers and employees at the level of the European Company. The Group also suggested that a set of 'reference rules' should apply if negotiations were to fail, their key provision being a 20% minimum two-seat worker representation on the board, with full voting status and board responsibility.

In 1998, the UK Presidency of the EU put forward a compromise text based on the findings of the Davignon report and re-launched the ECS onto the Council's agenda.

The UK compromise seemingly struck the right balance among all the countries' perspectives: the future European Company will not be able to circumvent existing information and consultation arrangements in Member States (eg, Germany). It appeared that the only remaining item blocking a conclusion to the saga was Spain's unwillingness to accept that employee participation be introduced in European companies formed by merger, holdings, or subsidiaries, when such participation covers less than 50% of employees in the European companies' founding companies.

Surprisingly, at the Nice summit in December 2000 a compromise was reached by authorizing a Member State not to implement the Directive on participation in the case of a European Company created by a merger. But in that case, the European Company could be registered in that Member State only if an agreement was concluded or when no employees were covered by participation rules before the European Company was created.

At the time of writing, the agreement on the European Company Statute is expected to be formally adopted in summer 2001 with an obligation to transpose the Directive into national law by June 2004.

Under the proposed Directive on worker involvement, the creation of a European Company would require negotiations on the involvement of employees with a body representing all employees of the companies concerned. If it proved impossible to negotiate a mutually satisfactory arrangement then a set of standard principles, laid down in an annex to the Directive, would apply. Essentially these principles oblige European Company managers to provide regular reports on the basis of which there must be regular consultation of and information to a body representing the companies' employees. These reports must detail the companies' current and future business plans, production and sales levels, implications of these for the workforce, management changes, mergers, divestments, potential closures and layoffs.

In certain circumstances, where managers and employee representatives were unable to negotiate a mutually satisfactory agreement and where the companies involved in the creation of a European Company were previously covered by participation rules, a European Company would be obliged to apply standard principles on participation of its workers. This would be the case of a European Company created as a holding company or joint venture when a majority of the employees had the right, prior to its creation, to participate in company decisions.

In the case of a European Company created by a merger, the standard principles on participation of its workers would have to be applied when at least 25% of employees had the right to participate before the merger.

Directive on National Worker Information and Consultation

Renault's closure of its Vilvoorde car plant in Belgium in February 1997 put the Commission under substantial pressure to launch an EU initiative aimed at setting up some fundamental rules on information and consultation at national level. In the Vilvoorde case, the existing national framework for worker involvement was found to be ineffective or only superficially applied by management. As the Commission regarded the social dialogue to be a more appropriate vehicle for initiating this type of legislation, the Social Partners (representatives of employers' and employees' organizations) were encouraged to establish these rules themselves. Under the provisions of the Social Chapter of the EC Treaty, the Social Partners can initiate social policy proposals and directly influence the outcomes. In this case, the employers' representative, UNICE, indicated its unwillingness to be involved, claiming it would run counter to the principle of subsidiarity, infringe on managers' prerogatives and make European industry less flexible and less competitive.

As the Social Partners could not agree to negotiate on this issue in the context of the social dialogue, the Commission issued its own proposals for a Council Directive on a general framework for informing and consulting employees in the European Community in November 1998 (COM (98) 612; OJ C 2 January 2, 1999), which is intended to fill in the gaps in existing national and Community provisions, in particular the European Works Council Directive. The Commission contends that because of the rapidly changing environment in which enterprises operate, particularly regarding consumer tastes and new technologies, reinforcement of the social dimension of these changes is essential in creating an adaptable yet motivated workforce. The principle elements of the proposal are:

- employee threshold - application to companies with 50 or more workers;
- definition of information and consultation - the timing, content and method (all responsibilities of the company) must ensure its effectiveness;
- the right for workers to information and regular consultation on economic developments and strategies (information only), employment trends and work organization or contractual relations within the enterprise and on decisions affecting them in all Member States;
- Social Dialogue - the possibility for the Social Partners to negotiate an agreement with the authorization of the Member States; and
- sanctions - in the event of serious violations, sanctions would apply comprising the legal nullification of decisions, which have a direct consequence on contractual or labor relations, and financial compensation in the event of bankruptcy.

The proposals are intended to leave some scope for transposing the rules to existing national regulations without compromising them (apart from the UK and Ireland, all Member States have national legislation or binding collective agreements giving employee representatives information and consultation rights). The Commission originally proposed that the Directive would apply to companies employing 20 or more emloyees. However, this threshold was raised to 50, as it was feared that the previous threshold would prove particularly difficult to implement and enforce within small and medium-sized enterprises (SMEs). As they stand, the proposals would affect almost 50% of all workers in the EU and 3% of companies.

A common position was adopted on June 11, 2001. The proposal now goes to the Parliament for its second reading.

European Works Council Directive: Multinational Companies
The Directive on European Works Councils (EWC) (94/45/EEC; OJ L 254 September 30, 1994) was adopted, following numerous modifications, on September 22, 1994. The objective of the Directive is to improve employees' rights to information and consultation, solely with regard to transnational issues which affect employees in at least two Member States. This information may relate to the structure of the business, the economic and financial situation, future employment trends, new methods and organizational changes, relocations, mergers and redundancies. To achieve this goal, Directive 94/54/EEC specifies that formal negotiations for the establishment of a works council must occur if a request is made by more than 100 employees of a company which operates in at least two Member States. If management begins negotiations with employees, results must be achieved within three years of making the initial request.

The Directive took effect on September 22, 1996, prior to which companies were able to set up voluntary arrangements with their workforce. It applies only to undertakings or groups of undertakings with more than 1000 employees and at least 150 workers in each of two Member States. Over 600 multinational companies are known to have put such agreements in place. US and other multinational companies operating in more than one Member State in the Union must also comply with the provisions of the Directive. The Directive does not apply to merchant navy crews.

Although the EWC Directive required an operational review by the Commission before September 22, 1999, an April 2000 report on the implementation of the Directive (COM (2000) 188 April 4, 2000) indicates that "the review process will continue taking into consideration the debates in the Council and in the Parliament on the dossiers closely linked with the Directive (ie, the proposed Directive on national information and consultation and the proposed Directive on employee involvement in the future European Company). On the basis of the results of this review as well as on the basis of the evolution of the other dossiers, the Commission will at a given moment decide on the possible revision of the Directive".

Thus, any future amendments to the Directive depend on the willingness of the Commission to take the initiative, which could easily be affected not only by the outcome of the above-mentioned dossiers but also by any possible new 'Renault' cases that come into the public spotlight. Also here, with the emergence of many new cases of company restructurings, a review late 2001, early 2002 is not at all unlikely.

The following issues have emerged for consideration in a review of the EWC Directive: definition of information and consultation, training of EWC members, numbers of meetings, experts, composition of the Special Negotiating Body (SNB), improvement of the information flow between transnational and the national level and adaptation of EWC agreements to structural changes within the company.

Business Perspective

With regard to employee involvement, business believes that the autonomy of management and employees and their freedom to agree solutions that are best suited to their needs and interests must be respected. The imposition of mandatory structures for the negotiation of employee information, consultation and/or participation arrangements would threaten the voluntary approach which enables management and employees to find the most appropriate information, consultation and/or participation model in line with their specific culture and needs.

In relation to the future European Company, observers believe, in general, that there is still one particular element missing, namely more attractive tax treatment. Optimists believe that between now and June 2004, when such companies become operational, a lot of progress should and could still be made.

Chapter VIII
Taxation

THE EU COMMITTEE
OF THE AMERICAN CHAMBER OF COMMERCE IN BELGIUM

1. Direct Taxation - The Tax Package

Background

The so-called 'Tax Package' was first published in a 1997 Communication outlining a package of measures to tackle harmful tax competition (COM (97) 495 October 1, 1997). It established the framework for a code of conduct for business taxation, as well as calling for proposals for regulating the taxation of savings and a Directive exempting interest and royalty payments from withholding tax in certain well-defined circumstances. Endorsed by a Council Resolution of December 1, 1997 (OJ C 2 January 6, 1998), this was the first time since 1990 that a consensus was achieved in the area of direct taxation, especially covering such a broad spectrum of issues.

The background to this breakthrough can be found in the Commission's Action Plan for the Single Market of June 1997. It was at that point that so-called 'harmful' tax competition between Member States was identified as one of the key factors leading to market distortions within the EU. Effectively, the Commission argued that the increasing use of supposedly over-generous tax breaks offered by Member States to attract investment on the one hand, and the existence of tax loopholes on the other, had led to significant losses of tax revenue, a divergence of tax regimes and distortions in employment levels from one Member State to another. In order to compensate for tax losses on the 'mobile production factors' (of capital, energy and natural resources), Member States increasingly resorted to placing a higher tax burden on labor (both through individual income taxation and social security contributions), notably as labor is less mobile and therefore less responsive to tax differentials. Small and medium-sized firms (SMEs) - which tend to create jobs - were seen to have been hit especially hard. Former Internal Market Commissioner Mario Monti's aim in promoting the Tax Package was to reverse this trend and thereby ease unemployment while attempting to converge tax regimes.

The overall commitment of Member States to tackle the issue of harmful tax competition, and their belief in the indirect, yet clearly negative impact on employment was confirmed at the Employment Summit held in Luxembourg in November 1997. The resulting Employment Guidelines foresaw that every Member State should aim for a step-by-step reduction in overall taxation. Taxation is also recognized as an important impediment to building a single market for financial services by 2005, as foreseen in the Financial Services Action Plan (COM (99) 232 May 11, 1999; see page 59).

Overall agreement on the Tax Package has been held up for some time due to the controversy surrounding the imposition of a withholding tax on income derived from savings by non-residents in other Member States. The 'tentative understanding' reached by European leaders and finance ministers at the Feira Summit on June 19-20, 2000, establishes a timetable for the final adoption of the package by December 31, 2002 (see below).

Code of Conduct on Corporate Taxation

The so-called 'Code of Conduct', introduced in the Tax Package, was appended to the Council's conclusions of December 1, 1997 (OJ C 2 January 6, 1998) and, as such, although not a legally-binding instrument, represents a political commitment on the part of Member States to reduce corporate tax breaks offered as part of investment incentives. As a first step, the Council decided to immediately place a freeze on any new laws or administrative practices which lead to 'significantly' lower levels of taxation compared with the average tax rates of the Member State in question. Furthermore, a Business Taxation Group (since known after the name of its chairperson as the 'Primarolo Group') comprising Member State and Commission officials was established to identify those particular tax measures which are 'harmful' and incompatible with the aims and requirements of the single market (OJ C 99 April 1, 1998).

The extent and nature of the issues that the above-mentioned group considered go some way in explaining the obstacles facing the entire Tax Package. Sorting out 'harmful' from 'harmless' incentives, for example, implies cutting across the areas of regional policy, state aids and fiscal sovereignty. It included examining a host of tax and investment incentives, a list which was eventually pared down to 66 legislative measures.

At the time, the then Internal Market Commissioner, Mario Monti, expressed great concern over the 'beggar-thy-neighbor' approach taken by the Member States, which was distorting competition by offering investment incentives which they themselves could not afford in the long run and which not all Member States could offer. Such 'tax-poaching' was viewed as not only discriminating against other Member State investments, but also leading to significant losses of tax revenue which would otherwise permit Member States to comply with various Community objectives such as increasing the level of environmental standards, reducing budget deficits and lowering the tax burden on labor (especially on those less skilled and mobile employees). In other words, such tax breaks were viewed as using up scarce financial resources which could be better spent elsewhere. At the same time, they tended to create tax systems which were diverging rather than converging.

A first report from the Primarolo Group emerged shortly before the Vienna European Council in December 1998, and summarized various procedural aspects as well as the focus of the group's deliberations, notably on intra-group services, financial services, offshore companies, and other sector-specific measures. It also set out to define the concept of 'harmful' taxes using five criteria. Tax advantages would be deemed harmful if they (i) are open to non-residents or (ii) are based on transactions with non-residents but not residents, (iii) are granted where no real economic activity takes place, (iv) deviate from generally agreed rules on transfer pricing, or (v) are not sufficiently transparent. A second interim report was submitted to the Council in May 1999, and offered preliminary assessments of the effective level of taxation of the potentially harmful measures put forward in the first report. The second report also indicated a broad scope for future discussions given the very large number of additional measures put forward by various Member States (most notably, the Netherlands). Among the themes identified at the time were timing differences, the taxation of SMEs, shipping regimes, and regional development aids.

The Group was supposed to draft a final report in December 1999, but failed to overcome the reservations of some delegations. It therefore re-convened in February 2000, in order to continue to review the 66 measures considered harmful and determine if any more such schemes had been introduced by Member States in the interim (as, in fact, has occurred). The report was eventually released setting out the various measures, with some extensive explanation, but taking no formal decisions. Further work has continued through the spring of 2001, always outside of public view or direct comment. However, the outcome of these efforts will really depend on the resolution of the dispute over the taxation of savings.

Taxation of Savings

This proposal is specifically aimed at taxing the interest earned by individuals from savings held in Member States where they are not resident (COM (98) 295; OJ C 212 July 8, 1998). The first proposals for a common system of withholding tax on interest date back to 1989. The basic issue has not changed much since then. Countries such as Germany, Belgium and France are preoccupied by the transfer of capital to bank accounts in other Member States such as Luxembourg where there is low or no taxation on savings of non-residents as well as a strong commitment to banking secrecy, which then stands in the way of any exchange of information between the tax authorities of the countries involved. This has led to concern over potentially massive tax evasion on such income. Indeed, as the introduction of the euro has further reduced cross-border transaction costs, an even greater incentive exists to resort to this kind of tax evasion.

The proposal is based on Article 94 of the EC Treaty, which requires the consultation of the European Parliament and unanimity in the Council. Because of the singular interests involved (notably the implications for bank secrecy practices), the scope of the original proposal was kept as narrow as possible. Specifically, the objective is to hinder the extreme cases of tax evasion. As a first step, the Member States were to accept a so-called 'co-existence' model, implying that every Member State should either, at the very least, impose a minimum tax of 20% on non-resident savings, or disclose information on non-resident savings to other Member States. A combination of the two would also be possible.

Despite hopes that this would prove to be an acceptable compromise, the proposal ran into considerable difficulties. Financial institutions raised objections to the extra administrative costs that compliance with the proposed Directive would entail, claiming it would mean the loss of thousands of jobs in financial centers around Europe. The Commission responded that a withholding tax on interest paid to investors and administered by 'paying agents' (which pay interest to savers), or 'custodians' (which hold bonds for institutions), was chosen instead of levying a tax on bond-issuers, which was felt to be an even worse solution for the City of London's € 3 trillion annual 'eurobond' market, in particular.

The June 19-20, 2000 European Council in Feira, Portugal, issued a report on the Tax Package as part of its conclusions. The report signaled a turnaround when stating that an exchange of information, on as wide a basis as possible, shall be the ultimate objective of the EU in line with international developments.

The result was the political agreement reached at the Ecofin Council in November, 2000. The key parameters of the Savings Directive are now as follows:

- all Member States (except Austria, Belgium and Luxembourg) are to immediately introduce an information sharing system regarding savings income earned by non-residents;
- Austria, Belgium and Luxembourg will be permitted to impose withholding taxes for a transitional period of seven years, at a rate of 15% for the first three years and 20% for the last four; and
- during this period, 25% of the tax received may be kept by the Member State where the paying

agent resides, with the remaining 75% to be remitted to the Member State where the investor is resident.

The information exchange regime should be in place everywhere within five years of the adoption of the Directive (ie, by December 31, 2007) at the latest. Austria will be required to amend its Constitution in order to move in this direction (although as this will apply to non-resident savings only, it is thought that it should prove politically acceptable). The full implementation of this Directive will be subject to the EU reaching similar agreements with third countries such as Switzerland, Liechtenstein and the US.

Interest and Royalty Payments between Associated Companies in Different Member States
The predecessor to the proposed Council Directive on interest and royalty payments (COM (1998) 67; OJ C 123 April 22, 1998) was officially withdrawn in November 1994. As had been the case with the proposed Savings Directive, the vested interests of Member States such as Belgium, Greece and Portugal proved to be too great to overcome at the time. Accordingly, the business environment continued to embody obstacles to trans-border capital flows, including widely varying withholding tax exposure and the necessity to deal with complex and time-consuming withholding and refund procedures.

In the context of interest, for example, Germany, the Netherlands and Denmark do not withhold taxes on interest from cross-border inter-company loans, while other countries, including Italy, Belgium, Portugal and Greece continue to do so, being reluctant to surrender what they consider to be an appreciable source of tax revenue. Unfortunately, the administrative burden and inconvenience resulting from the withholding system (even where refunds are available) is detrimental to the smooth and efficient operation of group financing and/or licensing activities.

Indeed, the current system of dealing with withholding taxes, in general, is a patchwork of domestic legislation and bilateral income tax treaties. Thus, the Commission has long recognized that action was necessary on a Community-wide basis.

Other than extending the scope of companies covered by the Directive, there are few overall changes to the original proposal. The proposal applies to all 25% directly or indirectly related companies and permanent establishments (branches), while the original proposal applied only to dealings between parent companies and their 25% owned subsidiaries (see OJ C 53 February 28, 1991). The basic concept is that both interest and royalties paid within a qualifying group will be free from withholding tax entirely. It is hoped that the initial concerns of some Member States will be overcome, by linking passage with the Savings Directive and the introduction of specific measures to combat fraud and abuse. Greece and Portugal had most to lose economically, however, they would be allowed to defer implementation for a transitional period. The overall aim continues to be the elimination of all withholding taxes on intra-(qualifying) group interest and royalties. At a later stage, the Commission may even seek to extend the Directive to include transactions between non-associated companies.

Even if there is a broad consensus within the Council on the proposed Directive, adoption depends on resolution of the rest of the Tax Package as a whole, and in particular of the Savings Directive. The actual implementation of the latter remains problematic.

Business Perspective

After what was literally a five-year hiatus, there was once again movement and direction to the Commission's efforts in the area of direct taxation. This may result in opportunities as well as potential pitfalls for business. On the one hand, the business community can contribute to the development of a constructive EU-wide tax policy to foster growth, employment and investment. On the other hand, the Code of Conduct might dismantle the favorite tax loopholes of many multinational companies.

Since the Tax Package contains something for everyone, it will most likely either stand or fall (with nothing inbetween). On balance, however, it could prove to be a step in the right direction from a business point of view, at least in the long run.

2. Indirect Taxation
VAT Harmonization

Background

There has been little far-reaching progress on the Commission's plans to propose the definitive Value-Added Tax (VAT) system since its Work Program for a Common System of VAT in 1996. The program foresaw an end to the transitional period (in force since January 1993) and the move towards a harmonization of VAT regimes within the EU. At the heart of the 1996 initiative was the intent to create a user-friendly VAT system that would end the co-existence of 15 separate tax areas, reduce the possibility of fraud and reinforce the single market. This firstly involves switching VAT charges to where goods and services originate rather than where they are consumed, thus introducing a single place of taxation, deduction and VAT control. Secondly, it involves either the approximation of VAT rates (through the setting of limits between 15% and 25%) or the establishment of a single EU-wide VAT rate.

There remains, however, strong opposition to the Commission's plans from some Member States. The setting of national VAT rates is regarded as an important income source and as an instrument with which governments can influence the economy. There are fears at both ends of the VAT scale. For example, Nordic Member States are less in favor of the establishment of maximum VAT rates and fear a flight of companies to countries with lower charges. At the other extreme, countries like the UK would no longer be able to set rates below a 15% threshold.

The European authorities agree on the fact that taxation in the Member State of origin would considerably improve the VAT system currently applicable in the EU and, as a result, help prevent fraud. However, as stated above, the shift to a system of taxation in the country of origin requires the standardization of tax rates and national legislation, which cannot be expected in the short term. As a result, although it is not the Commission's intention to question the idea of a definitive system of taxation in the county of origin as a long-term objective, the Commission considers that the functioning of the current system of taxation in the country of consumption has to be improved in the short term.

Current proposals

The debate surrounding the implementation of a uniform tax rate and therefore of a definitive VAT system exemplified the potential blockages in this area. A VAT Committee staffed by national experts was established in 1977 as an advisory board on EC VAT issues. In September 1997, the Commission proposed changing its status to a regulatory body (COM (97) 325; OJ C 278 September 13, 1997). The aim of the proposal was to attribute binding force to the opinions of the VAT Committee, allowing the Commission to take measures required for the uniform application of the Sixth VAT Directive (77/388/EEC; OJ L 145 June 13, 1977) on standard rates of VAT, which are binding on Member States. This proposal, however, falls under the consultation procedure which sets no time limit for the Council to discuss an issue or make a decision, and as of mid-2001 it remained blocked within the Council. However, the proposal is mentioned as a priority in a Commission Communication on a new strategy to improve the functioning of the current VAT system (COM (2000) 348 June 7, 2000; hereafter 'the Communication'). The Communication focuses on the modernization, simplification and a more uniform application of the existing rules. Besides the modification of the status of the VAT Committee, the implementation of three other long-standing proposals are mentioned in the Communication as being priorities in a first phase.

A first proposal for a Directive concerns the existing procedure regarding the refund of VAT paid by operators in another Member State and involves amending Articles 17 and 22 of the Sixth VAT Directive and repealing the Eighth VAT Directive (COM (98) 377; OJ C 219 July 15, 1998). A second related proposal for a Directive, released simultaneously, involves improved mutual assistance in the recovery of claims, an essential element of administrative cooperation and one of the Commission's major concerns given its importance for a smoothly running VAT system. A last proposal for a Directive concerns the determination of the person liable for the payment of VAT (COM (98) 660; OJ C 409 December 30, 1998), which aims to reform the current expensive and complex system requiring VAT payers established in one Member State to appoint a VAT representative wherever they conduct operations. This last proposal became a Directive (2000/65/EC) on October 17, 2000.

According to the Directive, a VAT taxable person who is not established in a EU Member State where he is liable to pay VAT is no longer obliged to appoint a VAT representative. Member States may therefore impose directly on non-established persons the same obligations as those which apply to established persons (VAT returns etc.). However, Member States may allow a non-established person to appoint a VAT representative as the person liable to pay VAT. This option shall be subject to conditions and procedures to be laid down by each Member State. Where non-established persons are nationals of a non-EU country with which no legal instrument exists which organizes mutual assistance similar to that laid down within the EU, it will be possible for the Member States to continue to require such non-established VAT taxable persons to designate a VAT representative to be the person liable for VAT.

As can be seen, the Commission has made attempts to ease the administrative obligations borne by traders and has embodied its suggestions in proposals that are still, for some of them, on the negotiation table. The new strategy also emphasizes that these simplification measures are wholly consistent with the Commission's 1996 SLIM initiative. SLIM (Simpler Legislation for the Internal Market) is an ongoing simplification exercise intended to bring greater clarity and coherence to all EU legislation, which is being carried out in parallel with the progressive realization of the Commission's work program for a new common VAT system. The Communication then envisages a second phase where new proposals are to be adopted. The first of these concerns the VAT treatment of e-commerce and has since been introduced in June 2000 (COM (2000) 349 June 7, 2000). Under this proposal, all on-line transactions should be deemed services and should be taxed in the EU if they are consumed in the EU (see page 120).

On November 27, 2000, the Commission introduced a proposal amending the Sixth VAT Directive (77/388/EEC) with a view to simplifying, modernizing and harmonizing the conditions laid down for invoicing in respect of value added tax (COM (2000) 650 November 17, 2000). Following a European survey and consultation with EU companies and VAT experts, the Commission proposes harmonized rules on invoicing that should put an end to the differences between Member States regarding invoicing rules, on the one hand, and common rules on the conditions under which traders can use electronic invoices, on the other.

A proposal on the taxation of postal services should also be presented by the Commission, according to the Communication. At present, some Member States still exempt postal services while others subject them to VAT. This situation creates distortion and unfair competition between postal operators within the EU. Therefore, the Commission intends to propose the taxation of postal services in all Member States.

Last but not least, the Commission will propose improvements regarding mutual assistance and administrative cooperation in order to improve the means of combating fraud.

As a follow-up to the Communication, in 2001 the Commission should file a report regarding the proposals introduced as from 2000. Based on this report, the Commission will determine its priorities for the future (third phase). These priorities will depend on the progress made by the Council in adopting the proposals of the first and second phases. However, it is expected that these priorities will concern the VAT treatment of subsidies, financial and insurance services, the supply of goods which are installed or assembled, sales by means of distribution networks and distance sales, as well as the improvement of cooperation between VAT administrations and the modification of Article 9 of the Sixth VAT Directive concerning the place of supply of services.

In March 2000 the Council adopted Decision EC/2000/185 (OJ L 59 March 4, 2000) authorizing, for an experimental period, a reduced VAT rate on certain labor-intensive services, such as small repairs to bicycles, shoes, leather goods, clothes and home washing machines; the restoration and repair of private dwellings; the cleaning of windows and private dwellings; and home care services and hairdresser's services. According to the Decision, Member States are allowed to opt for a reduced VAT rate on two or three services among those listed above, for a period of three years. Nine Member States decided to apply a reduced VAT rate on labor intensive services: Belgium, Spain, France, Greece, Italy, Luxembourg, Portugal, the Netherlands and the United Kingdom. This is significant in that it is the first time that VAT reduction has been used to boost employment in the EU. Participating Member States are required to submit to the Commission an assessment of the measures on job creation before October 1, 2002. Based on these assessments, the Commission will then decide whether or not to propose making this regime permanent.

Business Perspective

The business sector welcomes all measures proposed by the Commission that aim at simplifying the overly complex transitional VAT system, its complexity being a source of costs, delays and legal uncertainty for the business sector. In particular, it welcomes the Directive on the person liable to pay VAT which in many cases will do away with the obligation for a foreign VAT taxpayer to appoint a VAT representative, as well as the proposals regarding harmonization of invoicing, the modification of the status of the VAT Committee and VAT reimbursement to non-established taxpayers. With respect to the latter proposal, its implementation will provide a major simplification for EU-based companies regarding deduction of input VAT in Member States where they do not have a VAT number. It will require a (bilateral) refund compensation system between the Member States and can be considered to constitute a first, modest attempt by the Commission to introduce some kind of a final 'origin' system. Needless to say, it is likely to be a major challenge to bring these proposals to a favorable conclusion, particularly given the apparent opposition of some Member States to the proposed changes.

3. Taxation of E-Commerce

Background

The rapid growth of the internet and its increasing use as a means of conducting commerce has provided huge new opportunities for business and consumers worldwide. The business community has quickly understood the potential of electronic commerce (see page 127). However, national legislators have been faced with new challenges, not least in the field of indirect taxation, and thus the taxation dimension of electronic commerce is becoming increasingly important. Electronic commerce can be categorized in two major ways:

- by intensity of internet usage in commercial transactions (ie, goods ordered electronically but delivered physically, or services and intangible products ordered and delivered electronically); or
- by type of customer (ie, business-to-business, or business-to-consumer).

The Commission has felt that electronic commerce – where the goods are delivered physically - does not pose any major tax problems and should therefore not be considered a priority tax issue. The issues become more complex in the case of services and intangibles, where the internet may come to replace some existing forms of retailing and traditional tax collection points. The concern here is not about tax collection but about competitive distortion.

A key problem for tax administrations will be how to collect indirect tax from suppliers who do not have a physical presence within the Member States but sell directly to end consumers.

In response to these challenges, the Commission formalized its views by publishing a Communication on electronic commerce and indirect taxation in 1998 (COM (98) 374 June 17, 1998). The main purpose of this paper was to define guidelines for taxation on which to base further debate on the issues with other interested parties. As such, the paper formed the basis of the EU contribution to the OECD's ministerial conference on electronic commerce, held in Ottawa in October 1998. In this paper, the Commission proposed a number of general guidelines, specifically on adapting the EU's value added tax (VAT) system, in order to provide simple rules both to meet the needs and support the development of e-commerce in Europe. Taken as a whole, the Commission's proposals hinge on four key principles:

- no new taxation regime should be introduced;
- all efforts should be concentrated on adapting existing taxes, and more specifically VAT, to the developments of e-commerce;
- all types of electronic transmission and all intangible products delivered by such means should be deemed (for the purposes of VAT) to be services; and
- the EU's VAT system must be tax neutral (ie, the tax should be levied on the basis of where supplies are consumed rather than where they are produced).

At the above-mentioned OECD conference, member governments supported an approach whereby the internet should be tax neutral and e-commerce should be subject to traditional taxation. This OECD agreement effectively rules out the introduction of so-called 'bit' taxes (this tax would take the form of a flat-rate levy on information flows over the internet). Following this broad agreement, detailed work has been ongoing under the auspices of the OECD through joint industry and government working groups called Technical Advisory Groups (TAGs). The TAGs deal with a number of direct and indirect taxation issues.

In early June 2000, the Commission published a proposal for a Directive amending the Sixth VAT Directive (77/388/EEC) on the VAT arrangements applicable to certain services supplied by electronic means (COM (2000) 349 June 7, 2000). The proposed Directive is intended to modernize legislation concerning VAT on electronically delivered services and entails extending VAT compliance to all suppliers of electronic services to EU end consumers. Digital products (eg, video, software, music, electronic games, information, teaching programs and web sites) downloaded over the internet and/or broadcasts transmitted by subscription, or 'pay-per-view' channels, would be subject to VAT. All third-country (ie, non-established) suppliers of such services, would be required to register for VAT compliance in one EU Member State and adhere to its particular VAT regime, provided that they meet a minimum level of € 100,000 in annual sales. The Commission's proposal would only apply to non-EU based suppliers whose sole activity in the Community involves the supply of services by electronic means. Also, VAT will not be raised on business-to-business transactions (ie, more than three-quarters of all e-commerce transactions) provided by non-EU based suppliers.

The Commission had hoped that the proposed Directive would create a 'level playing field' for EU and non-EU suppliers. Currently, EU-based companies are required to apply VAT on sales within the Community and also on supplies outside the Community. Non-established suppliers based outside the EU, are not liable to assess, collect and remit VAT in the EU.

For intra-Community trade in such services, the company receiving delivery will be liable in the case of business-to-business transactions while the service provider will be liable in cases of business-to-consumer transactions.

Member States have rejected the Commission's original proposal on the grounds that it would have encouraged foreign companies to register in Member States with low rates of VAT like Luxembourg (rate of 15%). Member States have insisted on a regime that would ensure that non-established suppliers charge the VAT of the end consumer's jurisdiction. On November 27, 2000 the Council requested that the Commission come back in June 2001 with an amended proposal. The Swedish Presidency and the Commission have been working on an amended proposal in the Financial Questions Group with a common position expected to be reached by the end of June, 2001. If unanimity is reached then certain technical and implementation issues will need to be addressed under the Belgian Presidency.

The Directive requires consultation of the Parliament and unanimity in the Council. It is accompanied by a proposal for a regulation amending Regulation EEC/218/92 on administrative cooperation in the field of indirect taxation, in order to meet the requirements of the proposed Directive.

Business Perspective

Business supports the taxation principles endorsed by OECD governments in Ottawa in 1998. However, the business community remains concerned that legislative amendments risk creating a reporting and compliance regime that would be burdensome, WTO-inconsistent and restrict the growth of electronic commerce.

Substantive concerns remain regarding the non-neutral VAT treatment on online and offline products that are similar. In addition, the business community is concerned about the potential burdensome verification processes that Member States might wish to impose on third country operators as regards consumer jurisdiction and status.

4. Taxation of Energy Products

Background

In 1992, the Commission presented a proposal for an EU-wide energy tax which suggested the harmonized introduction of a specific tax on carbon dioxide (CO_2) emissions and energy content in the Member States. This proposal was based on a Commission strategy to improve energy efficiency and to maintain 1990 CO_2 emission levels by the year 2000.

The proposal was highly controversial because, by definition, it hit some sectors and companies harder than others. Many argued that it also ran the risk of damaging European competitiveness *vis-à-vis* the rest of the world in the short term. It was doubtful that other industrialized countries would take similar steps to cut CO_2 emissions. Despite the strong support of some Member States such as the Netherlands, Luxembourg, Belgium, Denmark, Italy and Germany, the proposal became bogged down in technical difficulties and in political recriminations in the Council, where it requires unanimity for adoption, over operational aspects.

In 1994 the proposal for an EU measure was shelved in the short term but Member States could still take independent action. The Commission promised to present some general guidelines in order to enable Member States to introduce CO_2/energy taxes based on common parameters, while taking on board elements of flexibility designed to overcome the obstacles which emerged during the Council discussions.

The Commission's amended proposal (COM (95) 172 May 10, 1995) envisaged that the implementation of a harmonized EU-wide tax be preceded by a transitional period during which the Member States, while respecting a harmonized tax structure, are free to set tax rates product by product.

Recognizing that the debate on the introduction of a CO_2 tax was stalled, the Commission began to examine new approaches to energy taxation (the CO_2 tax proposal still remains blocked). In May 1997 it submitted a proposal for a Directive restructuring the Community framework for the taxation of energy products (OJ C 139 May 6, 1997). This proposal does not introduce a new taxation system as such, but extends existing excise duties on mineral fuels to coal, coke, lignite, bitumens (and their products), natural gas and electricity. For all these products except electricity, only uses as motor fuel or heating fuel are taxable. Uses as raw materials in chemical reductions or for electrolysis, however, are not taxed. For electricity, the proposal provides for the taxation of output at the final consumption stage. It also sets minimum tax rates, but allows Member States to impose higher rates for environmental reasons. In order to remain competitive, Member States implementing this tax regime are encouraged to reduce taxation on labor at the same time.

In April 1999, the Parliament adopted its opinion. While approving the broad thrust of the Commission's proposal, it proposed introducing a number of amendments. Among others were the move to the second stage of minimum rates of duties as of January 2000 and automatically increasing these annually by the inflation rate, plus a further 2% for five years. A number of exemptions for products which use renewable sources of energy and other environmentally-friendly practices, were also called for. In addition, the Parliament left open the possibility of exempting the public transport sector from the scope of the proposal.

The proposal remains blocked in the Council. The 1999 German Presidency was unable to reconcile the opposing logic of environmental concerns, expressed primarily by Nordic countries, and economic competitiveness, upheld by Spain, Greece, Ireland and Portugal. The suggested use of transitional periods and exemptions or reductions in the level of taxation on certain products (eg, gas and electricity for private consumption) or even zero-level taxation for coal and lignite have failed to bring about compromise. Spain, in particular, remains opposed to the proposal on macroeconomic grounds, believing it would lead to increased inflation and unemployment, and injure competitiveness. Further, proponents of the tax (eg, Germany, Scandinavia) are beginning to raise objections over the 'dilution' of the proposal. Successive Presidencies have failed to make headway.

In response to fears that the EU is over dependant on imports of energy products the Commission issued a Green Paper on November 29, 2000 (COM (2000) 769 November 29, 2001): 'Towards a European Strategy for the Security of Energy Supply', that links energy taxes to the greater use of renewables, (in order to reduce the EU's reliance on imports of fossil fuels), measures to reduce CO_2 emissions in the EU and proposals to redress the EU's dependence on oils. The Commission's hope is, amongst other things, that this paper will kick-start the debate on energy taxes previously blocked at Council level. At present, no minimum level of energy tax has been suggested, with discussions largely focussing on the definition of energy intensive businesses that may be disadvantaged in the world market if energy taxes were introduced, without an exemption or rebate for such industries.

Indications are that Spain, for example, is softening its opposition to an energy tax provided that measures are contemplated that would guarantee the functioning of the internal market in electricity.

Belgium, which takes over the EU presidency in July 2001, is working closely with Sweden on the new talks, and is expected to continue the push for an early accord.

Business Perspective

Energy costs in the EU are already higher than in other competing regions. With the present high energy prices any debate aimed at encouraging even higher prices seems unlikely. Business would have much preferred any initiative which supports the downward approximation of excise duties, with an upper limit to avoid cross-border trade distortions. Among the possible negative impacts, competitiveness will be adversely affected if no viable alternatives to road transport are available, and if energy intensive industries have to bear high taxes not borne by EU manufactureres. In addition, a further increase in tax will also increase the existing problem of fraud often triggered by high duty rates, with an additional lack of sufficient mutual assistance and cooperation.

Chapter IX
Telecommunications & Information Technology

THE EU COMMITTEE
OF THE AMERICAN CHAMBER OF COMMERCE IN BELGIUM

1. The eEurope Initiative

Background

According to the European Commission, the changes set in motion by the information society 'are the most significant since the industrial revolution' and will profoundly affect the way we live and work. The general feeling in industry and government circles has long been that Europe is lagging behind the US in exploiting the potential offered by this electronic revolution. The US has been more successful in using the new technologies to create jobs and spur economic growth, whereas Europe is seen to suffer from a lack of entrepreneurial culture and an insufficiently pro-active public sector. In order to counter the fact that the EU was trailing the US in terms of internet penetration, the Commission published a working document called '*e*Europe, An Information Society For All' in December 1999. This was then updated into an Action Plan presented at the Feira Summit on June 19-20, 2000 (COM (2000) 330 May 24, 2000). The Action Plan sets out a strategy to address key barriers to the uptake of the internet in Europe and to ensure that the conditions are set for a decisive move towards the so-called new, or knowledge-based, economy.

The original *e*Europe initiative presented in December 1999 had covered ten fields of action. Redefined in the light of the conclusions reached at the EU Summit in Lisbon last March, the new action plan's objectives are to:

- develop a cheaper, faster, more secure internet;
- invest in people's skills and access; and
- stimulate the use of the internet.

The Commission has set 2002 as the deadline for achieving these three objectives.

A cheaper, faster, more secure internet - this goal is to be attained through a new pro-competitive regulatory framework which reinforces competition and takes account of the increasing speed of developments in this sector (see page 129). Actions include the unbundling of the local loop (Regulation 2887/2000; OJ L 336, see page 136) and ensuring the availability of the necessary frequencies for multimedia wireless systems.

Investment is further required to develop a faster internet for research and students. Lastly, the Commission is currently preparing a Communication on how to promote technologies allowing secure electronic transactions.

Investing in people - despite millions of jobseekers, Europe is experiencing an acute shortage of IT professionals. The Commission would like both the Member States and the private sector to help all workers become digitally literate through life-long learning in order to equip them with the necessary skills to perform in the 'knowledge economy'. One proposal of the action plan is to establish a European certificate for basic information technology skills.

Stimulating internet use - consumer confidence is a key factor in the development of electronic commerce so the Commission is recommending several initiatives to boost consumer confidence in e-commerce in partnership with consumer groups, industry and Member States. This will involve promoting alternative dispute settlement, trust marks and effective codes of conduct by working with stakeholders to develop general principles and by creating appropriate incentives, as well as an 'online e-confidence forum' managed by the Commission. The Commission is also addressing the issue of computer-related crime, in its Communication adopted in January 2001 (COM (2000) 890, see page 134). Computer-related crime is proving to be one of the biggest disincentives for individuals going online. However, the business community is worried about the length of time that they may be required to store traffic data.

On November 29, 2000, the Commission adopted a Communication (COM (2000) 783 November 29, 2000) on the progress of the *e*Europe initiative ahead of the European Council of Nice, which took place on December 7-8, 2000. The Communication noted that the *e*Europe initiative has had a broad impact in the Member States at European level and beyond. The Commission also released results of its survey of internet use, showing a 55% growth in internet penetration in the last six months. These indicated that internet penetration in EU households rose from 18% in March to 28% in October.

On March 13, 2001, in the run-up to the Stockholm Summit of March 23-24, the Commission adopted a Communication entitled 'Impact and Priorities of the eEurope 2002 Initiative' (COM (2001) 140 March 13, 2001). The document consists of two parts: 1) benchmarking on the take-up; and 2) use of the internet and priorities for future action, as requested at the Nice Summit in December 2000.

In terms of benchmarking, the Communication states that internet penetration has grown rapidly in the EU, with the EU now having about as many internet users as the US. The Communication highlights that the reason for this increase is that a greater liberalized market has lead to cheaper prices for internet access. Furthermore, 80% of EU schools are now connected to the internet for educational purposes.

The report also proposes some concrete measures to meet the remaining challenges. Key amongst these is the need, in education, to shift to the classroom itself now that all Europeans schools are about to be connected to the internet. The Commission proposes a new target of one PC for every five pupils. Furthermore, teachers should be trained to use the internet, curricula must be adapted and Member States should upgrade internet access for schools to high bandwidth. More also needs to be done to improve internet security. Furthermore, the legal framework for e-commerce needs to be rapidly transposed to national laws, Europe's lead in mobile communication needs to be maintained and Internet Protocol Version 6 (Ipv6) should be implemented to support the growing demands on the network.

Promoting European Content

At present, most web sites can be found in the United States and are in English, and most internet traffic is conducted across the Atlantic. Of the 100 most frequently visited sites, 94 are physically located in the US. According to the Commission, the global content market is estimated to be worth € 412 billion and provides work for four million Europeans. Council Decision 2001/48/EC (OJ L14 January 18, 2001), creating a multi-annual Community program to stimulate the development and use of European digital content, aims at supporting the production, use and distribution of European digital content (e-content) on the global networks. The first call for proposals under this program was adopted by the Commission on March 15, 2001. A related action under the *e*Europe initiative has been the request by the Commission to create a '.eu domain name' in order to strengthen European identity on the net and boost electronic commerce (COM (2000) 827 December 12, 2000).

E-learning

In March 2001 the Commission launched its *e*-Learning Action Plan (COM (2001) 172 March 28, 2001). The purpose of this Action Plan, which covers the period 2001-2004, is to present ways and means of implementing the *e*-Learning initiative, adopted by the Commission in May 2000 (COM (2000) 318 May 24, 2000). The intention is to involve education and training players, as well as the relevant social, industrial and economic players, in order to make lifelong learning, which is seen as the driving force behind a cohesive and inclusive society, within a competitive economy. The Commission hopes that it will help promote the employability and adaptability objectives under the European Employment Strategy (put in place following the inclusion of an Employment Title in the Amsterdam Treaty), rectify the shortage of skills associated with new technologies and improve social inclusion.

Business Perspective

Business was pleased to see the European Union confronting the challenges of the new economy through such a comprehensive policy initiative as this one on *e*Europe. This approach recognizes the digital economy both as a catalyst to the further development of the single market and as an opportunity to remove certain market rigidities while facilitating further social cohesion within Europe.

Europe needs a well defined technology-policy vision. This document attempts, maybe for the first time, to address the problems related to the deployment of a fast, dependable and secure digital infrastructure, no longer in isolation, but in relation to what this infrastructure needs to deliver to business and citizens. Business also encourages that the Action Plan be followed-up by concrete actions.

Attempts to place further burdens on telecoms operators and Internet Service Providers (ISPs) through a widened scope of the ISDN Directive (see page 132); standardization initiatives in the areas of authentication and data protection; failure to simplify the indirect taxation rules and to apply them to e-commerce transactions in a fair and efficient way are all policy directions that will indeed result in an increase in the administrative requirements of companies and of the costs of doing business in Europe.

The Commission and the Member States should, on the contrary, show the political will necessary to act together, achieving compromises in areas traditionally blocked by political imperatives, and promote openness on issues that will determine Europe's success in the new economy. They should commit the necessary financial resources to achieve the targets, and maintain an open and transparent decision-making process. Europe must now build on its strengths and ensure that it is a leader in the digital age.

2. The Electronic Communications Package

Background

On July 12, 2000 the European Commission adopted a package of legislative proposals aimed at creating a new regulatory framework for electronic communications. The package includes a Framework Directive (COM (2000) 393 July 12, 2000) and four specific Directives on:

- universal service and user rights (COM (2000) 392 July 12, 2000) (see page 130);
- access and interconnection (COM (2000) 384 July 12, 2000) (see page 130);
- authorization (COM (2000) 386 July 12, 2000) (see page 131); and
- data protection in the electronic communications sector (COM (2000) 385 July 12, 2000) (see page 132).

The package is a result of the full liberalization of the telecommunications markets in almost all Member States since January 1, 1998. The aim of the new regulatory framework is to ensure that markets become and remain competitive for all electronic communication services in what is a rapidly evolving technological environment.

2.1 Framework

The proposed Directive for a Common Framework for Electronic Communications (COM (2000) 393 July 12, 2000) addresses the convergence of the telecommunications, media and information technology sectors. The framework is designed to regulate, under a single framework, all electronic transmission networks and services while leaving the regulation of content to other Community instruments. The regulation of consumer equipment used for digital television will be covered under this Directive, while all remaining terminal equipment considerations will be governed by the RTTE (Radio & Telecommunications Terminal Equipment) Directive 99/5/EC.

The framework proposal also grants the Commission the ability to co-ordinate Member State positions on radio spectrum for commercial and non-commercial use. It also allows secondary trading of spectrum under certain conditions while safeguarding public interest objectives and guarantees non-discriminatory treatment on use of rights of way to ensure fair competition. Expropriation of property, however, is not an element of this Directive.

World Trade Organization (WTO) commitments on standards and on a telecommunications regulatory framework are recognized within the proposed Directive. However, international standards may be derogated from, on whole or in part, in order to assert 'compliance with specified standards at Community level to ensure interoperability in the single European market.'

The framework proposal aims to reinterpret the definition of significant market power (SMP) in line with the concept of dominance within EU competition law. SMP, which is the threshold test for *ex ante* regulation, can be invoked where technical, economic and legal barriers exist as a basis of special or exclusive rights or where an operator is vertically integrated and competitors necessarily require access.

The draft guidelines contained in the proposal will be used by National Regulatory Authorities (NRAs) to measure where effective competition exists, as well as to assess a transition from the existing SMP definition to the newly defined concept of dominance. The guidelines will also address the issue of newly emerging markets where a market leader is likely to have substantial market share but should not be subject to inappropriate obligations. The definition of relevant product and service markets will identify the markets which will be subject to analysis by national regulatory authorities and obligations by operators.

Highlights from the proposed draft guidelines:

- the guidelines address market definitions, assessment of significant market power, SMP designation and procedural issues;
- the guidelines will be applied by NRAs in markets identified in Article 14 of the Framework Directive on relevant product and service markets susceptible to *ex ante* regulation;
- the guidelines are to ensure consistency of approach by NRAs, as reproduced in the annex to:

  a) identify geographical product and service markets as well as trans-European markets;

  b) identify relevant product and service markets other than those identified in the Commission decision, in agreement with the Commission;

  c) analyze the characteristics of competition in the markets in the Decision and NRA's national markets using the guidelines methodology; and

d) identify undertakings having significant market power;

- the guidelines call for companies to comply with the obligation to provide information for NRAs to determine SMP and relevant markets; and
- the guidelines will assist NRAs to deal with confidential material from undertakings (authorization Directive), national competition authorities, information provided by the Commission and cooperation between NRAs.

Business Perspective

The increased powers provided to NRAs in this package need to be counterbalanced with a harmonized approach in defining relevant markets and assigning obligations under the significant market power definition. Industry supports co-ordination by NRAs at the Community level with Commission oversight and believes that this will create the legal certainty needed.

It is foreseen that the adoption of the framework package comprising the five instruments including the proposed Framework Directive could occur in January 2002 or by April 2002 at the latest.

2.2 Universal Service & Users' Rights

The proposed revision of the Universal Service Directive (COM (2000) 392 July 12, 2000) consolidates existing texts in telecommunications regulation (eg, Council Resolution of February 7, 1994 on universal service principles in the telecommunications sector (OJ C48 February 16, 1994)). The preposal strengthens the Commission's intention to provide, on a European stage, good quality electronic communication services at affordable prices, effective competition, and user and consumer choice on a basic set of services. The main aims of the proposed Directive are:

- to adapt and modernize existing measures on universal service so as to define the scope of this service, the rights of users and the measures for compensating providers of the service without distorting competition;
- to create a process for reviewing the scope of universal service obligations;
- to lay down specific user and consumer rights where necessary;
- to carry forward current measures on, and ensure the availability of, leased lines in the EU until competition in these services develops;
- to allows NRAs to take measures on behalf of users and consumers; and
- to underpin industry's efforts to ensure interoperability of consumer digital television equipment.

The proposal's scope focuses on consumer requests for a single subscriber line connection (non-ISDN) to the public telephone network at a fixed location and access to services. The proposal guarantees that service shall be provided by at least one operator in a territory and include provision of initiation and reception of local, national and international telephone calls, faxes and data communications at data rates allowing internet access. No specific data or bit rate is prescribed.

Business Perspective

Universal service, which aims to provide a minimum set of services to ensure ubiquity, quality and affordability for all consumers, is an objective supported by industry. Industry believes that the scope and approach should acknowledge market conditions along with public interest objectives to ensure that the appropriate provisioning of these services is attained. All obligations should be subject to a comprehensive review as set out in the Framework Directive. Furthermore, in view of the pace of technological change and innovation, the scope of this proposal should be measured to reflect actual market supply. Lastly, business recommends that where wholesale prices are set at the appropriate levels, this will have a downward effect on the level of the retail price.

2.3 Access & Interconnection

Another element of the Commission's communications package is the proposal for an Access and Interconnection Directive (COM (2000) 384 July 12, 2000). The proposal builds on existing legislation in this field, namely the Interconnection Directive 97/33/EC (as amended by Directive 98/61/EC) and Recommendation 98/511/EC (as amended by Directive 2000/263/EC) on interconnection in a liberalized telecommunications market.

The Interconnection Directive aims to strike an appropriate balance between the rights and obligations of players in accordance with their relative positions in the market. It enables designated organizations providing publicly available telecommunications networks and services to have rights and obligations and thus to negotiate interconnection with each other, on a non-discriminatory basis, in order to ensure national and European-wide services. In addition, operators with significant market power (SMP) are assigned certain obligations, in particular to compensate for an imbalance in negotiating power with much smaller new market entrants. Obligations for SMP operators include requirements for non-discrimination, for publication of a reference interconnection offer, including interconnect price lists, for cost-oriented interconnection tariffs supported by transparent cost accounting systems, and for accounting separation in certain cases.

Recommendation 98/511/EC deals with: interconnection pricing (recommending the use of long run average incremental costs as the most appropriate basis for meeting the requirement in the Interconnection Directive for cost oriented interconnection charges); and with accounting separation and cost accounting systems (for implementation of interconnection obligations with particular regard to the principles of transparency and cost orientation).

The current proposal for a Directive will establish a new regulatory framework for dealing with issues of access to, and interconnection of, electronic communications networks in the EU. It also provides legal certainty for market players by establishing clear criteria for regulatory intervention and clear limitations on what obligations concerning access and interconnection can be imposed in which circumstances. Moreover, it will allow for sufficient flexibility to enable regulatory authorities to deal effectively with new market problems that hinder effective competition.

The proposal also aims to harmonize the way in which Member States regulate the market between suppliers of communications networks carrying publicly available communications services. In summary, the regulatory framework set out in the proposed Directive will be characterized by:

- priority given to full commercial negotiations between parties to agree on the terms and conditions for access and interconnection;
- a defined framework for NRAs to address issues of access and interconnection;
- continuity with the current regulatory framework, with obligations for NRAs to review and, when possible, roll back certain obligations on operators with SMP; and
- possibility for NRAs to intervene in order to address identified market failures, acting in accordance with the principles of transparency, objectivity and proportionality.

In its first reading on March 1, 2001 the European Parliament made several amendments to the proposed Directive. In essence, whilst the initial text of the Commission promoted commercial agreements between operators and was not obliging operators to negotiate, the Parliament suggests promoting the new entrants, specifically in the mobile market.

On April 5, 2001, the European Council reached a political agreement on its common position. The main problem related to this proposed Directive was the question of whether the Directive should regulate solely interconnection negotiations or whether it should also extend to negotiations covering access. The Council rejected all of the Parliament's amendments and will wait until the second reading (expected in September–October 2001) and conciliation in order to find a compromise. Therefore, final approval on this Directive should be expected in March–April 2002 with the Directive being implemented into national legislation by mid–2003.

Business Perspective

The main issues related to this proposed Directive concern the telecommunication operators (and specifically mobile operators due to the mobile virtual network operators' (MVNOs) dossier) and the audiovisual sector. It is important for industry to consider the possibility of intervening in the legislative procedure because this proposed Directive represents the regulatory framework that will be valid in all the EU Member States from 2003 to 2008.

2.4 Authorization of Networks & Services

The proposal for a Directive on the authorization of electronic communications networks and services (COM (2000) 386 July 12, 2000) is intended to replace the current Directive 97/13/EC (OJ L 117; May 7, 1997) on authorizations and licenses. The aim of the new proposal presented by the European Commission is to simplify procedures for seeking authorizations by doing away with information requirements and by curtailing the scope of conformity controls.

The current legislation defines a regulatory framework for the procedures for granting authorizations to provide telecommunications services and the conditions attached to such authorizations. Two types of authorizations have been established by the EU institutions: general authorizations that allow undertakings to provide telecommunications services, with a Member State required to allow any undertaking meeting the relevant conditions laid down in a general authorization to provide the telecommunications service in question; and individual licenses that give undertakings operating under a general authorization specific rights or subject their operations to specific obligations.

The European authorization regime provides appropriate means to supervise access to the market and to monitor compliance with the requirements that are imposed on operators. At the same time, the development of competition will be served best by authorization regimes which do not impose undue burdens on operators, whether through conditions or through procedures. The key elements of the current Directive are the prohibition of any limitation in the number of new entrants (except to the extent required to ensure an efficient use of radio frequencies), priority given to general authorizations (NRAs) as opposed to individual licenses, the definition of harmonized principles, and the establishment of a one-stop shopping procedure to facilitate simultaneous applications for, and granting of, licenses in several Member States. The Commission has granted a mandate to the European Conference Postal and Telecommunications Administrations (CEPT) to put this procedure into place in the upcoming years.

The new proposal (COM (2000) 386 July 12, 2000) pushes for a significant further harmonization and simplification of national authorization rules and general authorization. The proposal:

- intends to cover all electronic communication services and networks under a general authorization and to limit the use of specific rights to the assignment of radio frequencies and numbers only;
- aims to ensure that no information is required as a prior condition for market entry and that systematic verification of compliance with conditions attached to authorizations is limited to those conditions for which this is objectively justified;
- would reduce administrative charges considerably by simplifying the authorization regimes, thereby reducing the regulatory workload and the attendant administrative costs; and
- foresees a continuing role for the CEPT in the harmonization of the radio frequencies.

In its first reading on March 1, 2001, the European Parliament emphasized that Member States should not introduce restrictions on licenses before expiry of the period for which they were granted unless this was necessary on grounds of public safety. In such cases, operators should be entitled to appropriate compensation. It also stressed that in order to ensure optimal development of a commercial radio market, efforts should be made to strike a better balance between the frequencies taken up by commercial and public service providers.

On April 5, 2001 the Council reached a political agreement on its common position on the proposed Directive. The biggest challenge concerned funding of the NRAs but agreement was reached without difficulty. Council rejected all of the Parliament's amendments and will wait until the second reading (expected in September–October 2001) and conciliation in order to find a compromise. Therefore, final approval on this Directive should be expected in March or April 2002 with the Directive being implemented into national legislation by mid-2003.

Business Perspective

The main issues covered by the proposed Directive concern all actors who need an authorization to operate, such as telecommunications clients but also broadcasters. Of concern to industry is the pursuit of a better harmonization of the national regimes, in order to reduce the administrative burden, and the different national legislations that could represent an unfair barrier to the entrance to a specific market.

2.5 Data Protection

There are two main Directives in the field of Data Privacy. The framework Directive on the protection of individuals with regard to the processing of personal data 95/46/EC (Data Protection Directive OJ L 281, November 23, 1995) and, in order to specify the requirements of this Directive for the electronic communication sector and complement it, Directive 97/66/EC (ISDN Directive) (OJ L 24 January 30, 1998) on the processing of personal data and the protection of privacy in the electronic communication sector. Despite incomplete implementation in the Member States, the Commission has undertaken to revise the latter (COM (2000) 385 July 12, 2000) as part of the electronic communications package

The main aims of the Data Protection Directive are to harmonize the national data protection rules applicable to privacy throughout the EU and to ensure the same high level of protection for individuals with regard to the processing of their personal data; and to ensure the free movement of personal data among the 15 EU Member States and the European Economic Area (EEA) countries.

The Data Protection Directive applies to all forms of processing (automated and manual) of personal data, being any information related to an identified or identifiable individual (data subject). It allows for the lawful and fair processing of personal data, if the data subject has given his consent, if such processing is necessary for the performance of a contract, or necessary for the compliance with a legal obligation.

It also sets specific rules applicable to the export of personal data to third countries that do not present an adequate level of protection. The Commission has adopted decisions recognizing the adequacy of regimes in the US (Safe Harbor), Hungary and Switzerland and is close to adopting a decision on the Canadian and Australian regimes. The safe harbor agreement (reached on May 31, 2000) provides a framework for transfers of personal data from the EU to the US for companies that have decided to abide by a set of seven principles, recognized as offering an adequate level of protection. The Commission is also working on draft standard contract clauses for data transfer to all countries that have not reached agreement on the adequacy of their privacy provisions with the EU.

The aim of the revised Directive is to update the ISDN Directive, and to adapt it to technological changes. The scope of the current draft proposal has now become all-encompassing and does not only include telecoms services but in fact all electronic communications. The main changes proposed by the Communication regard:

- new information requirements concerning the types of traffic data processed and the duration of such processing;
- a new article on location data, introducing prior consent for the processing of location data and processing limitations to the approximate duration necessary for the provision of a value added service; and
- introduction of prior consent for the sending of unsolicited commercial communications by email.

Completion of the legislative process and adoption of this draft proposal can be expected for the end of 2001. However, many questions remain open and Business is continually working on the issues. The Data Protection Directive is due for revision this year, and it would have been appropriate to undertake the review of Directive 97/66/EC at the same time. As this is not being done, the relationship between the proposed changes and the planned review remains unclear.

Business Perspective

Business supports the need for a uniform level of protection of personal data in the EU as well as for legislation that will remove obstacles to flows of personal data throughout the Union and worldwide. However, it has some reserves about the revision of the ISDN Directive and about the way the Commission seems to be assessing the adequacy of third countries systems of data protection. Although business welcomes the adoption of the Safe Harbor Agreement, the recognition of the adequacy of third countries and the work undertaken by the Commission on the model contract clauses, it believes that adequate should not be interpreted as identical and that the requirements for transfers should not go beyond what is in the Directive.

For privacy protection not to become a trade barrier, government and industry should seek to minimize the disruption of free flow of information consistent with privacy principles. Business would like to see a viable model contract that can be widely adopted. To achieve this, the Commission's proposed clauses on liability, on disclosure and on confidentiality of information need to have a viable business input. Business would welcome the opportunity to work with the Commission on viable alternatives.

For the 1997 Directive, in light of convergence between communication technologies, it is questionable whether the proposed changes fit within the context of a telecoms Directive. Applying principles of an outdated Directive intended specifically for telecommunications infrastructure to the entire internet will have a broad impact on e-commerce as well. A striking example is the information to be provided on the use of traffic data: the proposal fails to give a clear indication of what is understood by traffic data in the internet environment. Another example is the equal treatment of e-mails, automated calling machines and fax machines: by ignoring the special features of the internet and its global nature, the Commission does not recognize that a singular European opt-in requirement for commercial communications might disadvantage companies in Europe versus the rest of the world. In addition, there is a lack of consistency between the current proposal and existing legislation, which establish opt-out as a legal basis.

3. Cybercrime

Background

Europe's transition to an information society is having a fundamental impact on both the Union's economies and societies, bringing with it opportunities, challenges and threats to Europe's growth, competitiveness and employment levels. The information infrastructure now represents an important element of the backbone of Europe's economies, resulting in new opportunities for criminal conduct and thus far reaching implications in the social and legal fields.

Steps to protect intellectual property and personal data, to fight illegal and harmful content on the internet and to enhance the security of transactions have already been taken by the EU. In April 1998, computer-related crime was the subject of a Commission study (the COMCRIME study) with the result that the Tampere Summit of the European Council in October 1999 concluded that high-tech crime would be included in the agreements for a common approach to definitions and sanctions in the field of justice and home affairs. Following the *e*Europe initiative launched by the Commission in December 1999, the aim of which was to ensure that the EU will reap the benefits of digital technologies, the Feira European Council in June 2000 adopted the *e*Europe Action Plan (COM (2000) 330 May 24, 2000). The Action Plan marks an important step in the fight against electronic criminal activity, highlighting the importance of network security and providing for the establishment of a co-ordinated and coherent approach to cybercrime by the end of 2002. Much of the Commission's work in the field of cybercrime has focused around action taken by the G8, the Commission having actively participated within this forum. On May 15-17, 2000 the G8 held a conference in Paris on safety and confidence in cyberspace, urging law enforcement and industry to work together to fight cybercrime. A follow-up meeting was held in Berlin on October 23-26, 2000. In terms of bilateral discussions, a Joint EU/US Task Force on critical infrastructure protection has been established under the auspices of the Joint Consultative Group of the EU/US Science and Technology Cooperation Agreement.

Building on existing work in the international fora of G8 and the Council of Europe (CoE) and with the recognition of the need for industry participation, the Commission launched, on January 26, 2001, a Communication on creating a safer information society by improving the security of information infrastructures and combating computer-related crime (COM (2000) 890 January 26, 2001). The Communication focuses on the requirement for a balanced, multi-disciplinary approach to the problems of cybercrime which will take into account the needs of industry, individual citizens, and data protection authorities as well as those of law enforcement. To this extent, the Commission is proposing the creation of an EU forum to better facilitate the sharing of best practices and the raising of awareness. It would also allow law enforcement, industry and representatives of civil society to cooperate and realize better and more efficient ways to tackle computer-related crime.

The Commission has identified the following areas as points of action for the EU forum:

- developing, where appropriate, 24 hour points of contact between government and industry;
- developing an appropriate standard format for law enforcement requests for information from industry, increasing law enforcement's use of the internet when communicating with service providers;
- encouraging the development and/or implementation of codes of conduct and best practices and the sharing of such codes among industries and governments;
- encouraging the exchange of information on trends in high-tech crime between the various parties, particularly industry and law enforcement agencies;
- exploring law enforcement concerns in the development of early warning and crisis management mechanisms to prevent, identify and handle threats or disrupting events on information infrastructures;
- providing, where required, an enhanced expert contribution to work underway within the Council and in other international fora, for example the Council of Europe and G8; and
- encouraging cooperation between interested parties including principles shared by law enforcement, industry and users (eg, Memorandum of Understanding, Codes of Practice in line with the legal framework).

Other key principles of the Commission's Communication are:

- training - continuous, specialized training for both police and judicial staff is particularly pertinent, due to the rapidity of change in the fields of computer-related criminal techniques and capabilities;
- substantive criminal laws - development of comprehensive substantive criminal laws dealing with offences targeting critical network infrastructures associated with the internet, as well as those who use these network services;
- data collection and retention - the requirement of law enforcement to access and develop relevant data that industry keeps to develop criminal prosecutions; and
- a comprehensive and uniform approach - avoidance of a wide divergence of definitions concerning cybercrime, depending on the country, as well as preventing offenders from taking advantage of countries that lack criminal laws pertaining to cybercrime.

The Commission invited comments from all interested parties on the issues addressed in its Communication. It also organized a public hearing (held on March 7, 2001), which addressed several problems raised by the various stakeholders and industry. It is planned that the EU forum will contribute to finding solutions to these problems at its first meeting.

A further concern is to ensure harmonization in the EU with proposed or existing national legislation and to bring the proposed provisions of the CoE in line with existing EU legislation. A pressing issue which will need to be addressed by the Commission is the concern, expressed by many, that the Commission's Communication will lead to a conflict between EU law and the provisions of the Council of Europe Convention on cybercrime due to be adopted in June 2001. It is expected that all Member States and accession countries will sign this Convention, a move which may result in undue complexity, confusion and even conflict of the issue, begging the question of which rules will apply. It remains to be seen what the Commission intends to do to prevent such a conflict.

Business Perspective

For business it is important to ensure consumer confidence in the e-economy as without such confidence the development of *e*Europe will not continue at the envisaged pace. Business fully supports the fight against cybercrime. However, industry needs a harmonized legal framework in order to comply with activities requested from the law enforcement activities without bearing legal uncertainties. Only a fair and balanced approach which involves all parties will ensure further investments in Europe's future industry and markets. This requires legal certainty which can only be achieved by clear definitions, uniform minimum standards for interception, clear reimbursement rules for costs and limited liability for compliance with interception requests.

4. Local Loop Unbundling

Background

The local loop refers to the physical copper circuit between the customers' premises and the telecommunications operator's local switch in the local access network. On July 12, 2000, the European Commission issued its proposal for a Regulation on unbundled access to the local loop (COM (2000) 394 July 12, 2000). Regulation 2887/2000 was subsequently adopted by the European Parliament and Council and entered into force on January 1, 2001 (OJ L 336; December 30, 2000). Since that date, local loop unbundling has been a legal requirement across the EU for Member States to implement.

This proposal was a response to the conclusions of the June 2000 Feira Summit, where EU Heads of Government and State agreed on a number of actions and objectives related to the digital economy in Europe – the eEurope Action Plan. Among other things, the European Council called on the Commission and Member States to 'work towards introducing greater competition in local access networks before the end of 2000 and unbundling the local loop, in order to bring about a substantial reduction in the costs of using the internet'.

The proposed Regulation followed a Commission Recommendation (2000/417/EC, May 25, 2000) and a Communication (COM (2000) 237 April 26, 2000). These documents had been prepared after extensive consultation with industry. However, they were not legally binding, and therefore it was decided to issue the proposal for a Regulation. Several national regulatory authorities had indicated that it was necessary to establish a legal requirement.

The policy of unbundling was considered necessary in order to accelerate the deployment of high-speed internet access to citizens and small businesses across Europe. Fixed local exchange operators had rolled out their local access networks over significant periods of time through exclusive rights. The ubiquity of the copper local loop access infrastructure controlled by the incumbent operator was not economically feasible to duplicate, and alternative local access infrastructures (cable-TV, wireless local loops, satellite, etc.) could not be constructed with the same ubiquity and competitive conditions within a reasonable time. Regulatory intervention was therefore deemed necessary to ensure new entrants access to this infrastructure.

The unbundling Regulation mandates three means of opening up the local access network. These are:

- *full unbundling* - in the case of full unbundling of the local loop, the copper pair is rented to a third party for its exclusive use. The lessee has full control of the relationship with its customer for the provision of a full range of telecommunication services over the local loop, including deployment of digital subscriber line systems (DSL) for high-speed data applications;
- *shared access/line sharing* (unbundled access to the high frequency spectrum of the local loop for the competitive provision of DSL systems and services by third parties) - in this form of access, the incumbent operator continues to provide telephone service, while the new entrant delivers high-speed data services over the same local loop using its own high-speed ADSL modems. Telephone traffic and the data traffic are separated by means of a splitter before the incumbent's switch. The local loop remains connected to, and part of, the public switched telephone network; and
- *high speed bit stream access* (provision of DSL services by incumbent) - this refers to the situation where the incumbent installs a high speed access link to the customers' premises (eg, by installing its preferred ADSL equipment and configuration in its local access network) and then makes this access link available to third parties, to enable them to provide high speed services to customers. The incumbent may also provide transmission services to its competitors, to carry traffic to a 'higher' level in the network hierarchy where new entrants may already have a point of presence (eg, a transit switch location).

The Regulation mandates unbundled access to the metallic local loops only of notified operators that have been designated by their national regulatory authorities as having significant market power in the fixed local exchange market. Although commercial negotiation is the preferred method for reaching agreement on technical and pricing issues for local loop access, experience shows that in most cases regulatory intervention is necessary due to imbalance in negotiating power between the new entrant and the notified operator, and lack of other alternatives. Costing and pricing rules for local loops and related facilities should be transparent, non-discriminatory and objective to ensure fairness. Pricing rules should ensure that the local loop provider is able to cover its appropriate costs in this regard plus a reasonable return, in order to ensure the long term development and upgrade of local access infrastructure.

Business Perspective

The objective of the Regulation is supported widely among industry and consumers. It is recognized that unbundling of the local loop is a necessary condition for accelerating the deployment of broadband services and infrastructure competition in Europe. Although other infrastructures (cable, fixed-wireless access and others) are able to provide broadband access, none has the ubiquity which the local loop offers at this point in time. However, it is also clear that putting in place the legislation is only the first step; strong implementation and enforcement by national regulators and competition authorities is required. Current bottlenecks in the pricing and provisioning of leased lines as set out in Community law need to be enforced. At the same time, it needs to be recognized that there are many substantial technical and operational issues to resolve. Separating the real technical difficulties from obstructive behavior is a key task for regulators. If implemented correctly, unbundling has the potential to accelerate broadband deployment, infrastructure and service deployment in Europe substantially, a goal the entire industry is united behind.

5. Third Generation (3G) Mobile Communications

Background

The EU has become the world leader in mobile communications, in terms of technology and service development, competitiveness and consumer penetration. Mobile communications increased by 38% in the year 2000 and account for roughly 30% of total revenues in the telecom services sector in the EU. As in the case of the Global System for Mobile communications (GSM), penetration has reached 60% in 2000, and is expected to rise to 85% in 2003 and 120% in 2004. In comparison with the US, mobile penetration is only at 38%. Now with 11 of the 15 Member States having issued third generation of mobile communications (3G) licenses, the convergence of the digital economy and mobile communications (essential to the functioning of 3G) will warrant attention due to the social and economic implications of this introduction to an advanced mobile data service.

With the deployment of 3G networks across the EU expected to start within the next few months, the Commission has produced a report on the state of play and the way forward (COM (2001) 141 March 20, 2001). The report sets out four issues which will be closely monitored, due to the influence they will have on the future of 3G:

- the regulatory environment;
- the financial context;
- gaining experience with the new market; and
- outstanding technical issues.

Existing legislation governing licensing conditions provides the basis for regulatory conditions for the 3G system. Decision 128/1999/EC defined the capabilities of the new mobile service, called for harmonized spectrum use and set out a time frame for Member States to prepare their authorization systems by January 1, 2000. The Decision allowed each Member State to determine the mechanism for spectrum licensing and to define licensing conditions to be applied on its territory. This framework has led to divergence in licensing conditions across the EU, with different selection procedures being used: auctions, comparative selections, or a mixture of the two. The number of licenses made available varies between Member States as do their duration and entry into force. Such fragmented conditions, if followed for the implementation of 3G networks, would undoubtedly create distortions in a EU single market for mobile communications. In its legislative package for a new regulatory framework for all electronic communications services (see page 129), the Commission has set out the requirement that national authorities consult each other in advance of issuing licenses in order to ensure consistency in the licensing methods and conditions for services that are offered by operators in several parts of the Union. In particular, the proposal for a regulatory framework for radio spectrum policy (COM (2000) 407 July 12, 2000) aims to harmonize the allocation, assignment and conditions of use of radio spectrum for all non-military purposes in the EU. A mechanism would also be established whereby Member States and the Commission will be able to discuss the advantages of different spectrum assignment methods and conditions attached to licenses.

In 2000, both the UK and Germany auctioned their allocation of 3G licenses. In the UK, total charges collected for licenses amounted to £22 billion. However, since the summer of 2000, the interest in 3G licenses has diminished in Europe. France has attracted only two operators for four licenses and in Belgium three operators have applied for four licenses (compared to the 13 operators that participated in the UK auction to win one of the five licenses in play). This is due to two factors. Firstly, the recent downturn in the market for shares related to the internet and new technology has compounded the risk inherent in investing in 3G. Secondly, operators, after purchasing a license, are faced with comparable infrastructure costs for the deployment of new networks and for the marketing of 3G mobiles. Constrained by their reduced share valuation and the so far weak demand for 3G by consumers, companies are struggling to find the resources to make the necessary investments in 3G infrastructure, which are considerable. This has led to a demand on financial markets from the majority of telecom operators, reducing their credit-worthiness and, as a result, further reducing their ability to fund much needed infrastructure investment in new 3G services.

The ability of operators to successfully develop a market for 3G is dependent on the availability of spectrum. As the demand for mobile communication services grows, the question of availability of spectrum for 3G networks becomes a crucial one. Following a decision of the International Telecommunication Union (ITU) in 1992, a total of 215 MHz of the spectrum was designated for 3G services in Europe. Based on the anticipation of exponential growth, it has rapidly become obvious that additional spectrum will be required in order to be able to meet the demand. A number of studies conducted in different regions all concluded that about 160MHz additional spectrum will be required for 3G mobile services by the year 2010. This issue received attention at the World Radio Conference 2000, held in Istanbul from May 8, 2000 – June 2, 2000. The agreement reached ensures sufficient availability of radio spectrum to allow for further growth of third generation mobile communications. This assurance will allow for the furthering of the market by creating a more stable environment which will encourage investment.

In terms of outstanding technical issues, the Commission has singled out the need to introduce the new Internet Protocol (IPv6) which provides a much larger address space than the current system (IPv4) can cater for. The Commission has encouraged Member States to work together with industry in an *ad hoc* group, with the aim of producing suggestions to accelerate the introduction of IPv6.

Business Perspective

With considerable anticipation business and consumers await the introduction of the next generation of cellular phones known as 3G or UMTS (Universal Mobile Telecommunications System). Nevertheless the road toward providing this multi-functional service involving internet access as well as standard wireless telephony contains several pitfalls. Through the auction process the cost of issuing spectrum licenses in at least two Member States has been exorbitant, creating enormous capital pressure on operators with the effect trickling down to the manufacturers. For 3G, 70% of the costs have been related to licenses in contrast with other previous cellular services in which the licenses were well under 50% of the costs. The availability of capital impacts the speed and scope of network deployment.

The challenge rests with how to defray the costs of the licensing by recycling these funds to industry in a timely manner. For the European Commission it is imperative in the future that efforts are made to better harmonize spectrum allocation.

6. Internet Protocol (IP) Telephony

Background

IP (internet protocol) telephony, voice-over IP and internet telephony are terms that can be understood to mean a number of different things and are used in different contexts without much clarity. The International Telecommunications Union (ITU) has used this terminology as a 'generic term for the conveyance of voice, fax and related services, partially or wholly over packet-switched IP-based networks. IP Telephony may also include applications that integrate/embed the transmission of voice and fax with other media such as text and images' (Report of the Secretary-General on IP Telephony, ITU, January 31, 2001).

In the EU, the term most commonly used is 'voice on the internet'. The ongoing debate relates to how voice services, that are enabled by the internet, should be regarded in regulatory terms. The European Commission has issued two Notices on the subject (OJ C 6 January 10, 1998 and OJ C 369 December 22, 2000), both in relation to Directive 90/388/EEC on competition in the market for telecoms services. In these Notices, the Commission concludes that there is currently no need for revision of the regulatory framework to take account for 'voice on the internet'. When the new EU regulatory framework for electronic communications is adopted, the strict distinction between traditional Public Switched Telecommunications Network (PSTN) based voice telephony and internet voice services will disappear.

In 1998, the Commission adopted its first Notice defining its policy on voice telephony in respect of telephony via the internet. According to the Notice, telephony via the internet was not subject to the regulation applying to voice telephony until a certain number of conditions were met. This Notice was based on a public consultation. The Notice distinguished between three categories of voice services:

- commercial services provided from PC to PC;
- commercial services provided between PC and telephone handsets connected to the PSTN; and
- the provision of calls between two telephone handsets connected to the PSTN.

The conclusion was that only the third type was close to meeting the conditions of voice telephony.

Following on from this conclusion, internet telephony could therefore not be subjected by Member States to individual licensing procedures and other regulations such as universal service. The Commission concluded that internet telephony would be defined as voice telephony and therefore be subject to standard voice telephony regulation only if and when the following conditions were met:

- the communications must be the subject of a commercial offer;
- the service must be provided for the public;
- the service must be provided to and from public switched network termination points on the fixed telephony network; and
- it must involve direct transport and speech in real time.

As internet telephony did not meet all these criteria, the Commission concluded it could not be considered as voice telephony for the time being. This assessment was broadly endorsed during the public consultation. The Commission did, however, note that subsequent technological developments could make it necessary to review this decision, and set January 1, 2000 as the date for a new review.

After a further public consultation in the summer of 2000, the Commission adopted its second Notice, which basically concluded that the approach taken in 1998 was still valid. It restated the conclusion that voice services on the internet usually did not meet each of the conditions for the definition of voice telephony in Directive 90/388/EEC and should therefore not be treated as such from a regulatory point of view. The Commission's assessment does not preclude that case-by-case analyses could show that voice services on the internet might meet all the conditions laid down. In such cases, certain internet telephony providers could qualify as providers of voice telephony, and therefore be subject to the regulatory regime applicable to voice telephony, as soon as they would offer a quality of service equivalent to that of traditional voice telephony.

Further, the Notice attempted to clarify the differences between voice-over internet protocol and voice-over the internet. It stated, as a consequence of this distinction, that the conveyance of voice signals over dedicated private networks using the internet protocol was likely to produce a level of service comparable with that of voice delivered over conventional telephony networks.

The Notice also gave additional indications on the notion of integrated internet services contained in the 1998 text and emphasized the notion of substitutability with conventional voice telephony in the eye of the consumer.

Business Perspective

Generally speaking, business favors a minimalist approach to regulation of the communications sector and the internet, ie, regulation should only be applied in order to achieve clearly defined goals. Therefore, industry has, in the consultation procedures leading to the publication of the two Commission Notices on 'voice on the internet', advocated that so far there would be no need for a revision of the regulatory position of these services or of the providers that supply them. The Commission supported this view. In competitive, liberalized environments like Europe, the issue is of much less importance than in the developing world. Many developing countries explicitly ban internet-based voice telephony because it threatens the voice revenues of the national telecom operators. This issue is under continuing discussion in the ITU. In this context, there is some risk that the European approach, based on fairly strict 'technology neutrality' (ie, similar services to be regulated in similar ways), could be used by governments in some developing countries as an excuse to preserve the monopoly position of the national carrier. This would be detrimental for industry operating in such countries, as costs of communications would be higher than in a competitive environment.

7. Spectrum Clauses

Background

In light of the pivotal role radio spectrum plays in the fast-developing fields of wireless applications, such as 3rd generation (3G) mobile communications and satellite communications, a coherent regulatory framework at Community and international levels is required to address the major economic and strategic implications involved. The European Commission recognized this need in 1998 when it produced a Green Paper on Radio Spectrum Policy. On an international level, the European Conference of Postal and Telecommunications Administrations (CEPT) and the International Telecommunication Union (ITU) have undertaken a considerable amount of technical work in this field over many years. The impetus at the moment is for the EU to give policy guidance to the CEPT's work and to assure legal certainty by ensuring that radio spectrum is available in a harmonized manner. This requirement is made all the more urgent as legislation will cover the areas of communications, transport, broadcasting and R&D.

Following public consultation on its Green Paper and building upon continual cooperation both with Member States and the CEPT, the Commission published a proposal for a Decision on a regulatory framework for radio spectrum policy in the European Community (COM (2000) 407 July 12, 2000). It proposes to:

- establish a policy platform (Senior Official Spectrum Policy Group) which, on the basis of technological, market and regulatory developments and after consultation of relevant spectrum user communities, will advise the Commission on the use of radio spectrum in EU policy areas of a commercial and non-commercial nature;
- establish a legal framework which will allow the Commission, taking the advice of the Senior Official Spectrum Policy Group into account, to grant mandates to the CEPT and to secure implementation by the Member States of measures aimed at the harmonized availability and use of radio spectrum for EU policies;
- ensure EU-wide transparency through co-ordinated and timely provision of information related to radio spectrum use so that investment and policy decisions can be taken; and
- safeguard EU interests in international negotiations on radio spectrum by ensuring that common positions are adopted to reach EU policy objectives.

Scope and Definitions

Calls have been made for the Commission to encourage Member States to start (or in some cases) continue dialogue with the public sector spectrum users (such as the military and national emergency services), with a view to sharing spectrum or making it more available for commercial applications. The definition of the radio spectrum put forward by the Commission, as well as the allocation and assignment of spectrum, is limited in its substance; no reference being made to canceling current allocations and/or assignments to enable the introduction of different services and/or technologies.

Consultation with Industry

The Commission's proposal has received criticism for its lack of clarity concerning consultation with industry. The proposals for a Spectrum Policy Expert Group (SPEG), as set out in the Commission's communication on the results of its 1998 Green Paper on radio spectrum policy (COM (1999) 538), have not been taken up by the Commission in its proposal for a regulatory framework for radio spectrum policy. This is of particular concern as the Commission has not foreseen any mandatory consultation with interested parties, in particular industry, either within the framework of the newly proposed Senior Official Spectrum Policy Group, or within the Radio Spectrum Committee. Given the rapid and unpredictable development of convergence of technologies and the expected higher demand for bandwidth, mandatory dialogue with stakeholders is essential. Moreover, some confusion has risen between the regulatory role of the proposed committee of national experts and its link with the proposed Radio Spectrum Committee.

Spectrum Management

A definition of spectrum trading and refarming is provided in the Commission's proposal for a Directive on a common regulatory framework for electronic communications networks and services (COM(2000) 393 July 12, 2000). Trading of spectrum by National Regulatory Authorities (NRAs) will be limited to frequencies acquired through auctions with procedures for refarming subject to the licensing arrangements and obligations in the Member States.

Business Perspective

Business has argued that spectrum trading should not be limited to frequencies that were acquired through auctions. In practice, it may be necessary that the selling licensee of the spectrum notify the NRA concerned. In addition, given the reality of market developments, NRAs should have the flexibility to re-farm parts of the spectrum as they deem necessary.

Chapter X
Trade Policy &
International Agreements

THE EU COMMITTEE
OF THE AMERICAN CHAMBER OF COMMERCE IN BELGIUM

International Agreements
1. Transatlantic Relations

1.1 EU-US Relations

Background

The EU and the US are the two largest economies in the world. Their trading relationship generates almost 40% of global trade and constitutes the single largest bilateral trade and investment agreement in the world. This transatlantic partnership, therefore, is of vital global importance.

The EU and US are each other's largest trading and investment partners, with the flow of this transatlantic trade and investment amounting to $1 billion a day. The two-way trade has grown to account for nearly 20% of each other's trade in goods and services, more than half of each others total stocks of foreign direct investment; and an estimated seven million jobs (accounting for one in eight jobs in the US). Moreover, transatlantic trade is mostly concentrated in hi-tech areas such as information technology and aerospace, where the US holds approximately 52% of the EU market. As a result American and European companies have established deep roots in both economies and close political links have been forged.

The importance of this long-standing relationship was recognized with the signing of the 1990 Transatlantic Declaration, which laid the groundwork for closer EU-US cooperation in the changed international environment of the post-Cold War era, notably with the establishment of bi-annual presidential and ministerial meetings. Further to this agreement the EU and the US have launched a variety of bilateral trade liberalization initiatives. The key ones are the New Transatlantic Agenda (NTA), the Transatlantic Business Dialogue (TABD) (see page 149) and the Transatlantic Economic Partnership (TEP).

The New Transatlantic Agenda

Meeting in Madrid at the EU-US summit in December 1995, US and EU leaders signed the New Transatlantic Agenda (NTA) and adopted the EU-US Joint Action Plan, which took transatlantic political and economic cooperation a step further from simple consultation to joint action. The NTA was given the defined objective of establishing a 'transatlantic marketplace' designed to 'eliminate trade barriers and to expand trade and investment opportunities and to multiply jobs on both sides of the Atlantic'.

The process is an outward-looking program that commits both partners to issues of global importance. The documents contained both a set of agreed-on principles, common concerns and a wide-ranging list of joint actions to be taken by the parties. The Action Plan is comprised of 150 specific actions to which the EU and US have committed themselves, whilst the New Transatlantic Agenda's 'Framework for Action' sets out the four major goals of the agreement:

- promoting peace and stability, democracy and development around the world;
- responding to global challenges - fighting international crime, drug trafficking and terrorism, protecting the environment and combating diseases;
- building bridges across the Atlantic - working with business, consumers, environmentalists, educators and others to improve communication and ensure that future generations remain committed to developing a full and equal partnership; and
- contributing to the expansion of world trade and closer economic relations - strengthening the multilateral trading system and taking practical steps to promote closer economic relations between the two economies.

Moreover, in an effort to maintain the momentum of these initiatives the program is subject to a rolling process of review and renewal, at regular ministerial working groups as well as the bi-annual Presidential-level EU-US summits.

The potential benefits of this close, highly institutionalized relationship characterized by the NTA can be clearly discerned through the progress made between the EU and the US on closer trade harmonization. These regular sessions have fostered innovative ideas such as the Mutual Recognition Agreement (MRA), signed in June 1998, which is designed to eliminate duplicative regulatory processes by accepting each other's procedures. The governments have cooperated even further on developing mutual 'guidelines for regulatory cooperation', designed to provide for increased transparency in regulatory and legislative processes. These initiatives are unique to the EU-US relationship, and are built upon the working structure established by the NTA.

The most recent EU-US summit was held in Washington at the beginning of December 2000, with US President Clinton, Commission President Prodi, French President Chirac and Commissioners Patten, Lamy and High Representative Solana in attendance. Many of the issues discussed echoed those addressed at the Queluz summit in May 2000, insofar as the work from that summit was reviewed and progressed.

- a review of work initiated in the field of e-commerce by the last summit led both parties to stress that e-commerce, although novel, was still commerce and must be subject to judicious and proportionate legislation, especially regarding areas such as data privacy;
- EU-US cooperation in promoting democracy in the Balkans would continue, in particular initiatives to help sustain the recent positive developments in the region. Developments in the Middle East were also addressed; and
- the furthering of the humanitarian agenda in Africa to bring about access to affordable medicines to combat the global threat posed by communicable diseases (HIV/AIDS, malaria, tuberculosis) was reaffirmed by both sides.

Other results from the meeting included the signing of the renewed education agreement, increased cooperation on biotechnology, science and technology, and discussions on elements of the Transatlantic Economic Partnership (see below). A recommendation was also made that fundamental questions about the structure of the process should also be addressed, especially as the US stood on the brink of having a new administration. For example, a reassessment of key strategic themes for the future and review of ways in which the efforts of the partnership, particularly work resulting from the summits, could be more action-oriented and achieved more effectively.

In response to this recommendation, the European Commission adopted a Communication to the Council on 'Reinforcing the transatlantic relationship: focusing on strategy and delivering results' (COM (2001) 154, March 20, 2001). The Communication recognizes the growing role of the Union as an international actor and proposes that the framework of the NTA should be more structured and broad-based to reflect this increased scope of Union influence, especially with the advent of EU enlargement. In terms of structure, the Communication points to the dangers of the process becoming too bureaucratic and cumbersome and recommends that EU and US leaders build on suggestions that better-prepared and less frequent summits might give greater scope for more productive and significant actions. In terms of broadening the base of issues addressed, the Communication recommends that to increase the effectiveness of transatlantic efforts in confronting global challenges, all issues pursued should fall under clear and precise strategic priorities. Suggested themes include:

- security challenges;
- globalization and the multilateral trading system;
- fight against organized crime;
- energy issues;
- consumer protection;
- macroeconomics issues;
- fight against poverty in developing countries; and
- digital economy.

At the time of writing, the format and agenda of the next EU-US summit in Gothenburg on June 14, 2001 had yet to be determined.

The Transatlantic Economic Partnership (TEP)
A number of barriers to trade and investment continue to exist in the transatlantic marketplace. The impact of differing regulatory approaches in sensitive areas such as biotechnology, food safety, data privacy, to mention only a few examples, have demonstrated the need to increase the level and quality of bilateral cooperation.

In an effort to complement the economic objectives of the New Transatlantic Agenda, the Transatlantic Economic Partnership (TEP) was established on May 18, 1998 at the EU-US summit in London. As a major new initiative its aim is to break down the barriers to trade across the Atlantic and encourage both nations to work more closely together to pursue multilateral liberalization.

The TEP has sought the removal of bilateral regulatory barriers to trade in both goods and services by closer cooperation between regulators. The TEP has attempted to resolve the issues of government procurement, intellectual property, consumer, plant health, biotechnology, environment and food safety. At the December

2000 summit particular efforts were made in the fields of cosmetics, telecommunications equipment and consumer product safety and significant progress was made in 2000 by experts in the EU and US towards establishing reliable and consistent approaches to verification. Most recently, on January 17, 2001, regulations regarding electrical appliances and telecommunications equipment were annexed to the MRA.

In the multilateral field the program proposes regular dialogue with the US to reach a closer understanding on the key issues that will be tackled in new multilateral trade negotiations. These include implementation of WTO agreements, dispute settlement, liberalization in services and agriculture, trade facilitation, developing countries, electronic commerce, labor standards and WTO accessions (in particular the accession of China to the WTO). In the early part of 2001 the TEP focused on furthering already existing support amongst WTO members for an inclusive and balanced new round of WTO talks.

The TEP also has a political dimension, since it is clear that strengthening economic relations has and will continue to improve and reinforce the overall EU-US relationship. Despite, however, the harmonious trading relationship that exists, transatlantic trade disputes do arise. Although the NTA as a whole provides a framework for resolving any EU-US disagreements, efforts such as the Early Warning Mechanism, established at the 1999 summit, play an important role in alerting both governments to potential problem areas. A primary goal in EU-US relations is to avoid new trade disputes and one potentially very effective gesture would be to improve and reinforce the authority of the TEP along with the Early Warning Mechanism. Following the most recent summit in December 2000, the 1999 initiative was taken one step further when an examination was begun on how to refine the practical procedures that should govern the treatment of issues brought up under the Early Warning Mechanism.

Current EU-US Issues

A recently resolved dispute between the EU and the US involves the EU's banana regime. This long-running dispute centered around the preferential tariffs awarded to bananas from African Caribbean Pacific (ACP) countries by the EU, a system that was deemed to be incompatible with the EU's obligations within the WTO. After a failed reform of the import regime by the EU in January 1999, the Commission proposed a new import system introduced in two phases: a flat tariff would come into force in 2006 after a transitional period, beginning July 1, 2001, during which time a tariff quota system would apply, with preferential tariff access for ACP bananas. The proposal (COM (1999) 582 November 20, 2000), amending regulation 404/93/EEC applying to the common organization of the market in the banana sector, was adopted by Member States on January 29, 2001. The Commission recommended (COM (2000) 621 October 4, 2000) that licences under the transitional quota system be awarded under the 'first come, first served' basis. The regulation is due to alter slightly following the US and Commission talks, which concluded with a compromise agreement on April 11, 2001. The agreement proposes that the allocation of licenses during the transition period be carried out according to historic references and that the quantities of the various quotas be amended to expand access for Latin American bananas whilst still securing a market share for ACP produce. The US has pledged to suspend EU sanctions, with a view to a total removal of them, once these alterations have been implemented when the regulation comes into effect in July 2001 and the regime has received the formal backing of the WTO.

A second transatlantic dispute concerns beef and beef products. At present the EU is continuing its bans on the import of beef and beef products produced from animals to which certain hormones have been administered. The effect of the EU ban is to prohibit the import of significantly large amounts of US-produced beef and beef products. WTO panels have confirmed that the EU has no scientific basis for banning imports of US beef, and that the EU ban is inconsistent with the its WTO obligations. In response the Commission is carrying out an assessment in line with indications given by the WTO, other studies have been launched to gather further scientific information and the EU has adopted a regulation amending the 'hormone Directive', 2000/583/EC, which reduces the number of checks on US imported beef to Europe (OJ L 246 September 30, 2000). In the meantime, the EU has shown an interest in converting US sanctions into a compensatory tariff reduction and the US has shown signs of willingness to open its market to non-hormone treated beef products. There are hopes that a trade-enhancing compensation package might be negotiated.

In response to the EU's failure to comply with the WTO rulings over bananas and beef, the US has imposed a 'carousel' system of regulatory tariffs (whereby the goods facing restriction are rotated on a regular basis) against the EU. The latest 'carousel' list was due to appear in July 2000, however, this did not happen due to internal disagreements in the US. The EU believes that the US is in breach of WTO rulings and lodged a complaint therein on June 5, 2000. The issue was addressed at WTO consultations on July 5, 2000, but pending the application of legislation, the EU will only request the establishment of a WTO panel once the sanctions have been rotated. However, following developments over the banana dispute (see above), it appears these sanctions may be removed by summer 2001.

In 1997, the EU launched a case under the WTO's Dispute Settlement Procedure, claiming that the US's Foreign Sales Corporation (FSC) provisions constituted import substitution subsidies under the Subsidies Agreement and that they violated the export subsidy provisions of the Agreement on Agriculture. A WTO panel, established in 1998, ruled in favor of the EU and in February 2000 the WTO Appellate body condemned the income tax exemption afforded to US exporters by means of FSCs as an export subsidy inconsistent with WTO provisions. In May 2000, the US proposed a solution to FSC which included a new tax regime which would apply to foreign income from all foreign sales, rentals and leases regardless of whether the goods were manufactured in the United States or abroad. However since its launch in November 2000, the EU has continued to argue that the system remains WTO incompatible. By the end of November 2000 the EU had requested WTO authorization to implement countermeasures to preserve their own rights. These countermeasures, however, will not be put in place until the WTO has concluded that the new legislation does indeed constitute a prohibited export subsidy, which is anticipated to be spring-summer 2001. To date the dispute involves by far the largest amount in damages to EU transatlantic trade.

Following the adoption of Council Regulation 925/1999/EC (hushkits legislation) which aims to limit some of the noisier re-certified aircraft registered or flown in the EU, the US initiated a procedure on the basis of Article 48 of the Chicago Convention. At a meeting on January 26, 2001 between the International Civil Aviation Organisation Council (ICAO) and the EU Transport and Energy Commissioner Loyola de Palacio, however, a dialogue was held on the definition of an international standard for aircraft noise. The discussions indicated that an agreement to end the dispute could well be made when the ICAO Assembly meets in September, 2001 (see page 188).

The 1992 EU-US Agreement limiting both direct and indirect aircraft subsidies has been at the heart of an ongoing dispute over the European governments financing of Airbus. America was the first to bring allegations against the EU, when Boeing drew attention to Airbus debts being written-off by European governments in the late 80s and early 90s which allow them to channel funds into developing new aircraft. Outgoing president Bill Clinton warned that the US would be closely analyzing the funding of Airbus' new A380. The latest turn in the dispute has come with Commission claims that indirect government aid to Boeing over the same period was in breach of the 3% limit set in the 1992 bilateral agreement. Calls are now being made on both sides of the Atlantic for there to be more transparency in the application of subsidies to the aircraft industry.

Business Perspective

While a great deal of the attention given to the EU-US relationship focuses on disputes, the business community has actively promoted the positive side of the relationship. The current transatlantic and WTO disputes amount to less than 3% of the world's largest two-way trade relationship. Both the EU and US business communities have urged the governments to focus on the positive, and on growing areas for trade and to cooperate on resolving disputed issues. Through the TABD (see page 149), the business communities have encouraged governments to continue to remove barriers to transatlantic trade and investment. Furthermore, the communities are working with the US and EU administrations to re-create a cooperative global trade agenda, and to reinforce the multilateral rules-based system.

1.2 The Transatlantic Business Dialogue (TABD)

Background

A clear objective of the EU-US Joint Action Plan adopted in 1995 to enhance transatlantic economic and political relations (see page 145), was to 'build bridges over the Atlantic' by establishing practical frameworks for enhanced cooperation between transatlantic civil society and the governments of the European Union and United States. The Transatlantic Business Dialogue (TABD) is one of four dialogues (the others being labor, consumer and environmental dialogues) and was launched in Seville in November 1995 at a conference attended by EU and US Chief Executive Officers (CEOs) and top government representatives led by European Commissioners for Trade and for Industry and by the US Secretary of Commerce. The aim of the process is to remove costly inefficiencies caused by excessive regulation, duplication and differences in the EU and US regulatory systems and procedures, as well as to identify areas in which the US and the EU can enhance cooperation in meeting the challenges of the global marketplace.

The TABD is unique because of the personal involvement of CEOs, working closely with officials from the highest levels of government from the EU and the US. It operates through an informal process whereby European and American companies and business associations aim to develop joint EU-US policy recommendations for action by the European Commission and US administration, as well as the US Congress and the European Parliament, which might boost transatlantic trade and investment opportunities. With no membership fees or bureaucracy the TABD is open to a wide range of companies - from multinationals to small and medium-sized enterprises (SMEs) - keen to support strengthened EU-US cooperation in the development of global trade policy, particularly within the World Trade Organization (WTO) (see page 168). By bringing together active participants in transatlantic trade, the TABD is able to apply the technical expertise of business leaders to the political agendas of the EU and US administrations. For example, during the latest EU-US Summit in Washington in December 2000, the TABD co-chairs presented the participants with recommendations which strongly urged the governments to improve their early warning system, redouble their efforts to conclude the Mutual Recognition Agreements and resolve the various disputes in the WTO.

How the TABD Works

There are more than 40 issue groups that cover different sectors (eg, medical devices, telecommunications services) and horizontal issues (eg, customs, climate change, intellectual property). Each issue group, led by a business executive from both the US and the EU, is responsible for making joint trade recommendations and tracking their implementation. The issue development process remains flexible to accommodate new challenges that arise in transatlantic business.

The issue groups are divided amongst five working groups, under the active leadership of a US and EU CEO and a co-ordinating manager. This format is designed to ensure effective co-ordination, raise visibility of the issues and maximize results. The TABD working groups are:

Standards and Regulatory Policy - this working group promotes a new regulatory model based on the 'approved once, accepted everywhere' principle on both sides of the Atlantic. It develops detailed action plans to remove obstacles associated with duplicative standards, testing and certification procedures. It approaches this in two ways: by targeting specific horizontal issues such as mutual recognition, conformity assessment and greater use of international standards; and by targeting issues of special importance to individual sectors. To date, more than 18 sectors have actively participated in this group.

Business Facilitation - this working group focuses on intra-company issues affecting business' ability to operate across the transatlantic marketplace. Its objective is to ensure the smooth operation of the new transatlantic marketplace in the following areas: accountancy standards, personnel mobility, taxation, export controls, customs, sanctions and international business practices.

Global Issues - this working group promotes development of the global trading system through cooperative actions that stimulate and strengthen the multilateral framework, particularly with respect to the WTO. The group focuses on the positive benefits of transatlantic and global trade liberalization. Its issue committees cover the WTO agenda, services, government procurement, intellectual property, investment, competition and climate change.

Small and Medium-sized Enterprises (SMEs) - this working group ensures that the perspective of small and medium-sized companies is incorporated directly into the overall TABD recommendations. The group also promotes greater partnering opportunities for small US and EU businesses.

Digital/New Economy - since 1997, the TABD has adopted detailed positions promoting an industry-led, market-driven approach to the development of e-commerce (see page 127). This fifth working group is charged with ensuring 'the continued and rapid growth of electronic commerce' and addresses the traditional range of policy issues (eg, tax liability, privacy, electronic authentication). This year, the TABD will also tackle bottlenecks in the e-commerce 'value chains' by focusing on the access and regulatory issues that currently impede smooth, efficient transactions. This proactive business agenda will set an example for countries around the globe on how to promote the economic and social benefits of e-commerce.

Issue Priorities for 2001-2002

The TABD seeks a progressive, step-by-step removal of trade and investment barriers and the convergence of US and EU regulatory policies.

Each year the TABD hosts a CEO conference that brings together company CEOs and senior-level government representatives to formulate trade recommendations and measure progress on outstanding problems. This unique gathering of CEOs and senior government representatives provides an ideal opportunity to foster understanding and to achieve breakthroughs on challenging issues. At the conclusion of each conference, the company CEO attendees produce a joint report listing trade recommendations.

Previous conferences have produced significant advances, including mutual recognition agreements (MRAs) and harmonization of standards; development of global positions on e-commerce issues; progress toward a single international accounting system; and integration of smaller businesses into the trade policy process.

At the most recent annual CEO conference held in Cincinnati on November 16-18, 2000, over 150 CEOs and senior government officials from the US and EU produced a list of progressive trade liberalization measures. Many of the issues were carried over from recommendations made at the last TABD meeting in Brussels in May 2000. The following were amongst the key priorities proposed in Cincinnati:

- Globalization - discussion focused on the great prospects globalization held in terms of economic growth, job creation and access to new goods and services. At the same time it was recognized that trade disputes (whilst only accounting for 3% of transatlantic trade) absorb a disproportionate amount of government resources and attract a disproportionate amount of adverse publicity. It was also acknowledged that the benefits of globalization are not distributed evenly. A commitment was made, therefore, that TABD members would play a more active role in informing the wider community of the benefits of a globalized economy and work not only with governments, but also with international organizations and citizens' groups out of the conviction that globalization is not incompatible with their concerns.
- Regulatory transparency - this approach was highlighted as a means of improving the transatlantic trade and investment environment. Such a policy would also have the advantage of increasing the speed and efficiency of the approvals process, bringing the EU and US to the TABD objective of 'approved once, accepted everywhere'. Similarly, it was stressed that 'the bedrock of early warning is transparency' in that open regulatory and legislative systems permit greater involvement by all stakeholders in identifying potential problem areas.
- Early Warning System - the conference emphasized the responsibility of businesses to take full advantage of this system. It recommended that they should make efforts to raise the concerns of interested stakeholders and attempt to resolve problems before they become economically damaging trade disputes. Specific emphasis was placed on preventing protracted trade disputes and creating clear criteria for the system in this regard. The report also exhorts both governments to resolve outstanding disputes.
- WTO New Round - in the interests of greater global trade and prosperity both business communities were united in their desire for a new round of negotiations and continued progress on the built-in agenda for services and agriculture (see page 168).
- Digital Economy - the conference produced specific recommendations on mechanisms to ensure continued growth in this area and also supported business-led government-driven initiatives to ensure that computer skills become part of the education and training programs on both sides of the Atlantic.

Business Perspective

Business was pleased to note that the conference recognized and affirmed the great value of international trade and foreign direct investment in a rules-based system and was also in agreement with its concluding remark which stressed that the transatlantic trade disputes color the trade landscape. Important disputes have gone on too long and minor impediments have been allowed to get in the way of real progress. Business also supports the sentiment that accomplishments are needed to reinforce the value of the entire dialogue process.

2. Enlargement - Wider Europe

2.1 Enlargement of the European Union

Background

Between April 1993 and June 1996, ten Central and Eastern European countries (CEECs) made formal applications for EU membership, thus joining Cyprus, Turkey and Malta. For the CEECs, the prospect of EU membership has meant undertaking a difficult transition to (or a return to) independent states with functioning market economies. Similarly, for the EU, enlargement has brought pressing challenges mainly regarding the need for internal institutional reform (see page 86). However, for both sides the potential benefits of EU enlargement are great. For the applicant states, EU membership will bring with it potentially huge economic benefits, particularly as the EU has rapidly become the most important trading partner for almost all CEECs. For the EU, enlargement offers the prospect of new markets and of wider political and economic stability in Europe.

It is clear therefore, that enlargement is very much a two-way process. Without solid commitment and progress from both sides (the candidate countries and the EU) enlargement will continue to be an aspiration rather than a reality. For the CEEC states, this means that (in partnership with the EU and particularly the European Commission) they must work towards the furthest possible degree of convergence between their own and the EU's economic, political and legal structures. For the EU meanwhile, the possibility of enlargement necessarily means that it must undertake meaningful institutional reform as was begun at Nice in order to avoid future political deadlock in a Union of up to 28 states.

First Steps

The first step towards enlargement was the conclusion of Europe Agreements with each CEE applicant. These govern trade relations, economic aid and political cooperation. This includes the adoption of EU legislation on the free movement of capital, and general compliance with WTO rules (see page 168). The bilateral bodies set up under these agreements continue to monitor the accession process.

The June 1993 European Council in Copenhagen defined the criteria according to which applications are judged (the Copenhagen Criteria). These are:

- political - stability, democracy, rule of law, human rights;
- economic - a functioning market economy, capacity to cope with competitive pressure within the Union; and
- legal - the adoption of the EU body of law *(acquis communautaire)*.

In December 1994, the Essen European Council gave the go-ahead to a gradual accession strategy focusing on the adoption of EU legislation. A White Paper presented in June 1995 identified minimum requirements for accession and listed 899 pieces of internal market legislation to be transposed into the national law of the applicant countries.

Finally, the Madrid European Council in December 1995 called upon the Commission to assess the applicants and the impact of enlargement for the Union. 'Agenda 2000' was the Commission's response to this challenge.

Agenda 2000 & Opinions on the CEECs

Agenda 2000 addressed the EU's accession strategy, the effects of enlargement on EU policies, and how enlargement is to be financed. Adopted by the Berlin Council of March 1999, it tackled the question of EU internal reform in preparation for enlargement (see pages 86 - 87) and set the new financial perspectives for 2000-2006. This foresees a stable annual € 3.1 billion in pre-accession aid for all applicants, subdivided into the main aid instruments of PHARE (Poland and Hungary Assistance for Economic Restructuring Program) (€ 1.5 billion), the Instrument for Structural Policies for Pre-Accession (ISPA) (€ 1.04 billion) and agricultural aid (€ 500 million).

The Commission's evaluation of applicants against the Copenhagen Criteria was appended to the Communication on Agenda 2000. The Commission concluded that all but Slovakia met the political criteria, but applicants did not meet the economic and *acquis* criteria, each to a different extent. Despite these shortcomings, the Commission recommended individual negotiations to start with the Czech Republic, Estonia, Hungary, Poland and Slovenia (known as the 'Luxembourg Six' (plus Cyprus), because the recommendation was approved by the Luxembourg European Council in 1997).

In July 1993, the Commission had delivered a favorable opinion on Cyprus' application for membership, stating that the prospect of EU accession for the whole island could be an incentive for a political settlement between Turkish and Greek Cypriots. Direct negotiations with Cyprus started together with the five CEECs in 1998.

At the Helsinki European Council in December 1999, the EU extended the invitation for formal negotiations to the rest of the applicant countries: Slovakia, Latvia, Lithuania, Bulgaria, Romania and Malta (the so-called 'Helsinki Six'). Malta reactivated its membership bid following a change in government in 1998 (COM (99) 69 February 17, 1999). Turkey was also invited to be a formal candidate. On March 8, 2001 the Council adopted a Decision on the principles, priorities, intermediate objectives and conditions contained in the Accession Partnership with Turkey (OJ L 85 March 24, 2001).

The Accession Process

The accession process takes place in stages, and each applicant country proceeds at its own pace. For analytical purposes, the accession process can be divided into two separate yet complementary processes: the pre-accession strategy and the accession negotiations. Principle instruments of the pre-accession strategy are the Europe Agreements (see page 151), the Accession Partnerships, pre-accession aid and more recently participation in Community programs and agencies. The Accession Partnerships are tailored to each applicant country (see OJ L 335 December 28, 1999) and contain the short and medium-term priorities for each applicant country as proposed annually by the EU. National programs for the adoption of the *acquis* are the applicant countries' response. They must offer a realistic plan to fulfil conditions and respect priorities in the Accession Partnerships.

Another key measure is EU aid. PHARE funding focuses on the reinforcement of administrative and judicial capacity or 'institution-building' and on adoption and implementation of the *acquis*. ISPA finances transport infrastructure and environmental projects (COM (98) 138 March 18, 1998 & COM (98) 294 May 20, 1998). Common agriculture policy (CAP) funding concentrates on improving the structure of agricultural holdings, phytosanitary and veterinary inspection, the quality of foodstuffs and rural infrastructure. SAPARD (Special Accession Program for Agriculture and Rural Development) aims to help candidate countries with structural adjustment problems in these areas and in the implementation of the CAP.

Finally in terms of the pre-accession strategy, applicant countries are able to participate in certain Community programs (eg, SOCRATES) and agencies (eg, the Trademark Agency) in order to smooth their eventual transition into the Union (see COM (99) 710 December 12, 1999).

Accession negotiations with the 'Luxembourg Six' officially started on March 31, 1998 and with the Helsinki Six in February 2000. The first round of talks is essentially informative, during which the Commission's Enlargement DG explains what lies behind each element of the *acquis* in the various areas. The EU and applicants then exchange positions and negotiate on each of the 31 EU policy areas, the so-called 'chapters'. It is important to note that the parties involved are not negotiating the *acquis* itself, only the manner and timing of its transfer into the national law of applicant states (ie, derogations and transition periods). 'Closure' implies that the *acquis* has been presented, the applicants have responded to this and preliminary negotiation agreements have been reached. Final negotiations cannot, however, be concluded with an applicant until the Accession Treaty is finalized. The Council Presidency and the Council are also closely involved, especially in areas such as Justice and Home Affairs. Yearly 'progress reports' on the negotiations are submitted to the Council, the most recent being the one presented in November 2000 (COM (2000) 700 November 8, 2000). The European Parliament is informed of developments during the negotiations by the Commission and Council. The Council may consider the opinions of the European Parliament before making major decisions during the negotiations, it is however not obliged to do so. Accession itself will require Parliament's approval.

Negotiating under Differentiation

The Helsinki European Council approved a new approach to enlargement negotiations. The Commission and EU Member States will manage future accession negotiations on the basis of 'differentiation'.

Differentiation varies from the previous 'wave' approach to enlargement. Under the new differentiation system, any country now has the right to join the EU as and when it has completed negotiations and met all requirements. This implies that the former 'pre-in' countries now may catch up with the countries that have been in negotiations since March 1998.

The negotiating chapters open at any given time can also differ from country to country, and will be reduced in number compared to past years. Rather than open several chapters with all candidates uniformly every six months, the EU will now open chapters for which they deem individual candidates can rapidly complete negotiations.

The basic criteria for accession to the EU, however, have not changed. Applicants will still be required to meet the Copenhagen criteria, and to implement (not only adopt) all Community legislation. Derogations and transition periods are to be limited in time and scope.

At the Nice Summit in December 2000, the EU adopted a timetable or 'road map' for enlargement negotiations in the form of a sequenced approach to the chapters of the negotiations. The strategy suggests taking up the outstanding issues in the negotiations, except those with the greatest budgetary implications. These, together with the 'institutional chapter' and remaining unresolved issues, will be addressed in the first half of 2002.

Negotiations have slowed down somewhat since the start of 2001 as negotiators have tackled the more thorny issues such as free movement of persons (EU Member States fear the uncontrolled influx of workers) and agriculture (large farming sectors of countries such as Poland could further inflate CAP expenses). Moreover, the EU has yet to start dealing with the most difficult aspect of enlargement: the financing of the new Member States who, according to a new study by Dresdner Bank, will require another twenty years before they reach 50% of the average EU living standard. The study says that the financing of agricultural and regional policies in ten new members (excluding Bulgaria and Romania) would require € 44 billion from the EU in 2005 alone.

The most recent enlargement negotiations, held on May 17, 2001, saw the EU close a number of chapters with the 'Helsinki Six'. Negotiations with the 'Luxembourg Group' were postponed until June 1, 2001 due to a deadlock between Member States on the common position on the free movement of workers (see below). At the end of the May negotiations, Cyprus had closed the largest number of chapters (21 out of 30), followed by Slovenia and Estonia (18 chapters closed). Apart from the rescheduled June 1 meeting, there will be one more negotiating round under the Swedish Presidency, scheduled for June 11-12, 2001 at ministerial level.

Prospects for the Future

The negotiating process should reach the most crucial phase in 2002, most likely after the general elections in France and Germany. The Commission has said that it should be possible to conclude negotiations with the most advanced candidate countries some time in 2002. The Accession Treaty, resulting from negotiations, will then undergo the parliamentary ratification process that is expected to take at least 18 months. Most of the candidate countries expect to hold referenda before joining the EU.

The 'Luxembourg Six' originally expected to be able to join the EU on January 1, 2003, while the EU committed itself to completing the enlargement process with the most advanced candidates by 2004 so that they could participate in the 2004 European Parliament elections. Enlargement Commissioner Günter Verheugen says that ten out of twelve negotiating countries can seize this opportunity. Only Bulgaria and Romania are considered too far behind with their reforms to compete for early membership of the EU.

However, concerns have been expressed by some applicants that the EU is slowing down the enlargement process. At a meeting in the Estonian capital of Tallinn on April 9, 2001, negotiators said the EU was too slow in clarifying its positions on key issues, such as agriculture. These concerns have not been helped by delays, in mid-2001, in the enlargement negotiations with the 'Luxembourg Six'. The delay comes after Spain blocked the adoption of the common negotiating position of the EU on the free movement of workers from the new Member States after enlargement. The current proposal under discussion would curb employment of workers from the new Member States for 5-7 years, as requested by Germany and Austria. However, Spain is not willing to agree to transition periods for Eastern European workers until it receives a guarantee from its European partners that EU aid to Spain's less developed regions will not be reduced because of enlargement.

Enlargement discussions will be further complicated when Member States start discussing agriculture. France is likely to insist on subsidies for its farmers. However the Common Agricultural Policy will require a radical overhaul if it is to survive the Union's eastward expansion – Poland alone has as many farmers as the entire EU.

The responsibilities of the EU in this regard are clear. While the prospect of accession continues to act as a major incentive for reform, the aid given by the EU only constitutes a drop in the ocean for most applicant countries. Preparation for EU membership is very demanding for governments, the economy and civil society and the rewards are not always immediate. In such a situation, concerns about possible delays are causing political difficulties in the applicant countries and are provoking tensions in their relations with the EU.

A further problem related to uncertainty surrounding accession is the waning of popular support for enlargement, both in the Member States and candidate countries. The final results of the Eurobarometer opinion poll, released in April 2001 shows that only 44% of EU citizens support enlargement, while 35% are opposed to it. However, in contrast, business in both the EU and CEE is still very keen on enlargement. A survey released by Eurochambres on May 11, 2001 showed that on the whole CEE companies are quite optimistic about enlargement. 50% believe they will benefit from joining the EU.

Business Perspective

The business community fully backs the enlargement of the EU and in particular the rapid adoption by applicant countries of EU single market legislation. This will enable the gradual creation of a true pan-European market which will significantly contribute to the economic growth and competitiveness of European-based investment. Investment in the applicant countries will be facilitated by the removal of remaining tariff and non-tariff barriers both between the EU and applicant countries and between the applicant countries themselves. It will also be enhanced by fast and sensible application of EU rules and standards with the objective of keeping administrative burden to a minimum.

In this regard, business is still very concerned by the frequent discrepancy in applicant countries between the status of formal adoption of the *acquis communautaire* and the actual enforcement of EU legislation. Government procedures, for example regarding safety and conformity assessment with existing regulations, are often still very bureaucratic and time-consuming, thus negatively affecting market access for EU exporters as well as local manufacturers. More specifically, further efforts are needed to replace the pre-market clearance and notification systems with a true in-market surveillance approach, as advocated by both business and the Commission.

Business is also further encouraging transparency in government policy-making and the legislative process and a better and more focused government/business dialogue in all applicant countries. The role of local American Chambers of Commerce and other business organizations in this regard is essential.

Finally, the business community is concerned about the future effectiveness of the EU in deciding and implementing future policies in an enlarged Union. The importance of a successful IGC on institutional reform cannot therefore be sufficiently stressed. Moreover, particularly in light of the financial consequences of the reconstruction of South Eastern Europe, a significant reform of the CAP is necessary prior to requiring the applicant states to adopt EU agricultural policies.

2.2 New Independent States (NIS)

The NIS are the 12 states that emerged after the break up of the former Soviet Union (less the Baltic states) - Russia, Ukraine, Uzbekistan, Belarus, Kazakhstan, Kyrgystan, Azerbaijan, Moldova, Georgia, Armenia, Turkmenistan, Tajikistan. Together they created a Commonwealth of Independent States, a loose framework for political and economic cooperation between them based mostly on bilateral agreements. With the exception of Tajikistan, Partnership and Cooperation Agreements govern relations between the EU and the NIS. Nine are now in force. During the Swedish Presidency the EU has in particular focused its attention on relations with Russia and the other NIS Member States. A Troika led by Swedish Foreign Minister Anna Lindh, and normally including the EU External Relations Commissioner, Chris Patten, and the EU High Representative for the Common Foreign and Security Policy and Secretary-General of the Council Javier Solana, visited Ukraine, Moldova, Russia, including Kaliningrad which is also a sovereign Russian territory, in mid-February 2001. And only days later, the same trio visited Armenia, Azerbaijan and Georgia.

Partnership and Cooperation Agreements
Partnership and Cooperation Agreements (PCAs) aim to establish relations between the EU and the former Soviet republics. They focus on environment, cross-border and customs issues, justice and home affairs, transport, education and intellectual property protection. They are intended to help stabilize emerging democracies by contributing to their move towards market economies. PCAs are managed within a hierarchical institutional framework, comprised of an annual Cooperation Council (foreign ministers' level), a Cooperation Committee (senior officials' level), thematic subcommittees, and a Parliamentary Cooperation Committee with the European Parliament and the national parliament of each partner country.

Common Strategies
Introduced by the Amsterdam Treaty, under the Common Foreign and Security Policy chapter of the EU Treaty, Common Strategies set the general lines of EU policy towards specific countries and issues. They cover political, trade and economic relations, and cooperation in the field of justice and home affairs. The Common Strategy for Russia was the first to be adopted in June 1999 at the Cologne European Council. At the Helsinki European Council in December 1999 a Common Strategy for Ukraine was also adopted. Common Strategies are unilateral policy documents, unlike bilateral agreements such as PCAs that have to be ratified by national parliaments of all parties to the agreement. Implementation of the Common Strategies however is done through the instruments of the PCAs.

TACIS
In December 1999, the EU Council adopted the new TACIS (Technical Assistance for the Commonwealth of Independent States) Regulation, covering the period 2000-2007 (OJ L 12 January 18, 2000). TACIS is increasingly used in support of PCA and Common Strategy implementation aiming to reinforce the rule of law, to strengthen the economic and financial framework, to promote industrial cooperation and partnership, and to improve the business climate.

The TACIS annual report for 1999 (published in January 2001) reveals some improvements in the financial performance of the program. As well as efficiency and management improvements, the report highlighted the fact that TACIS became more closely integrated into EU policy in the region, with tighter links between TACIS programs and the principles set out in the EU PCAs - particularly democracy building and market economy reforms as well as protection of human rights.

Cumulatively TACIS commitments in 1991-1999 total € 4.2 billion with Russia receiving € 1.3 billion and Ukraine € 468 million. The EU is also a large provider of humanitarian aid to the NIS. In late August 2000, the Commission cleared a package of humanitarian aid worth € 7.85 million to assist the most vulnerable sections of the populations in seven of the twelve NIS member countries.

Russia
The EU is Russia's largest trade partner, accounting for 36.7% of Russia's imports and 33.2% of its export trade. In 1999 Russia was the EU's sixth largest trading partner. The importance of Russia to the EU is particularly evident in the energy sector with energy supplies representing 45% of Russia's exports to the EU. The first country to enter into a PCA with the EU, Russia remains by far the largest beneficiary of TACIS aid. In 1999 it received € 101 million which was aimed at providing support for economic and democratic reforms undertaken in Russia after collapse of the Soviet Union in 1992. Aid is specifically concentrated on restructuring public enterprises and the private sector.

Key issues for the future development of EU-Russia relations include: EU investment in Russia, particularly in the energy sector, WTO accession, talks on resolving bilateral trade issues (eg, steel, spirits) and eventually a possible free trade area, environmental protection and nuclear safety (particularly through the conclusion of the MNEPR - Multilateral Nuclear Environmental Program), justice & home affairs (especially organized crime, European stability) and non-proliferation of weapons.

The Common Strategy for Russia of June 1999, adopted for an initial period of four years, aims to further develop democracy and the rule of law, cooperation in the field of environment and health protection, and to strengthen stability throughout Europe by giving Russia a more important role to play in European Affairs. It also envisages systematic judicial cooperation to deal more effectively with organized crime.

The EU is increasingly keen to improve EU-Russia relations especially in the field of economic cooperation, a point demonstrated by the EU's 'Northern Dimension' initiative which brings together the EU, Scandinavian and Baltic states and Russia to discuss areas of potential cooperation in areas of shared interest such as environmental protection, fishery and trade development. However, the EU still insists on an improvement of the situation *vis-à-vis* Chechnya, stressing in particular that a political solution must be reached on the conflict, the affected population must be given assistance and the accusations of crimes against human rights must be thoroughly examined and dealt with in the relevant courts of law with strict adherence to democratic procedures. The Swedish Presidency has also spoken up regarding concerns about signs of increased pressure on the independent media in Russia.

Another current area of importance in EU-Russia relations is the question of Kaliningrad. The talks on Kaliningrad are focusing on how the upcoming EU enlargement to the East will affect the one million residents of the isolated Russian enclave on the Baltic coast sandwiched between Poland and Lithuania. In January 2001 the Commission released a Communication on the Kaliningrad situation (COM (2001) 26 January 17, 2001), while high-level discussions on the subject have also been held at the highest political level. Russian President Vladimir Putin and EU leaders spent a significant part of the 2001 EU summit in Stockholm discussing the future status of Kaliningrad after EU enlargment. Key issues to be resolved include transport and transit, visas, energy, supplies, fisheries, veterinary agreements and contract law.

Ukraine

The EU signed a PCA with Ukraine on June 14, 1994, which entered into force on March 1, 1998. The PCA arrangements cover goods, services, labor and capital and introduce the possibility of creating a free trade area between the enlarged EU and Ukraine at some point in the future. Separate agreements govern trade in steel and textile sectors. Ukraine is also the second largest beneficiary of TACIS aid and in 1999 received € 46 million.

The Helsinki European Council in December 1999 decided on a Common Strategy for Ukraine. Its main priorities are support for the democratic and economic transition process, stability and security and strengthened cooperation between the EU and Ukraine within the context of EU enlargement. In a speech to the European Parliament in March 2001, Commissioner Patten reaffirmed the importance of the values set out in the PCA and the Common Strategy, in light of certain recent incidents putting into question the principle of press freedom in Ukraine.

There are a number of additional issues which are of key importance to EU-Ukraine relations. These include the closure (or otherwise) of the Chernobyl nuclear reactor, intellectual property rights, migration/human trafficking and security of energy supplies (particularly gas) between Russia and the EU.

Other NIS

A special strategy is currently being defined for the Caucasus region. The Communication on relations with the South Caucasus (Georgia, Armenia and Azerbaijan) (COM (99) 272 June 7,1999), is designed to counter instability in the region caused by the incomplete transition processes and conflict.

Meanwhile relations with all other NIS states are governed by PCAs - except Tajikistan for which no PCA has been proposed. PCAs are in force between the EU and Armenia, Azerbaijan, Georgia, Kazakhstan, Kyrgyzstan, Moldova and Uzbekistan and remain to be completed with Belarus and Turkmenistan.

Business Perspective

International businesses active in the NIS markets trust that international agreements such as PCAs and the EU's country-specific Common Strategies start resulting in successful projects that can be translated into tangible business opportunities for both Western and local companies. The long-term objectives set out under TACIS or USAID are very challenging, but perhaps the pilot-project approach - based on small projects that can be completed within reasonable periods - could be a better way to help develop the local NIS markets to the benefit of business.

Overall, based on the experience in the NIS region thus far, it is clear that in order to better assist the NIS countries in the development of free markets and democratic institutions, business representatives need to be more involved. This includes involvement in setting the goals of the programs financed by international organizations and working closely with TACIS and USAID to develop concrete projects with clear objectives. In such cases, policymakers and business representatives can learn on a day-to-day basis through trial-and-error and, in-so-doing, increase the productivity of projects and also the rewards for both business and the local community.

2.3 South-East Europe

Background

The various countries and regions which make up the Balkans region of South-Eastern Europe have come a long way since the signing of the Dayton Peace Accords on November 21, 1995 signalled the end of the conflict which had torn through the region in the early 1990s. While progress has been neither smooth nor geographically symmetrical, it is nevertheless true that the prevalent situation as we move forward into the 21st century is markedly better than that which faced the Balkans in the last decade of the 20th.

With the fall of the Milosevic regime in the Federal Republic of Yugoslavia (FRY) on October 5, 2000, perhaps the greatest remaining obstacle to a lasting peace in the Balkans was removed. This in turn meant that, while numerous challenges remain (witness the spread of violence in the Former Yugoslav Republic of Macedonia (FYROM)) there are increasing signs that other Balkan states are beginning to follow Slovenia into a reorientation of national policy toward engagement and cooperation with the European Union.

The EU is, in turn, committed, for obvious geopolitical and economic reasons, to help this reorientation, with eventual EU membership as the ultimate goal. At an EU-Balkan summit in Zagreb in November 2000, the EU laid out, for the first time, a 'road map' to EU membership before the countries of the Balkans. The EU, along with five South-East European countries signed a Declaration agreeing to strengthen regional cooperation, including plans for a free trade zone. Albania, Bosnia and Herzegovina, Croatia, FYROM and FRY were recognized as 'potential candidates' for EU membership. However, although regional cooperation was stressed, the route to association and membership for each country will follow 'an individualized approach'.

As well as providing impetus and support for the democratic transition of the Balkan states, the EU also provides substantial financial and technical assistance to the countries of South-Eastern Europe. The EU is by far the largest assistance donor to the region as a whole. Since 1991, through its various aid programs, the EU has provided more than € 4.5 billion, while for the year 2000 over € 520 million has been made available for the principal aid programs - PHARE and Obnova.

Moreover, in order to improve the effectiveness of this aid, in November 2000, the EU reformed the process by which financial assistance is channelled to the Balkans. Obnova, established to assist reconstruction in the former Yugoslavia, and the PHARE programs for the Western Balkans were joined together to form Community Assistance for Reconstruction, Democratization and Stabilization (CARDS). CARDS will concentrate on building up and modernizing institutions and administrations so as to strengthen democracy, rule of law and respect for minority rights. The Council also extended the range of the European Reconstruction agency, which previously only dealt with Kosovo, to all of the former Yugoslavia.

For their part, the countries of South-East Europe are committed to developing an area of free trade amongst themselves as a first step towards the full liberalization of trade with the EU. At a meeting in Geneva on January 18, 2001 organized by the Stability Pact for South Eastern Europe, representatives of Albania, Bosnia, Bulgaria, Croatia, the Federal Republic of Yugoslavia (FRY), Macedonia and Romania committed themselves to regional free trade. In their Joint Statement of Intent, the governments promised to 'prepare a Memorandum of Understanding' by the end of June 2001, on concrete trade liberalization measures.

Stability and Association Agreements

For obvious geographical, political and historical reasons, the EU has a special interest and responsibility towards the stabilization and development of the South-Eastern Europe region. However, despite major efforts by the EU to stabilize individual countries and the region as a whole over the last decade, the progress made so far has been limited and fragile. Thus there was a clear need for a stronger initiative for the region. This led the EU to introduce, in 1999, a substantial innovation: the Stabilization and Association Process.

The Stabilization and Association Process offers Albania, Bosnia and Herzegovina, Croatia, FRY and FYROM the prospect of EU integration based on a progressive approach adapted to the situation of each country. The Process offers major incentives to these countries, but also sets political and economic conditions. The need for regional cooperation is stressed particularly strongly.

In order to develop a closer relationship with the EU, the countries will have to gear their political, economic and institutional development to the values and models underpinning the European Union: democracy, respect for human rights and a market economy. The EU will assist them in introducing the reforms necessary to progress in these areas.

So far the EU has opened negotiations for a Stabilization and Association Agreement (SAA) with FYROM (agreement signed in April 2001) and Croatia. Bosnia and Herzegovina, Albania and FRY may also be invited in the future provided all political and economic conditions are met.

The Stabilization and Association process will include as appropriate:

- Stabilization and Association Agreements (SAA): a new kind of contractual relationship offered by the EU – in return for compliance with the relevant conditions. This represents a new dimension of relations, offering for the first time a clear prospect of integration into EU structures;
- asymmetric trade liberalization;
- economic and financial assistance, budgetary assistance, and balance of payment support;
- assistance for democratization, and civil society;
- humanitarian aid for refugees and other persons of concern;
- cooperation in justice and home affairs; and
- development of a political dialogue.

Stability Pact

The Stability Pact for South-Eastern Europe, adopted in June 1999 in Cologne, is an EU initiative. It aims to bring peace stability and economic development to the region. Although the Pact is not a direct instrument of the EU, the EU is nevertheless a major contributor to its work. It lays down a framework for cooperation between the EU, the European Commission, the US, Russia, Japan, South-East European countries, Turkey and other countries and international organizations including international financing institutions.

In May 2001, Bodo Hombach, the Co-ordinator of the Stability Pact for South-Eastern Europe, presented the results of the Stability Pact's € 2.4 billion Quick Start aid package to the Council. The package, which ran from March 2000 to March 2001, contained 244 projects of which 201 were, according to Mr Hombach, "under way".

Individual Countries

Serbia

Following the fall of the Milosevic regime on October 5, 2000 and the ensuing democratic changes in Belgrade (including the subsequent arrest of Milosevic by Serbian authorities in April 2001), the EU has radically changed its policy with regard to Serbia in an attempt to ensure that recent progress becomes irreversible.

Only a few hours after the democratic transition, EU foreign ministers announced a lifting of sanctions, and the immediate repeal of the oil embargo and flight ban. The general feeling of goodwill was mirrored in Belgrade where new President of Yugoslavia Vojislav Kostunica, stated that: "The major goal of Yugoslavia's foreign policy is to approach in a comprehensive manner the family of nations comprising the European Union and then join it".

The EU later announced the extension of the European Reconstruction Agency to Serbia and Montenegro and, moreover, asked the European Commission to propose an extension of the recently announced trade preferences for the Balkans to the whole of Yugoslavia. Also, at the Biarritz European Council in October 2000 Commission President Prodi announced an emergency package for Serbia totalling € 200 million.

However, the relationship between the EU and Serbia is very much a two-way process, and EU assistance is conditional on progress being made in Belgrade. After a visit to Belgrade in February 2001, the EU Troika stressed its expectations of the new leadership in Belgrade whom, they advised, must undertake a comprehensive economic, legislative and political reform program.

FYROM

On April 9, 2001 a Stabilization and Association Agreement was signed between FYROM and the EU (COM (2001) 90 February 19, 2001) which will eventually provide fully liberalized access to the markets of the EU. This was the first such agreement to be signed with a country in the Balkans.

Croatia

Croatia's Stabilization and Association Agreement negotiations, which were opened at the Zagreb summit in November 2000, were completed in May 2001 when Commissioner Patten and Croatian Foreign Minister, Tonina Picula, initialled the Agreement. Technical requirements such as translation will delay the signing of the SAA for a few months, after which areas like trade will come into effect through an interim agreement. Political elements (for which the Member States retain responsibility) will have to wait for up to two years while the Agreement is ratified by the 15 national EU parliaments.

At the initialling ceremony in May 2001 Commissioner Patten stated that the SAA "reconfirms Croatia as a potential candidate for membership of the EU". The Croats would like to prepare a credible EU membership application possibly by the start of 2002 with a view to joining the Union by 2006.

Albania

Albania's progress towards a Stabilization and Association Agreement was also established at the Zagreb Summit in November 2000. A High-Level Steering Group (HLSG) has been charged with preparing the country to begin negotiations for the Agreement. For its part, the EU has indicated that Albania is proceeding reasonably well with the reforms necessary before negotiations for a SAA can begin, but that it must improve in certain areas such as legislation implementation.

Business Perspective

The business community fully backs the EU policy of cooperation with the Balkan countries with EU membership as the ultimate goal. Economic integration between the Balkan countries and the EU will become more and more important. Therefore, business is in favor of the fast introduction of a regulatory framework in line with the EU rules and standards. This will reduce costs for producers, allow lower prices for consumers, facilitate exports for producers in the Balkan countries and make attracting foreign investment easier. While this process goes on, further economic integration through regional trade agreements is also key to the development of the Balkan countries. Consequently, business supports the conclusion and implementation of regional trade agreements.

3. Regional Cooperation

3.1 Euro-Med Partnership

Background

The Euro-Mediterranean Partnership was launched during the Barcelona Conference in November 1995. The aim was to create a multilateral forum for developing closer political and economic links in the southern Mediterranean region. The Barcelona Declaration adopted at the conference consisted of three sections, the first dealing with security, pluralism and human rights aspects, the second with the gradual creation of a free trade area and the third with cultural exchange programs (COM (95) 235 May 31, 1995). The declaration was adopted by the EU and 12 Mediterranean countries (Algeria, Cyprus, Egypt, Israel, Jordan, Lebanon, Malta, Morocco, the Palestinian Territories, Syria, Tunisia and Turkey). As a result of the declaration, several follow-up Association Agreements have been signed or have come into force.

The declaration also called for the establishment, by 2010, of a Euro-Mediterranean trade area, linking together the 15 Member States and the 12 Mediterranean Partners.

The three sections for action outlined in the Barcelona Declaration remain fundamentally valid and relevant. However, delivery of the objectives has been slow, in particular as concerns the process of negotiation and ratification of the Association Agreements. The spirit of partnership has failed to ignite dialogue in areas such as human rights, prevention of terrorism or migration. South-South trade (ie, between the Mediterranean partners) has not increased and financial assistance through the MEDA program (the financial program which provides support for the objectives of the Association Agreements, through bilateral, national allocations and through regional programs) has been hindered due to complicated procedures in both the EU and the partner countries.

Against this background the Commission produced a Communication on 'Reinvigorating the Barcelona Process' (COM (2000) 497 September 6, 2000). Used as a discussion tool at the Euro-Mediterranean meeting of Foreign Ministers in Marseilles in November 2000, the Communication set out the Commission's plans to give impetus to the Euro-Mediterranean Partnership. The proposals include:

- speeding up the negotiation, signature and ratification of the Association Agreements. The slowness of Member States to ratify the Agreements has been particularly lamented (the Agreement with Jordan signed in 1998 has still to enter into force);
- developing South-South trade. In order to meet the objective of an EU-MED free trade area by 2010, the Commission wants all countries signing an Association Agreement with the EU to conclude free trade arrangements among themselves. This should be accompanied by sub-regional cooperation, developing, *inter alia*, the interconnection of transport, energy and telecommunications;
- harmonizing measures relating to the single market. A deadline of 2002 is to be put in place for priority measures relating to such issues as customs, norms and standards, with the year 2004 set as the date for the start of implementation (between both the EU and the partners and between the partners themselves); and
- improving the delivery of MEDA. The revised MEDA Regulation (MEDA II, agreed upon in September 2000) will help streamline decision-making procedures in the Union and should help remedy the current discrepancies between commitments and actual payments made for projects.

The amount made available through the MEDA program for the period 2000-2006 is € 5.35 billion. This will be used to maintain the Union's current efforts. Together with EIB lending, nearly € 13 billion will be available over this period.

The Euro-Med Association Agreements represent a step forward towards peace and political stability in the Mediterranean area. Apart from the aid package, they provide for the gradual exposure of the economy to more competition. Nevertheless, the Euro-Med program has come under increasing criticism, due to an alleged lack of interest and long-term strategy on the EU side. The Partnership is also deemed to favor the EU. The reduction of trade barriers increases market access for the EU, given the lack of progress in the creation of free trade agreements among the Euro-Med countries themselves, and as such could well divert non-EU trade flows towards the EU. The challenge ahead is to create larger and more open markets, and to improve support under MEDA to increase the attractiveness of the region to investors.

With a view to achieving the goal of establishing a Euro-Mediterranean trade area by 2010, Euro-Med trade ministers met in Brussels on May 29, 2001 for the first Euro-Med meeting on trade. The ministers pledged to intensify efforts they hope will result in a free trade area between Euro-Med partners.

3.2 African, Caribbean & Pacific Countries (ACP)

Background

In June 2000, the 71 ACP and 15 EU Member States concluded a new Partnership Agreement on political and economic cooperation. The new ACP-EU Partnership Agreement replaces the Lomé Conventions that, for the past 25 years, have framed the cooperation between African, Caribbean, and Pacific (ACP) countries and Member States of the European Union. The new agreement sets out a comprehensive and integrated approach to alleviating poverty, contributing to sustainable development and assisting ACP countries integrate into the world economy. The Agreement however excludes trade issues, for which negotiations will start in 2002.

The Agreement reinforces the political foundation of ACP-EU cooperation. Political dialogue is supposed to be deeper and wider than at present. It will cover a broad range of political issues that fall outside traditional development cooperation, including areas such as peace-building, the arms trade, conflict prevention and resolution, drugs and organized crime, as well as the sensitive issues of repatriation or re-admission of illegal immigrants.

These new areas for dialogue join the ongoing dialogue on the three existing 'essential elements' - the consolidation of democratization processes, respect for human rights and recognition of the rule of law.

Another new feature of the Agreement concerns participation by non-state actors and local authorities. The new arrangement encourages the integration of all sectors of society in the development process and actively solicits their participation. The measures to achieve this include: participation in consultations on cooperation policies and strategies; access to the financial resources of the European Development Fund; involvement in, and ownership of, project and program implementation; and access to institutional development and capacity-building support.

The Agreement also explicitly recognizes the role of the private sector as an engine for development. A comprehensive and integrated program of action to support the business sector is outlined at the macro, meso and micro levels.

The ACP-EU trade regime will undergo a profound transformation although its exact nature is still to be defined. The all-ACP preferential regime will be split into several trade and economic cooperation agreements, each of which will be treated differently by the EU. This is a clear response to the concerns of the WTO which threatened the very survival of the Lomé preferences. In essence, the final text is 'an agreement to agree' on new trade regimes to be implemented at a later date. The current all-ACP non-reciprocal tariff preferences are maintained until December 31, 2007. Starting in 2008, a set of Economic Partnership Agreements (EPAs) will replace them, which will be reciprocal and WTO-compatible (exceptions will be made for Least Developed Countries (LDCs)).

The ACP-EU Joint Parliamentary Assembly, meeting in Libreville (Gabon) from March 19-22, 2001 kick-started discussions on trade agreements. The assembly produced a resolution which underlined the EU's commitment to ensure that in future trade negotiations, each ACP country will be accorded treatment consistent with the level of economic, administrative, institutional and political development of the country. The Resolution also demands that the high food and animal feed standards applying within the EU should be extended to exports to the ACP. A resolution on 'everything but arms' (see page 165), reached at the same assembly, welcomed the EU Council approval on February 26, 2001 of the Commission's proposal to eliminate quotas and duties on all products except arms from the Least Developed Countries (LDCs). This plan will make the EU the world's first major trading power to commit itself to opening its market fully to the world's 48 poorest countries, 39 of which are ACP countries. However, the full liberalization of sugar, rice and bananas, which constitute very important export products for many of the LDCs, will not be implemented until 2009.

A fourth innovation is that future aid will be allocated according to an assessment of each country's needs and performance, combined with regular adjustments though a system of 'rolling programing'.

In terms of the amount of aid received by the ACPs, the Commission has committed itself to significantly increase disbursements to the ACPs, perhaps doubling the current rate to reach € 3.5 billion per year.

Once signed, the 20-year agreement will not enter into force until it has been ratified by ACP and EU Member States - a process that may take up to two years. Addressing the Joint Parliamentary Assembly in March, 2001, Commissioner Poul Nielson criticized delays in ratifying June 2000's Cotonou Agreement. As yet, no Parliament in the EU Member States has ratified the Agreement, with only a few of the ACP states having done so.

3.3 Mercosur & Mexico

Background

The four Mercosur countries (Argentina, Brazil, Uruguay, Paraguay, plus Chile and Bolivia as associate members) form the world's third largest free-trade block. A web of trade arrangements tie Mercosur members to the rest of the American sub-continent, especially to the Andean Community (Colombia, Venezuela, Ecuador and Peru). The EU and Mercosur are linked through a Framework Agreement for Inter-regional Cooperation, signed on December 15, 1995 (OJ C 14 January 19, 1996). Calling for the preparation of gradual and reciprocal trade liberalization, it encompasses cooperation in trade (eg, customs facilitation, intellectual property), promotion of investment and advanced political cooperation.

Closer cooperation is spurred by rising trade flows. The EU is Mercosur's biggest trading partner, with trade between the two regions (plus Chile) totaling € 49 billion in 1998. Of Mercosur's total imports, 33% originated in the EU countries, and 30% of its exports went to the EU in 1998. Moreover the establishment of Mercosur in March 1991 has coincided with considerable increases in EU exports to the region (up 340% in ten years). The EU is also the single largest provider of foreign direct investment (FDI) in Mercosur. EU FDI in Mercosur countries went from $ 650 million in 1993 to $ 8 billion in 1998.

Both sides indicated a willingness to move towards a free trade zone at the first-ever Latin America-EU meeting in June 1999. Following on from this decision, April 2000 saw the first of three meetings planned for 2000 to form the world's largest free trade zone linking 680 million people by 2005. The first phase of talks concluded with the adoption of 'negotiated documents' setting out the agenda for the trade negotiations and the structure of the working groups. A second round of talks started on June 13, 2000 in Brussels, with the third round held in November, 2000. These three negotiating rounds have led to progress in the political and cooperation (both social and cultural) fields, with trade negotiations forming the main point for discussion throughout 2001. Indeed, following the fourth meeting held in March 2001, both parties agreed to the launching of negotiations on tariffs and services as soon as possible after July 1, 2001 (the start of the fifth round). The Commission has also proposed the launch of a Business Facilitation Initiative with the aim of meeting the desire of business communities on both sides of the Atlantic to facilitate trade and ensure effective market access. This would be framed within the context of the Mercosur Europe Business Forum (MEBF), which last met in Buenos Aires in May 2001. An important step in the overall objective of liberalizing trade between the EU and Mercosur and Chile, the proposed initiative would give priority to addressing customs issues, cross-border procedures, standards, sanitary and phytosanitary measures, e-commerce and competition.

The proposed free trade agreement (FTA) recognizes the growing importance of Latin America as a trading partner for the EU. For the first time ever, Latin America and the Caribbean received more FDI than Asia in 1999 with $ 97 billion vs. $ 91 billion. The Agreement is also in response to EU concerns that US exports and investments may overtake their lead in the Mercosur customs union, especially in the light of the agreement signed at the Third Summit of the Americas (April 20-22, 2001) which aims at creating a hemispheric Free Trade Area of the Americas (FTTA) by December 2005. This point is highlighted by reference to the effects of the 1994 North American Free Trade Agreement (NAFTA) which has seen US exports to Mexico double since 1994.

On March 23, 2000 Mexico and the EU signed a wide-ranging accord on free trade which came into force on July 1, 2000 (COM (2000) 9 January 18, 2000) and will be fully phased in by 2007. The FTA guarantees that by 2003 over 50% of EU exports of industrial products will enter Mexico duty free, while all duties will disappear at the latest by 2007. Mexican exports of goods to the EU will enter duty-free by 2003. Mexico has become the second biggest trading partner with the EU in Latin America since it began to implement the free trade agreement. The FTA also provides progress in the areas of services, public procurement, intellectual property and competition. EU exports to Mexico increased from $ 4.5 billion in 1995 to $ 10.4 billion in 1999, while imports from Mexico jumped from $ 3.2 billion in 1995 to $ 4.7 billion in 1999.

The FTA is part of a wider Economic Partnership, Political Co-ordination & Cooperation Agreement between the EU and the United Mexican States. The first session of the EU-Mexico Joint Council, meeting under the auspices of the Agreement, took place on February 27, 2001. It allowed for the entry into force of the whole of the Agreement with its three pillars: political, commercial and cooperation. The Joint Council adopted the results of the negotiations concerning trade in services, capital movements and related payments and intellectual property, which subsequently came into effect on March 1, 2001. Cooperation activities between the EU and Mexico in the coming years will focus on: consolidation of the rule of law and institutional support; economic cooperation; fight against poverty and social development; and cooperation in the fields of science, technology, education and culture.

3.4 Asia

Background

EU relations with Asia are covered by a series of bilateral arrangements and multilateral fora. The most active multilateral forum has become ASEM (Asia-Europe Ministerial Meeting). ASEM consists of 26 members: the 15 EU Member States plus the European Commission, Japan, China, Korea and seven ASEAN countries (Singapore, Malaysia, Indonesia, Brunei, Thailand, Vietnam and the Philippines). It is organized around three pillars: political dialogue, economic cooperation, and cooperation in the social and cultural fields.

The first ASEM summit took place in Bangkok in 1996, in the aftermath of the EU's adoption of its new strategy towards Asia (COM (94) 314 July 13, 1994) and in the midst of a boom for Asia's emerging economies. The summit focused on establishing a political dialogue and reinforcing economic cooperation.

The second ASEM summit in London in April 1998 decided to establish an ASEM Trust Fund at the World Bank 'to help finance technical assistance and advice both on restructuring the financial sector and on finding effective ways to redress poverty, drawing on European and Asian expertise'. The ASEM Trust Fund became operational on June 29, 1998 with the signature of the first donor agreement with the World Bank. Nine donors - Denmark, Finland, France, Italy, Luxembourg, Netherlands, Sweden, UK and the European Commission - have so far pledged approximately $ 41.5 million. The Fund will operate until the end of 2001.

The Third ASEM summit was held in Seoul in October 2000 and addressed, *inter alia*, the future directions of the ASEM process into the first decade of the new century.

The Summit agreed a total of 16 joint cooperation projects to bond the two regions together. The plans were contained in the Asia-Europe Cooperation Framework (AECF) 2000, or the ASEM Charter, the key document outlining the course of ASEM for the coming ten years, which includes various cooperative projects and guidelines for new admissions. The plans were aimed at raising the level of educational, cultural and intellectual exchanges.

The AECF states that democracy, human rights and the rule of law are the ultimate visions of the ASEM. The AECF also reveals the much-anticipated guidelines for admitting new members into ASEM – some 20 countries have shown an interest in joining ASEM since its inception but lack of membership guidelines have delayed their entry. The AECF also adds a commitment to intensify high-level political dialogue, as well as discussing transnational crime like smuggling, 'human trafficking' and the illegal arms and drugs trades. Among the economic priorities are a commitment to intensify the the dialogue in high-tech sectors like agro-tecnology, e-commerce, transport, energy and environmental engineering. Under the heading of social and cultural activities it lists plans for promoting mutual awareness including university cooperation and electronic networking between schools.

The Fourth ASEM will be held in Copenhagen in the second half of 2002.

ASEAN

The Association of South East Asian Nations (ASEAN) was created in 1967 and encompasses all of the South East Asian countries since the accession of Cambodia in April 1999. The member countries who make up ASEAN have a combined GDP of € 550 billion, but with large disparities among them. ASEAN is the fourth largest trading region in the world and, with a population of 400 million people, is one of the largest regional markets. Relations between the EU and ASEAN are based on a Cooperation Agreement (1980) which aimed to reduce trade barriers, facilitate market access, enable industrial cooperation between firms and promote development programs.

EU and ASEAN officials met most recently at a Ministerial Meeting on December 11-12, 2000 in Vientiane, Laos. The dialogue had been suspended since 1997 when Burma was admitted to ASEAN despite its military regime which was seen as antidemocratic and had a poor human rights record. But after a three-year freeze in political discussions, and despite continued concerns over Burma (or Myanmar), EU governments decided that their ties with ASEAN were too important to be jeopardized by disagreements with Burma. The meeting ended with both sides pledging to continue dialogue and further existing cooperation in many areas. The Vientiane Declaration also reiterated both sides' commitment to promote human rights. Also on the agenda at Vientiane were Asian security issues and the launch of a global trade round.

China

China's rapid economic development in the past twenty years has had a significant impact upon EU-China trade relations. Total two-way trade has increased more than twenty-fold since reforms began in China in 1978, and was worth € 70 billion in 1999. At the moment, China is the EU's third most important non-

European trading partner after the US and Japan. In 1999, the EU was the largest foreign direct investor in China, excluding Hong Kong, as European companies invested $ 4.5 billion. The EU believes that further reform and liberalization will help China to attract foreign investment and technological know-how, and to sustain rapid growth.

To strengthen and enhance this developing economic relationship, in May 2001, the Commission adopted a Communication on EU-China relations (COM (2001) 265 May 15, 2001). The Communication suggests ways of developing EU-China relations by defining short and medium-term action points for EU policy: strengthening of political dialogue, support towards creation of an open society, better integration into the world's economy, better use of EC cooperation programmes and raising the EU's profile in China. On May 21, 2001 External Relations Commissioner Chris Patten undertook a five day visit to China where he promoted both the Communication and EU-China relations in general.

The new Communication recalls the long-term EU policy objectives as defined in the 1998 Commission Communication 'Building a Comprehensive Partnership with China'. While the strategic orientations contained in that document remain valid, there has been a realization that there is scope for making EU policy more effective by broadening dialogue and cooperation and fine-tuning existing instruments. The new Communication makes proposals on key issues where EU policy could be adjusted or where new elements could be added, presenting a new setting for EU-China relations.

The EU is also a strong supporter of China's early accession to the WTO. The EU considers that a WTO without China is not truly universal, while for China, accession to the WTO will symbolize the crowning point of its integration into the global economic order. China has been negotiating terms of entry to the trade-rules body since it struck bilateral market access deals with the US in November 1999 and the EU in May 2000.

China has made a major effort in recent years to undertake the necessary reforms in order to join the WTO – for example cutting tariffs, reforming its currency and developing a legal system - although a number of obstacles still need to be removed before accession can take place.

The WTO Working Party on China's accession last met in January 2001, and important progress has been made toward finalizing the multilateral commitments that China will accept in its Protocol of WTO accession and the annexed Working Party report. Progress has in fact been quite significant, and the currently outstanding issues are limited in number. All countries negotiating in Geneva are now negotiating with a view to concluding the talks.

In February 2001 EU Trade Commissioner Pascal Lamy confirmed that negotiations with China regarding WTO entry have narrowed to just a few issues, such as agriculture and services. With its agricultural sector particularly unprepared for international competition, China dug in its heels in defense of its farming subsidies at the January 2001 meeting. This met with stiff resistance from the US who has voiced strong opposition to China's agricultural protection policies. EU concerns relate mainly to services and it has asked for more assurances that China will maintain stability and transparency in its service sectors, especially insurance.

The exact date of China's accession is still not known, but many countries hope it will be before November 2001, when the WTO meets to discuss launching another global trade round. However, diplomats say China's WTO entry is unlikely before late 2001 at the earliest.

The EU-China agreement on the WTO (designed to resolve certain EU-China issues in order to ease progress within the actual WTO accession negotiations) mainly concentrated on the liberalization of the telecommunications sector, tariff reductions, and market access in the automobile, distribution and agricultural sectors. There were also a number of horizontal agreements regarding measures which distort trade (eg, local content rules), public procurement rules and domestic preferences (eg, in the tobacco industry). The final Council of Ministers and European Parliamentary approval will follow after the completion of the multilateral process at the WTO.

4. Developing Countries

Background

Articles 177 and 181 of the EC Treaty call for the promotion, application and monitoring of the development and cooperation policy of the European Union. The EU is a major player in the promotion of development policy. Approximately half of worldwide public aid to developing countries is currently provided by the EU, not to mention the fact that the EU is the main trading partner for the developing world.

In its Communication of April 26, 2000 (COM (2000) 212 April 26, 2000), the Commission proposed new guidelines for the EU´s development policy. The principal aim is to eradicate poverty. To achieve this objective, attention and support must be given to sustainable economic, social and environmental policy, and the promotion of human rights, democracy, the rule of law and good governance. More precisely, the Communication identifies the need for action in the following six areas:

- trade and development;
- support for regional integration and cooperation;
- support for macro-economic policies;
- transport;
- food security and sustainable rural development; and
- institutional capacity-building.

An assessment of the implementation of this general policy declaration and an action plan is to be subject to review by the Commission in the form of an annual report on Community development. The first such report will be presented during the second half of 2001.

EU Development Policy and the World Trade Organization (WTO)
Globalization, which involves a rise in trade and private investment flows, offers opportunities to increase employment, development and general quality of living. However, it also entails the risk of marginalization. The 49 least developed countries (LDCs) still account for less than 0.5% of world trade. Ironically, developing countries now make up a majority of the World Trade Organization (WTO) membership. The EU believes that the new Round of global trade negotiations, expected to be launched at the Fourth WTO Ministerial in Qatar in November 2001 (see page 168), should reflect the concerns of developing countries. The EU believes that the WTO should establish a framework to facilitate development and the new Round should reflect developing country concerns of:

- participating in all WTO procedures;
- implementation of WTO agreements;
- improving market access and trading opportunities;
- negotiations on new WTO disciplines such as competition, investment and trade facilitation;
- capacity building – human resources, institutional constraints; and
- promoting greater coherence in global economic policy-making.

The WTO provides the ideal forum and the new Round provides the opportunity to promote the interests of developing countries.

'Everything But Arms' (EBA) and the Third United Nations Conference on Least Developed Countries
In February 2001, the European Union approved the European Commission´s proposal to eliminate quotas and duties on all products except arms from the world´s 48 LDCs. The plan will make the EU the world´s first major trading power to commit to opening up its market fully to the LDCs.

Duty and quota elimination for all products took effect on March 5, 2001, with the exception of sugar, rice and bananas which will have a transition period. Specifically:

- duties on bananas will be reduced by 20% annually starting January 1, 2002 and eliminated at the latest on January 1, 2006;
- duties on rice will be reduced by 20% on September 1, 2006, by 50% on September 1, 2007, by 80% on September 1, 2008, and fully eliminated by September 1, 2009; and
- duties on sugar will be reduced by 20% on July 1, 2006, by 50% on July 1, 2007, by 80% on July 1, 2008 and fully eliminated by July 1, 2009.

To compensate for the delay in liberalization, the EU will offer duty-free quotas for sugar and rice, based on the best figures for LDC exports during the 1990s plus 15%. This figure will increase by 15% each year during the interim period. Further, the Commission had agreed to closely monitor the imports of rice, bananas and sugar and to report to the Council in 2005 on the impact of trade within the EU and for the LDCs.

Further to the 'everything but arms agreement', at the Third United Nations conference on LDCs, held in Brussels from May 14-20, 2001, the international community adopted a Program of Action for the LDCs for the decade 2001-2010. The Program of Action calls for concrete initiatives to stop the marginalization of LDCs. It outlines a range of measures to be taken by developed nations and the LDCs. The commitment on trade and development, includes:

- commodities;
- regional arrangements;
- services; and
- reducing the impact of economic shocks.

Developing countries are to aim at improving preferential market access for LDCs by working toward a duty-free and quota-free market access for all LDC products in the markets of developed countries. The full and special measures for LDCs as outlined under the Uruguay Round are to be implemented, and new measures for LDCs are to be considered in a new Round of global trade negotiations. Lastly, it was agreed that technical assistance for the implementation of multilateral trade agreements is to be strengthened.

Human Rights and Democratic Principles

The European Union promotes human rights and democratic principles as laid down in the Universal Declaration on Human Rights, the International Covenant on Civil and Political Rights, the International Covenant on Economic, Social and Cultural Rights, and the European Convention on Human Rights. These agreements enshrine the international commonly recognized values for fundamental freedoms and human rights.

With the entry into force of the Treaty of the European Union in November 1993, further steps were made to integrate human rights and democratic principles into EU policies. Within the Treaty, the section on the Common Foreign and Security Policy refers to 'democracy, rule of law, and respect for human rights', while the new section on development co-operation includes the statement that, 'community policy in this area shall contribute to the general objective of developing and consolidating democracy and the rule of law and to that of respecting human rights and fundamental freedoms'.

The coming into force of the Treaty of Amsterdam on May 1, 1999 was another step forward in integrating human rights into the legal texts of the EU. Article 6 specifically refers to principles of liberty, democracy, respect for human rights and fundamental freedoms, and the rule of law common to all Member States.

Since the early 1990s, the EU has systematically included a human rights clause in its bilateral trade and cooperation agreements with third countries, including association agreements and the Cotonou Agreement with ACP countries of 2000. A Council Decision of May 1995 explains the basic modality of this clause, with the aim of ensuring its consistency in application.

On April 29, 1999 the Council adopted two Regulations on the development and consolidation of democracy, the rule of law and respect for human rights and fundamental freedoms under Articles 179 and 308 EC (Regulation EC/975/1999 and Regulation EC/976/1999). Both Regulations provide the legal basis for all human rights and democratization activities in the EU. Operations financed under these Regulations are to be completed by 2002. The Regulations expire on December 31, 2004.

On May 8, 2001 the Commission issued its Communication on the EU´s role in promoting human rights and democratization in third countries (COM (2001) 252 May 8, 2001). The Communication identifies three areas in which the Commission can play a more active role in the pursuit of human rights and democratization:

- through promotion of coherence and consistency in EU policies;
- through placing a higher priority on mainstreaming human rights and democratization principles in the EU´s relations with third countries; and
- through the adoption of a more focused and strategic approach to the European Initiative for Democracy and Human Rights (EIDHR).

Within Annex 1 of the Communication, a more detailed analysis is made as to how democracy and human rights principles are incorporated into current agreements with third countries, such as:

- The Cotonou Agreement with ACP States (signed June 23, 2000);
- Communication in follow-up to the Rio Summit with Latin American countries (COM (2000) 670 October 31, 2000); and
- Communication on Reinvigorating the Barcelona Process (COM (2000) 497 September 6, 2000).

Annex 2 provides the list of Action Points stemming from this Communication. One of the key actions being that a human rights dimension will be incorporated into the Green Paper on Social Responsibility to be adopted in June 2001.

Fair Trade

The Commission issued its Communication on Fair Trade on November 29, 1999 (COM (99) 619 November 29, 1999). Although there is no legal definition of fair trade, the Communication gives an overview as to what the concept of fair trade entails and how it works in practice.

The fair trade concept applies especially to trade between developing countries and more developed countries. The objective of it is to ensure that producers receive:

- a price that is reflective of an adequate return on their input of skill, labor, and resources; and
- a share of the total profit commensurate with their input.

The objective is achieved via an agreement for a fair price, on a case-by-case basis, by the participants in the fair trade initiative. In situations where the price of goods is agreed internationally (coffee and cocoa), a minimum price is established so that producers receive a return above the world price for their produce. In 1994 it was estimated that the total turnover of fair trade products in the EU was around € 175 million, while in 1997 the figure was estimated at € 200-250 million.

Fair trade initiatives remain private initiatives and operate through voluntary participation – to this extent fair trade is consistent with a non-discriminatory multilateral trading system, as it does not impose import restrictions or other forms of protectionism. If governments were to introduce regulatory mechanisms based on fair trade concepts, then they would have to take into account their WTO obligations. Fair trade is an example of how to bridge the gap between developed and developing countries and to facilitate integration of the latter into the world trading system.

Business Perspective

Business is convinced that the EU and other multilateral organizations can play a vital role in providing technical support and expertise for the development of legal and regulatory infrastructures in developing countries, including implementation and enforcement at all levels.

Business advocates a 'better trade than aid' policy. Open trading systems provides access to developed markets, thereby offering opportunities for LDCs and other developing countries to exploit their competitive advantages to the full. Reform of tariffs is an essential element of this. In particular, there must be a re-examination of tariff escalation for processed goods as they move up the value chain. Orderly markets require that the damaging effects of export subsidies, especially the CAP on agricultural markets, should be removed. In this respect, the 'everything but arms' initiative is to be welcomed, although the opt-out demanded by some Member States is regrettable.

Business supports development aid and poverty alleviation initiatives. It urges the EU and other multilateral organizations to set up aid programs with clear objectives and transparent, accountable procedures for tendering and disbursement. This clarity of process is necessary whether funding is directed to the governments of developing countries or channeled via NGOs.

At a more advanced and long-term level, in order for business to thrive in emerging markets they must have functioning democratic institutions and guarantees for human rights. Business realizes the growing importance of the interaction of trade, social and ethical issues. However, it does not agree with initiatives that use companies for extra-territorial reach into areas where the EU is reluctant to deal with developing countries.

However, this applies in both directions and the business community continues to argue for greater liberalization of trade and less restrictions on Foreign Direct Investment (FDI) in the developing countries, in particular the ACP countries and LDCs. A co-ordinated approach towards trade issues, including investment, competition and market access questions, can and does provide an important contribution to poverty alleviation.

Trade Relations
5. The World Trade Organization (WTO)

Background

The World Trade Organization (WTO) was established in January 1995 to implement and administer the new trade framework set out during the Uruguay Round negotiations (1986-94) of the General Agreement on Tariffs and Trade (GATT). The WTO has 140 members (as of November 30, 2000), with a number of additional countries currently negotiating to join, including China (see page 163) and Russia. Based in Geneva, the WTO has the following functions:

- to administer WTO trade agreements;
- to act as a forum for trade negotiations;
- to handle trade disputes;
- to monitor national trade policies; and
- to provide technical assistance and training for developing countries.

The WTO's Dispute Settlement System

A strengthened multilateral dispute settlement system was one of the key outcomes of the Uruguay Round. The dispute settlement mechanism is based on clearly-defined rules and timetables for completing cases. Priority is given to settling disputes through a preliminary consultation procedure. This first consultation settlement stage seeks to avert trade disputes by enabling the parties to discuss a case under the WTO umbrella. Around 30% of cases are settled 'out of court' in this way.

However, if consultations fail to lead to conclusive results, a panel of experts is invited to consider the case and forward recommendations. First rulings are made by the panel, and endorsed or rejected by the WTO's full membership. It has become increasingly difficult to overturn the panel's decision, despite the possibility of a subsequent appeal. The appeal can be accepted or rejected by the so-called Dispute Settlement Body (DSB). Sanctions, in the form of limited trade sanctions, are only imposed if the parties cannot agree on compensation or if they are not prepared to implement the recommendation of the DSB.

The EU makes full use of the WTO system to enforce its rights. Between January 1995 and January 2001, 222 dispute settlement cases were initiated in the WTO. Of these, the EU has been actively involved in 140 cases, almost three-fifths of the total. A significant number of these cases are between the EU and the US. This reflects the amount of bilateral trade flows and trade interests between the two biggest trading blocks in the world. One well-known Atlantic trade dispute involving banana imports was resolved in mid-2001. On May 2, 2001 the European Commission adopted a regulation to implement the banana import regime in line with the understanding arrived at with the US before Easter 2001 and later with Ecuador. The new rules cover the management of import licence arrangements and apply from July 1, 2001. This demonstrates the willingness on both sides to find amicable solutions to trade-related disputes, however, it should be borne in mind that trade disputes between the EU and the US in fact affect only a very small fraction (around 1%) of the bilateral trade.

The 'Millennium Round'

The Ministerial WTO Conference held in Geneva on May 18, 1998 gave its backing to the concept of a new round of world trade talks to begin at the end of 1999. This new 'Millennium Round' was expected to take up from where the Uruguay Round left off and include a wide range of additional areas. Negotiations aimed at launching the new round and finalizing its content, took place at the end of November 1999 in Seattle. The negotiations broke down, with WTO ministers unable to resolve differences over key issues such as agriculture, anti-dumping regulations and labor standards. The EU and US both pledged to continue to work to find a way forward and re-launch "an inclusive new round as soon as possible".

A number of important lessons were learnt at Seattle which have been largely taken on-board by the WTO. These include:

- better opportunities for wider participation by all members in the WTO decision-making process;
- greater transparency both within the WTO and *vis-à-vis* the rest of the outside world; and
- enhanced consultation procedures with civil society.

However, for the moment it still remains unclear when a new round will be launched. WTO Members are not currently assessing whether or not there is sufficient consensus to launch a new Round at the 4th Ministerial this November in Doha, Qatar.

Trade Commissioner Pascal Lamy has been advocating the case for launching a new round as soon as possible. Lamy's and similar calls for the commencement of talks are being echoed by other important groups such as the OECD, the Asia-Pacific Economic Cooperation Forum and the G-8 Group

The Commission's Position

It is now widely held that international trade is the engine of global economic growth - thanks to the multilateral trading system. Over the 50-year lifespan of the WTO and its predecessor, the GATT, global trade has grown 17-fold, production has quadrupled and per capita income has doubled. Within this picture, the EU is the world's largest trading block, accounting for over a fifth of all world exports in 1999 and, following completion of the 'internal single market' in 1992, one of the world's most open markets. The EU is also the biggest single market in the world and will expand further in the next decade, after candidate countries from Central Europe and the Mediterranean have become members - extending the world-wide benefits of the open EU single market even further. The rule-based, open, multilateral, international trade system is a key factor for EU (and global) prosperity.

The Commission laid out its general approach and the items it wanted to promote in the new trade round in July 1999 (COM (99) 331 July 8, 1999). In the Communication, the Commission confirmed its intention to pursue a 'single-undertaking' approach to the new trade round. It believes this approach allows for gains and concessions covering numerous areas to be balanced out by each actor and 'packaged' into a general agreement which is acceptable for all.

The Communication 'sets out a possible EU agenda' for a 'comprehensive trade round, conducted as a single undertaking and offering a balance of benefits to all WTO members'. Its agenda aims at:

- securing further trade liberalization and market access which accommodates the needs of developing countries;
- strengthening the WTO multilateral system;
- promoting the developmental role of the WTO; and
- ensuring that broader issues such as health, environment and social concerns are addressed.

More specifically, the Commission listed 14 core items which it wanted to address during the trade round, some of which are described in the following pages. These comprise the so-called 'built-in' agenda items (ie, where the Uruguay Round already foresaw further negotiations), new issues partly based on existing WTO work group discussions, and other items.

Since Seattle, the EU has continued to push for a comprehensive round. By 'comprehensive' the EU means that the round needs to cover the vital interests of all WTO members - so that each member can point to real gains from the negotiations. The EU considers that a new round should be comprehensive enough to include not only the 'built-in agenda' (eg, agriculture and services) and market access, but also the strengthening of the existing rules and disciplines such as anti-dumping. The establishment of additional rules for investment, competition and trade facilitation is also regarded by the EU as necessary, as are the formulation of new rules to cope with the global growth in electronic commerce (see page 127). Non-trade concerns, as well as factors such as the sustainable use of exhaustible natural resources and environmental aspects, again, are issues to be decided upon by the new round.

In short, the four basic components which the Commission would like to see addressed by the trade round if and when it takes place, are:

The improvement of market access and the further liberalization of trade - the improvement of market access in key areas such as agriculture (see page 171), services (see also page 172) and tariffs is vital for the improvement of the multi-lateral trading system.

The strengthening of the WTO rule-based system - with regard to investment, competition and trade facilitation. Progress on these issues is essential if the EU is to underpin any improvements in the market access elements of any agreement. It is also essential, in the opinion of the Commission, to update the WTO rule book to ensure that it remains relevant in the twenty-first century (eg, *vis-à-vis* electronic commerce).

The improvement of the integration of developing countries into the multilateral trading system - the EU considers it vital that the WTO becomes more pro-active in terms of promoting a more equal distribution of the benefits of international trade. This involves helping developing countries expand their economies, and develop in a sustainable manner. Since Seattle, the EU and US have taken several initiatives together on this point including a package of market access arrangements for the Least Developed Countries (LDCs) (see page 165 - Everything But Arms (EBA) initiative).

The construction of a more active dialogue with civil society - a key factor in the EU's post-Seattle strategy is to respond more effectively to the opinions of civil society, particularly regarding environmental and consumer issues, for which purpose the Commission has been holding regular meetings with representatives of civil society and NGOs.

As stated above, the promotion of market access continues to be one of the principle aims (and *raisons d'être*) of the WTO and its new trade round, and is therefore discussed here in more depth. Market access stands for the totality of government-imposed conditions under which a product may enter a country. Access for goods can be hindered through tariffs, quantitative measures or non-tariff barriers. Under the 1994 GATT agreement, the raising of tariffs should be the only instrument adopted by a state to regulate the inflow of goods. Tariffs therefore constitute a 'justified' measure protecting a domestic economy. Tariff rates are preferred by the WTO, as they are visible and predictable measures which can be negotiated and reduced. Hence the attempts to first transform non-tariff barriers into tariffs before negotiating a reduction (see for example 'agriculture'). Quantitative restrictions set limitations on the amounts of goods imported or exported and were prohibited under the GATT. With the gradual removal of tariff barriers, a growing variety of less obvious forms of protection such as technical standards and regulations (Technical Barriers to Trade (TBTs)) or subsidies have gained greater importance. Here the aim is to identify these and then to develop rules and disciplines able to limit their trade restrictive effects. The Commission would like to extend the sectors currently covered by market access regulations, as well as strengthen the existing provisions.

A final point regarding the EU's position *vis-à-vis* the new WTO round involves the danger of a repeat of the Seattle failure, which would do immeasurable damage to the long-term welfare of the global multilateral trading system. In order to protect against such an eventuality, it is necessary to make progress on a number of fronts.

Firstly, it is vital that the WTO wins the support of the general public for the international trading system, with key components of this being the need to demonstrate that trade and the environment can be mutually reinforcing and secondly to show that the economic benefits of trade are universal and not just confined to large multinational companies.

Secondly, it is important to restore confidence in the WTO after the shock of Seattle. The WTO has been working towards this goal by regaining some of the lost momentum in Geneva (including groundwork talks on agriculture, services and the full implementation of the Uruguay Round).

However, it seems clear that there needs to be a far deeper convergence of views between WTO members before a full and effective round can begin. Making this point, WTO Director General Mike Moore has stated that there is no point in calling ministers together for another round of free trade talks until there is almost complete consensus on the key issues at stake. Four of these key issues are discussed in depth below. They are environment and labor issues, which were the source of much of the disagreement at Seattle (see page 174), trade in services and trade in agricultural products (both key issues currently under discussion in Geneva; see pages 171-173).

Business Perspective

The transition from the GATT to the WTO has made the Geneva-based trade body much more relevant to business. For instance, the new binding nature of WTO dispute settlement offers greater legal certainty in public international trade law, allowing business to more clearly understand the market access commitments they should expect in foreign markets. Similarly, the significant post-Uruguay Round expansion of the WTO into services and intellectual property has increased the relevance of the WTO far beyond the GATT confines of trade in goods.

Furthermore, the success of the WTO in negotiating market-opening agreements in telecommunications, financial services, and information technology have provided further legal certainty and incentive to businesses wishing to expand their international presence in these sectors. Looking ahead, if and when it takes place, the new round of trade negotiations should result in increased liberalization in sectors such as agriculture, industrial goods and services.

5.1 Trade and Agriculture

Background

The 1994 Uruguay Round Agreement on Agriculture for the first time effectively tackled the difficult question of agricultural protectionism. WTO members agreed to cut tariff barriers by 36% by 2000, to prohibit new export subsidies and to cut existing ones. Limits were also put on the amount of domestic support for agriculture which could distort trade.

Yet the Agreement's impact on trade has been limited. Agricultural tariffs remain high with average bound tariffs of over 40% (some going up to 500%), compared to only 4% for manufactured goods. Many WTO members apply complicated tariff structures, and levels of price support remain high, particularly for sensitive commodities such as sugar, dairy and rice. In addition, food safety and health arguments are increasingly used to set standards and production processes that can easily act as non-tariff barriers. Recent food scares (BSE, foot-and-mouth disease) could tempt policy-makers to erect even more such barriers, using the 'precautionary principle' (see page 81) as a pretext. Finally, agricultural trade has been at the center of some bitter trade disputes, particularly between the EU and US, and the issue will remain controversial with the future WTO accession of both Russia and China (see page 173) with their large, partially state-owned agricultural sectors

The 'Agenda 2000' reform of the EU's common agricultural policy (CAP) was intended to prepare the EU for enlargement towards Central and Eastern Europe, and to provide flexibility for the next WTO negotiations. However, the reform turned out to be much less ambitious than anticipated, reducing the scope for liberalizing the EU's agricultural market. A mid-term review of Agenda 2000, foreseen for mid-2002, is unlikely to result in ambitious CAP reform, thus making substantive negotiations in the WTO more difficult.

The Uruguay Round Agreement provided for an in-built agricultural agenda to make further progress towards substantial and progressive reductions in agricultural support and protection. As a result, and in the absence of a full WTO Round, discussions on trade and agriculture began in March 2000, based on the 'built-in' agenda. After WTO Members submitted negotiating proposals, a stock taking in March 2001 highlighted that some players, such as the EU and Japan, are unlikely to engage in more substantial agricultural negotiations in the absence of a more inclusive WTO Round.

On the question of market access, the EU favours overall average reductions of bound tariffs and a minimum reduction per tariff line. The EU is willing to negotiate reductions in export refunds provided that other export-enhancing instruments are also disciplined, such as subsidised export credits, food aid or state trading enterprises. On domestic support, the EU favors further reductions of 'amber box' (ie, trade distorting) supports. But it insists on the continued possibility to use 'blue box' measures, (ie, trade distorting support that is linked to supply control measures). Finally, in addition to special treatment for developing countries, the EU wants the 'multifunctional' role of agriculture to be recognized, allowing for measures promoting the environment, rural areas or animal welfare to be exempted from reduction commitments. The EU position is therefore far away from the 'almost agreement' reached in 1999 at the WTO meeting in Seattle, before the meeting broke down.

The EU's limited flexibility became apparent most recently in the Commission's failed attempt to abolish tariffs and quotas for agricultural goods from least developed countries as of March 2001. In its 'Everything but Arms' initiative (see page 165), sugar, rice and bananas were exempted from immediate liberalization, postponing full market access to 2009 for rice and sugar.

This failure demonstrates the extent of opposition the EU – but also other WTO members, such as Japan or the US – faces from domestic farm lobbies, particularly in sectors which remain semi-isolated from market forces, such as sugar and dairy. The new WTO round, possibly to be launched in Qatar in November 2001, will be a key opportunity to overcome such opposition, to advance agricultural reform and to reduce protectionism on agricultural goods and processed foods.

Business Perspective

Agricultural trade remains a sensitive issue because of the links with domestic support policies. But liberalization is the route to economic efficiency, growth and welfare both in industrialized countries and the developing world. The 'built-in agenda' talks in Geneva and any new WTO Round must be used to advance agricultural liberalization.

In addition to freer trade in agricultural raw materials, trade in processed food products is of growing importance. But trading processed food is often difficult if food manufacturers are forced by policy measures to pay high prices for agricultural raw materials, which make their exports uncompetitive without export refunds to compensate for those costs. Moreover, barriers to processed food exports often remain high due to 'tariff escalation' and it would be appropriate for the next WTO round to open up a new focus on this area in terms of market access.

Finally, more needs to be done to facilitate trade in food by bolstering the Sanitary & Phytosanitary (SPS) agreement and finding agreement on new areas such as trade in genetically-modified organisms (see page 33).

5.2 Trade in Services

The services sector is central to the future of the European and world economy, as it contributes more to world-wide economic growth and job creation than any other sector. The EU is a world leader in services – largely due to the degree of competition within the internal market. The EU is a leading proponent of efforts to liberalize trade in services world-wide.

Promoting the liberalization of cross-border trade in services forms an integral part of the so-called 'built-in' agenda (see page 171) of the WTO. The 1994 General Agreement on Trade in Services (GATS) forms the basis of WTO initiatives to introduce multilateral rules in the services sector and represents the first ever set of multilateral, legally-enforceable rules covering international trade in services. With GATS, trade in services was no longer simply considered as an ancillary to goods, but was acknowledged as the world's fastest growing sector in terms of international trade, contribution to GDP and job creation.

The main principles of GATS include the following commitments: total coverage of all services sectors as defined in the agreement; application of most-favored-nation (MFN) treatment with limited exemptions; the principle of 'national treatment' concerning foreign companies' market access; ensuring transparency in policies; maintenance of objective and reasonable regulations for affected services; no restrictions to international payments; and a commitment towards progressive liberalization through further negotiations.

GATS has also already led to further sectoral agreements in services:

- negotiations on basic telecommunications (eg, voice telephony, certain data transmission services, telex, fax) were concluded in February 1997 and entered into force in February 1998. A total of 69 countries representing more than 93% of world revenues in telecommunications services made binding commitments in most basic sub-sectors (local, long-distance and international);
- in December 1997 a major liberalization result was concluded on financial services. Altogether, 102 countries with a share of world-wide financial services trade of around 95% agreed to open their domestic markets to foreign suppliers, binding themselves to a set of multilateral rules enforceable through the WTO dispute settlement mechanism; and
- in December 1998, the WTO's Council for Trade in Services adopted the 'disciplines on domestic regulation in the accountancy sector', applicable to all WTO members who have scheduled specific commitments for accountancy under GATS. This was a first step in the development of GATS disciplines on the domestic regulation of services, to ensure that measures relating to qualification requirements and procedures, technical standards and licensing requirements do not constitute unnecessary barriers to trade in services.

GATS 2000 (Built-in Agenda)

As a result of the Uruguay Round negotiations, WTO members committed themselves under Article XIX of the GATS to resume negotiations ('GATS 2000') no later than five years from the date of entry into force of this agreement. On this basis, all WTO members are committed to negotiations to further reduce barriers to trade in services in line with the principle of progressive liberalization. The need to take into account the interests of all participants on a mutually advantageous basis to secure an overall balance of rights and obligations is emphasized. In particular, this means that the particular situation of developing country members should be given due consideration.

The run-up to GATS 2000 saw the completion of an information exchange program in the Council for trade in services followed by the assessment of trade in services required by Article XIX section 3 of GATS. Under the terms of Article XIX of the GATS agreement, further negotiations on trade in services began as scheduled in the context of 'GATS 2000' in January 2000. The negotiations, mandated, as already mentioned, as part of the WTO's 'built-in agenda', cover all services sectors, including financial services, telecommunications, express delivery, energy, professional services, and travel and tourism.

On the basis of the contributions of members to the information exchange program and the background notes from the secretariat, the WTO's Council for trade in services gathered all the necessary elements required to establish negotiating guidelines. These guidelines were subsequently completed on March 23, 2001. The objectives of these guidelines are as follows:

- that negotiations should proceed on the basis of progressive liberalization as a means of promoting the economic growth of all trading partners and the development of developing countries, and recognizing the right of members to regulate, and to introduce new regulations, on the supply of services;
- liberalization shall be achieved through the reduction or elimination of adverse measures in order to promote the interests of all participants on a mutually advantageous basis;
- the negotiations shall aim to increase the participation of developing countries in trade in services, with special priority given to least-developed countries;
- the process of liberalization shall take place with due respect to national policy objectives, the level of development and the size of the economy of different members; and
- due consideration shall be given to small and medium-sized service suppliers, particularly those of developing countries.

In terms of scope, the guidelines stress that:

- there shall be no *a priori* exclusion of any service sector or mode of supply. Special attention shall be given to sectors and modes of supply of export interest to developing countries; and
- MFN exemptions shall be subject to negotiation according to paragraph 6 of the Annex on Article II (MFN) Exemptions. In such negotiations, appropriate flexibility shall be accorded to individual developing country members.

Business Perspective

The GATS is the only framework that will provide services companies with access to other markets. The liberalization achieved in 1997 in the basic telecoms and financial services sectors have shown that the GATS can achieve some liberalization. However, outside of these two areas liberalization has been inconsistent at best and there is significant room for improvement in the new round of negotiations in all services sectors.

Electronic commerce has accelerated the capability of services companies to trade cross-border. Business cannot wait for the 50 years that it took to achieve liberalization of trade in goods (ie, reduction of customs tariffs). New and innovative negotiating methodologies such as model schedules, clusters, horizontal commitments and the like are key to driving the fundamental and significant liberalization that is so urgently needed across all services sectors.

Some areas of particular interest to the business community include:

- the movement of natural persons across borders should be treated as a priority in the GATS negotiations. Too often national boundaries are an obstacle to those service providers who need to move personnel across borders for trade and investment-related purposes;
- the development of disciplines regarding domestic regulation and the need to ensure that they do not create barriers to trade in services. Domestic legislation should be transparent, non-discriminatory and least-trade restrictive;
- the broadening and deepening of commitments in financial services and telecommunications as well as across a host of services that have been enabled by electronic commerce (ie, legal, medical, educational, entertainment, advertising, travel and tourism);
- postal and express delivery services should be liberalized under the GATS to promote liberalization; and
- finally, the liberalization of government procurement of services through its inclusion in WTO negotiations would constitute a welcome step in the right direction for business.

5.3 WTO Electronic Commerce Work Program

In September 1998, the WTO established a comprehensive work program to examine all trade-related issues pertaining to global electronic commerce, and to help WTO members understand how existing commitments apply to electronic commerce (for a more detailed discussion of e-commerce initiatives at EU level, see pages 127-133). The Council for trade in services, the Council for trade in goods, the Council for trade-related intellectual property rights (TRIPS) and the Council for trade and development have all undertaken work on electronic commerce. After Seattle, countries agreed to resume discussions on the WTO Work Program on Electronic Commerce on May 3, 2000.

E-commerce has numerous influences within the multilateral trading system. Among these are issues such as market access for goods and services, intellectual property rights, customs valuation, application of technical standards and other regulations.

With respect to services, it is necessary to recognize the relationship between e-commerce and specific services sectors. International trade in services is conducted to a large and increasing extent through electronic means. Therefore, e-commerce cannot reach its full potential without significant commitments in virtually all services sectors.

One of the key questions facing WTO members is to what extent domestic laws (eg, taxation, cultural preservation, social services, security, content regulation, consumer protection and privacy) will have to adjust in order to obtain the benefits of the internet economy. As more and more economic activity becomes international, more elements of 'domestic' policy have the potential to affect multilateral trade. However, it is quite possible that these potential trade barriers can arise simply because of different, totally legitimate approaches toward any given e-commerce-related policy matter. Presently, there is no multilateral organization or mechanism for reaching a common approach or mutual recognition with respect to domestic regulatory regimes.

Business Perspective

E-commerce accelerates global economic integration. Unfortunately, there is no similar initiative by national governments to integrate governance models. The most significant public policy threats to the growth of e-commerce will come from this mismatch of global economics and governance.

The ability to provide services across borders is a necessary prerequisite for the robust development and growth of e-commerce. If service provision across borders is not permitted, then the ability to deliver those services electronically will be constrained and fragmented in national markets.

In the absence of rules to the contrary, WTO members could use national regulations and laws in a multitude of ways to impede e-commerce.

5.4 Environment, Labor & Trade

Among the most vocal protesters during the Seattle WTO Ministerial were those expressing concern about the impact of globalization and trade liberalization on environmental protection and on the fate of workers. Indeed, environmental NGOs captured much of the media attention paid to the Seattle meeting, and the sharp split among WTO member countries on whether a new negotiating round should address labor standards was one of the key obstacles to a successful launch. More than a year later, these issues remain among the most contentious in the quest for a new negotiating round which potentially will start at the Fourth Ministerial in Qatar in November 2001.

Environmental Protection and Global Trade

The EU's own charter commits itself to ensuring a high degree of environmental protection, and EU institutions advocate this position forcefully in the context of international trade and economic relations. Thus, the European Commission pursues strong environmental standards not only in the context of the WTO, but across a broad range of EU trade and commercial relations (including, for example, enlargement arrangements and bilateral free trade agreements).

At a meeting in WTO headquarters in March 2001 (not attended by the US), some members recognized a need to clarify the rules on the environment. However, concerns were voiced over protectionism 'through the back door' and members indicated the need to ensure that any clarification of trade and related environment rules would not be discriminatory and would not allow unnecessary trade restrictions.

The EU's negotiating position has shifted in since then. Traditionally, it included a specific demand for acceptance of the precautionary principle (see page 81) as a basis for potentially trade-restrictive measures. The Commission argues that adherence to the precautionary principle is a key tenet of its approach to setting a high level of protection for the environment and for human, animal or plant health, as allowed by GATT Article XX. Since February, however, the EU has diluted its negotiating position in an effort to address the concerns of developing countries and the US. It is now promoting a plurilateral, opt-out approach whereby members could discuss environmental issues without being obliged to adhere to rules in this area. The Commission has stressed that the EU only wants to clarify existing WTO rules, not to impose new restrictions. Moreover, the EU also advocates the use of multilateral environment agreements as a preferred means of achieving environmentally beneficial policies, whilst avoiding conflict between trade and environmental rules.

While the Commission has advocated an enhanced dialogue with civil society on trade issues generally, it has been particularly active in engaging environmental NGOs on their trade concerns. The EU has played a leading role in helping to organize WTO sessions at which civil society can address the inter-relationship between trade and environment roles, and environmental NGOs have taken full advantage of the Commission's recent efforts to strengthen its own broad outreach program. These contacts will help to reinforce the Commission's emphasis on ensuring that WTO rules allow member countries the leeway to enforce a high level of environmental protection, even if this raises the risk of impeding trade flows.

Labor Standards and Global Trade

The long-simmering disagreement between key developing countries and some leading developed economies over the inclusion of labor standards in world trade rules came to a head at the Seattle Ministerial. Developing country leaders, long concerned that such initiatives would deprive them of the few comparative advantages their economies enjoy, reacted furiously to suggestions that the US could envision a trading system that included sanctions for countries whose labor protections were deemed inadequate. The rift was one of the principle causes of the failure to launch a new round. However, at their recent meeting in Geneva, members (including the EU) ruled out a sanctions-based approach to any discussions. The current position of the new US administration is to support the discussion of labor issues on the international stage, but not in the WTO.

Until now, the inter-relationship between trade and labor has been addressed mainly by the United Nations Conference on Trade and Development (UNCTAD) and the International Labor Organization (ILO). In 1996, WTO member countries agreed that the ILO (because its membership included governments, employers' and workers' representatives) was the most appropriate forum for progress on the issue. The ILO has long campaigned for international recognition of certain basic worker rights, and succeeded in incorporating the right of association and collective bargaining, and an end to forced labor, child labor and discrimination, into the 1998 Declaration on Fundamental Principles and Rights at Work.

While the EU has pressed for the creation of a working group on trade and labor standards within the WTO (of the kind that exist on trade and the environment, and on trade and investment) and more recently for a standing forum between the two organizations, it appears to accept that developing countries' opposition to such a step has not lessened. Nevertheless, the Commission continues to advocate increased collaboration between the ILO and WTO (including granting the ILO formal observer status at WTO meetings), and has made the trade and labor issue another priority for its stepped up dialogue with civil society.

Business Perspective

Business recognizes that legitimate concerns about public health and the environment need to be reflected in setting and enforcing trade policy, and it is at the forefront of the push for liberalizing trade in environmentally friendly products and services, which can help to further the goal of sustainable development. With regard to the adoption of health and environment measures by governments, business favors an approach that relies upon science-based decision-making, thus eliminating the scope for political interference. It is essential that any such measures should cause the minimum distortion possible to normal flows of trade. This necessarily means obtaining a broad international consensus on the quality, reliability and scope of scientific information used to justify claims that a measure is necessary for protection of health or the environment, and on whether trade-restrictive actions may be taken before such information is available.

Trade liberalization offers important economic benefits by expanding employment opportunities and raising incomes, including in developing and least-developed countries where the need is most acute. Business agrees on the importance of ensuring that such benefits are accompanied by adherence to internationally recognized norms for the treatment of workers, including, for example, the ILO Declaration on Fundamental Principles and Rights at Work. Many companies have considerable doubts, however, as to whether it would be appropriate or effective to use the WTO framework to establish and enforce such norms.

6. Export Control on Dual-Use Goods

Background

Dual-use refers to goods or related technologies with both civil and military uses. Their availability for export is controlled by governments in order to protect essential security interests. Export controls in the EU were harmonized in 1994 by Council Regulation EEC/3381/94 and Council Decision 94/942/CFSP.

Given the sensitivity of issues related to the export of dual-use goods, Member States retain a high level of autonomy in establishing export control regimes. This has led to considerable variations between export controls in different Member States which can result in difficulties for companies involved in cross-border cooperative arrangements. Trade distortions can also result when exporters in one country face more complex controls or licensing procedures than exporters of the same product in a neighboring Member State. Differences between the EU and US export control regimes also cause significant problems for business. There is, therefore, a significant need for harmonized controls.

Following two years of application, the Commission came to the conclusion that it had not been possible to establish a credible common system of export controls accepted by exporters and routinely enforceable by customs (COM (98) 258 May 15, 1998). It acknowledged that confidence among industry had fallen and industry associations did not feel they had a level playing field in comparison to their American and Japanese competitors. Operations had proved especially difficult for companies established in different Member States. The practical problems all appear linked to the fact that the present export control regime is limited to a mutual-recognition exercise, essentially caught between the aims and requirements of the EU's common commercial policy (common export promotion) and the common foreign and security policy (eg, commitment to non-proliferation). Problems persist such as delays and information gaps at borders and the lack of results in terms of combating proliferation. These are caused by the complexity of co-existing national, global and general licenses, often with the same destinations but a slightly different product scope.

The regime has led to split and unclear EU and Member State competencies, which was also criticized in a European Court of Justice (ECJ) ruling in October 1995. The problems prompted the Commission to propose the establishment of a new dual-use goods Community regime. A new Council Regulation (EC/1334/2000) was adopted on June 22, 2000 (OJ L 159 June 30, 2000), replacing the previous Regulation EEC/3381/94.

The Regulation is now based only on Article 133 *(ex Art.113)* of the Treaty (common commercial policy). For this purpose, the previous Council Decision CFSP/942/94 was repealed, ie, the control list of dual-use goods and technology is now integrated in the new Regulation (single pillar versus two pillar system, see page 5).

The Regulation forms part of the measures in the Commission's plans relating to the European defense industry (COM (97) 583 December 4, 1997) and aims at simplifying and strengthening the present regime with a view to facilitating legitimate trade while allowing resources to be focused on the control of sensitive exports and of fraud. It therefore foresees a combination of common policy and reinforced administrative cooperation between Member States.

The Regulation mainly consists of:

- the creation of a Community general license for certain exports in order to consolidate the *de facto* convergence of Member State licensing policies *vis-à-vis* certain third countries (Australia, Canada, the Czech Republic, Hungary, Japan, New Zealand, Norway, Poland, Switzerland and the US);
- the extension of the 'catch-all' to all military end-use goods for shipments to countries subject to a UN, OSCE or EU embargo (at present the catch-all clause is limited to programs with weapons of mass destruction);
- the coverage of dual-use technology transfer by PC, fax and telephone, extending the previous Council Decision 94/942/CFSP of December 19, 1994 (OJ L 92 March 25, 1998) to cover more modern 'intangible forms' of data transmission;
- the reduction and simplification of licensing procedures for intra-Community trade whilst ensuring that trade can be monitored and exports controlled. Some limited controls are still maintained because of the particular sensitivity of the products, eg, nuclear and ballistic devices. For encryption products, intra-EC trade is liberalized completely, except for a few very specialized products (development and cryptoanalysis items);

- the reinforcement of administrative cooperation, in terms of reinforcing information exchange and consultation between Member States; and
- the effective unification of procedures, allowing decisions currently falling under the CFSP to be dealt with under the EC Treaty (Article 133).

While the new Regulation abolishes the previous two-pillar system, it does not cover one particular aspect of technology transfer ie, the technical assistance by natural or legal persons. For this purpose, a separate Council Joint Action was adopted on June 22, 2000 which regulates such transfers - including in oral form - related to certain military end-uses (2000/401/CFSP; OJ L 159 June 30, 2000).

Other than the initiatives taken at EU level, there are also wider international fora in which the export of dual-use goods is an important issue. In July 1996, 33 countries from Europe, the Americas, Japan, Australia and New Zealand agreed to cooperate in restricting the transfer of conventional arms, dual-use goods and technologies by participating in the Wassenaar Arrangement (WA). This agreement is the successor to the Co-ordinating Committee on Multilateral Export Controls (COCOM), set up to limit exports to communist countries during the Cold War, which was discontinued in 1994. It co-ordinates efforts to restrict exports of sensitive or destabilizing conventional arms or dual-use technologies to 'states of serious concern' and is not a treaty, but an executive agreement among exporters to co-ordinate their national export controls. The WA has a dual-use and a munitions list and has made some progress on common standards for export controls and cooperation among national export authorities. This leads to regular updates of the list which need to be adopted by the EU (see OJ L 18 January 23, 1999 and OJ L 73 March 19, 1999).

Business Perspective

The business community has continued to argue for greater harmonization and transparency of export control. Within the EU there is also a need for greater transparency in the implementation of export control rules. Problems have arisen in the past due to the limitations of the various mutual recognition regimes between EU Member States, with some being more restrictive than others or requiring individual authorizations rather than global or general licenses. These differences have caused confusion, delays and distortions of competition and have especially affected companies established in different Member States. Furthermore, the system placed European firms at a disadvantage to their US and Japanese counterparts. Business therefore sees the new initiative as a step in the right direction. However, it remains to be seen whether the final results will meet the concerns of business. The issue of export controls is also being treated within the TABD; here particular focus is being placed on avoiding unilateral embargoes with extraterritorial impact.

Whilst the creation of a Community general license is welcome, its benefit could be widely increased by extending its scope to a far larger number of destinations than the current ten countries. Furthermore, as growing focus is put on regulating intangible transfers of technology (by phone, fax, electronic means) the business community needs clear and realistic guidelines as to the implementation and enforcement of these controls.

European and US businesses require guidance from all governments on catch-all provisions, emphasizing the need for regular revisions of export control lists, and generally welcome a constructive dialogue between governments and business in this area.

7. Reform of the Transit System

Background

Transit - movement of goods under duty suspension through several customs territories - is in essence a trade facilitation measure. It is based on the designation of a legal entity that provides a guarantee to ensure the collection of duties and other charges due in the event of irregularities. Transit procedures are governed by two main systems: the EU's Community transit system and the Common Transit Convention (23 contracting parties: EU, EFTA and Visegrad countries). Procedures are based on a series of documents which have to be validated at the customs office of departure and produced at the customs office of destination within a prescribed time limit.

In March 1995, the Commission noted that since the opening up of borders in Central and Eastern Europe to international trade, the transit system had been targeted by criminal networks for highly profitable fraudulent activities. Fraud had indeed become a major and growing problem not only resulting in high revenue losses, but also in substantial economic damage due to the illicit competition from fraudulent goods. This prompted the European Court of Auditors to review the Community transit system in November 1995. It identified a significant number of irregularities and deficiencies resulting in financial loss to the Community and Member States. In December 1995, the European Parliament (EP) decided to set up its first ever Committee of Inquiry to examine the Community transit system and the allegations of fraud and mismanagement associated with it.

The first remedial measures to counter fraud in transit were taken in 1996 and dealt with issues such as suspending the access to guarantee facilities for so-called sensitive goods (alcohol, cigarettes and certain agricultural products). Subsequently, the Commission's Action Plan for Transit in Europe was published in 1997 (OJ C 176 June 10, 1997). This took on board the Parliament's recommendations calling for an early-warning system for sensitive goods, a reform of the guarantee system and improved control mechanisms - all under the roof of a merged Pan-European customs transit system. The plan's main elements were:

- commitment to the swift implementation of the transit system's computerization;
- boosting cooperation between customs administrations by improving the prior information system;
- developing a common risk management policy allowing customs to define precise criteria for targeting inspections, record checks and inquiries;
- modulating access to simplified procedures and guarantee facilities according to the reliability of operators;
- securing the movement of goods in transit by reducing the risk of goods being unlawfully removed from customs supervision or en route;
- developing a policy for detecting and dealing with small and large-scale fraud; and
- in the long term, merging the Community and the Common Transit System.

The Action Plan was subsequently endorsed by the Council. This was followed by the first amendment proposals of the Common Transit Convention in June 1997.

Amending the Community Transit system firstly means modifying the Community Customs Code (CCC). This was achieved in February 1999 by Regulation EC/502/1999 (OJ L 65 March 12, 1999). It allowed for new proposals on implementing regulations, the first of which was adopted in April 1999 (OJ L 119 May 7, 1999) regarding the full computerization of transit procedures. Amendment of the provisions governing the Common Transit Convention was also achieved in February, 1999 (OJ L 65 March 12, 1999).

The legislative reform process launched in 1997 was completed at the end of 2000, with the adoption of the reform proposal for the Community transit system (Regulation EC/2787/2000 December 15, 2000; OJ L 330 December 27, 2000) and the adoption of Decision N. 1/2000 of the EC-EFTA Joint Committee on common transit of 20 December 2000, (OJ L 9 January, 12 2001). The reform will be fully implemented by July 2001. A transit manual, providing guidance for customs and operators on the interpretation of the rules will be finalized by the end of 2001.

The Transit Contact Group, a consultative body set up by the Commission and composed of customs and operator representatives, will meet in June and December 2001 to discuss progress in implementing the reform and New Computerized Transit System (NCTS).

The reform left one issue outstanding: the type of data needed by customs and operators for management and control of transit procedures. To identify the specific data that could be provided by operators to meet those needs, the Commission set up a 'data subgroup', composed of representatives from customs and operator associations. The subgroup will formulate recommendations with regard to transit legislation of the Community and the Common transit systems. The final report from the data subgroup is expected at the latest for the December 2001 meeting of the Transit Contact Group.

Business Perspective

The business community is supportive of measures aimed at securing the transit systems against abuse by fraudsters such as restricting access to guarantee facilities and simplified procedures to reliable operators and the computerization of the transit systems. It therefore welcomes the adoption of the transit reform.

As regards the type of data needed for the management and control of transit procedures, there is some degree of concern about the proposed inclusion in the transit documents of the Harmonized System (HS) code of all goods shipped, as this measure could potentially place a heavy burden on operators. The business community welcomes the setting up of the 'data subgroup' that hopefully will allow for a practicable approach to meeting the need for data.

The business community has also called on the authorities to ensure a uniform application of the rules throughout the Community and to maintain the dialogue established with operators until the reform is fully implemented. The business community has stressed the need for the development of the transit manual as a means to seek more uniform application of the rules. A first draft has been circulated to operator associations in May 2001 and operator input will be discussed at the June meeting of the Transit Contact Group.

Business is also concerned with progress on NCTS. Whilst computerization is moving ahead according to schedule, connection of operators to NCTS is still not in place in the countries already participating in NCTS. The business community intends to stress the need for consultation at national level about NCTS implementation.

Chapter XI
Transport & Energy

THE EU COMMITTEE
OF THE AMERICAN CHAMBER OF COMMERCE IN BELGIUM

Transport
1. Maritime Safety

Background

The Commission published a Communication on a common policy for safe seas in February 1993 (COM (93) 66 June 8, 1993) which analyzed the main causes of accidents at sea with a view to identifying crucial areas which call for specific measures at the international, Community, regional or local levels. The document recognized the central role of the International Maritime Organization (IMO) in developing international safety and environmental regulations.

With the Council's support, legislation was brought forward by the Commission and has since entered into force. Much of this built on, or complemented, already existing international regulations in the framework of the IMO or of the International Labor Office (ILO) in regard to working conditions for seafarers.

In March 2000, in response to the sinking of the tanker Erika off the coast of Brittany, France, the Commission issued a Communication on the safety of seaborne oil trade (COM (2000) 142 March 21, 2000), setting out the broad lines of future EU action and accompanied by three legislative proposals. The first batch of proposals aim at reinforcing port state control, introducing more stringent criteria for classification societies and accelerating the international timetable for the phase-out of single-hull tankers. In amending the Port State Control Directive (95/21/EC), the Commission seeks in particular to improve inspections with respect to those vessels which present greater risks on account of their age or the nature of their cargo. It therefore recommends that ships over 15 years old, which have been detained more than twice in the preceding two years be banned and black-listed. Oil tankers over 15 years old will be subject to expanded inspections (the prevailing limit being 20 and 25 years). The proposal on classification societies imposes stringent qualitative criteria to be met by recognized organizations and gives the Commission the right to withdraw the recognition of classification societies if shortcomings in their performance are identified. As regards the phase-out of single-hull tankers, the EU is proposing to accelerate the IMO timetable for the banning of single-hull tankers and begin the gradual phase-out of certain categories of tankers in 2005, as opposed to 2007-2012 in the case of IMO and 2010 under the US's 1990 Oil Pollution Act.

The current status of the "Erika I" package is as follows: the proposals on port state control and classification societies are pending their second reading in Council. As regards double-hull tankers, in accordance with the Ministerial agreement in late 2000, the matter was referred to the IMO - an agreement at international level having been deemed preferable. In April 2001, the IMO agreed on a phase-out schedule for single-hull tankers, close to that advocated by the Commission, with a final phase-out date of 2015.

A second package of measures was brought forward by the Commission (COM (2000) 802 December 8, 2000), comprising a monitoring system for maritime traffic, the setting up of a maritime safety agency and a new EU pollution compensation fund (COPE fund; Council Decision 2000/409/EC June 19, 2000), to complement the existing international liability regimes. A first exchange among Transport Ministers in early April 2001 indicated wide support for the creation of a maritime safety agency. As regards traffic monitoring, most Member States favored action in the IMO framework, such as strengthening international rules and accelerating the timetable for mandatory fitting of black boxes on board vessels. The Commission's proposal requires all ships to have this equipment on board as from entry into force of the legislation. As regards the EU compensation fund, most ministers advocated pressure being placed on the IMO to have the ceiling raised for the international compensation fund (IOPC) and payment mechanisms improved.

Business Perspective

The Oil Companies International Marine Forum (OCIMF), representing the world's major oil companies on marine safety and technical matters, has supported the Commission's proposals regarding classification societies and port state control. It also welcomes the principles behind the proposals on reporting and monitoring ships in EU waters, although with reservations about some of the details. OCIMF actively contributed to discussions in the IMO on the issue of double-hulls and are similarly engaged with regard to the discussion on compensation regimes and liability issues. Conversely, OCIMF is not in favor of the COPE Fund proposal which, the organization fears, could well be counterproductive and, at worst, act as a disincentive in preventing future accidents. Many ship operators and users of shipping services share the concerns over safety in shipping which have arisen following recent tanker spills and are strong supporters of measures to enhance safety in maritime transport. Wherever possible, international rather than regional solutions are to be favoured, given the global nature of shipping.

2. Community Railways

Background

Under the Common Transport Policy, the Commission is seeking to develop a single market and promote sustainable mobility, efficiency in the transport system, intermodality and a transfer of freight and passengers to rail. Due to the traditional organization of rail as state-owned and state-run national companies, the liberalization measures described below imply a radical rethinking and restructuring process. Deregulation and the introduction of competition remain key elements. Competition implications regarding the EU's anti-trust provisions will only begin to apply towards the end of liberalization, ie, as state rail monopolies face increased competition from private undertakings and as some are being privatized. Until this occurs, the rail sector is being treated under aspects of state aid control and anti-monopoly provisions in the Treaties.

The only country to have undergone a radical restructuring is the UK and with very mixed results. Some Member States see the UK model as an example of too radical a liberalization with little increase in efficiency, quality or competitiveness and few cost-reduction bonuses. It has been particularly controversial in the passenger sector where small yet significant improvements by some operators have been greatly overshadowed by the well-publicized failure of others. On the freight side, developments in the UK have been more encouraging. However, efforts in the other EU Member States have been frustratingly static. The creation of a Single European Transport Market is already advanced in road, sea and air. Rail alone remains the mode of transport in which the least progress in terms of liberalization and quality improvement has been made.

At the EU level, rail transport has experienced a steady decline for nearly thirty years. According to the Commission the proportion of goods moving by rail around the EU and across its borders fell from 32% (1970) to 14% (1996); the share of the passenger market in the same period dropped from 10% to 6%. In its White Paper on the 'revitalization of the railways' (COM (96) 421 July 30, 1996) the Commission insisted that liberalization is the only way to halt and reverse the steep decline of rail transport.

In March 1998 the then Transport Commissioner Neil Kinnock put forward an ambitious schedule by proposing an opening of the rail freight sector by 5% of the market as soon as possible and by 25% over the following ten years. However, a November 1998 strike in six Member States alongside continuing French resistance to liberalization forced Commissioner Kinnock to reiterate that progress would be slow and phased, with the emphasis on liberalization, not deregulation. The Commission suffered another setback to its efforts of revitalizing rail in 1998 when the Rail Freight Freeways program, which allows uninterrupted cross-border cargo services, had less takers than expected - only four have been opened and only one actually operates.

On July 27, 1998 the Commission proposed a package of specific measures in a general Communication on rail transport (COM (98) 480; OJ C 321 October 20, 1998). This so-called railway package comprises three proposals for Directives on:

- certain access rights to infrastructure and the separation of infrastructure management and transport operations, at least in accounts (amendment of Directive 91/440/EEC);
- a common scheme for licenses in order to ensure free circulation of services and fair treatment of undertakings, while ensuring that they are safe and dependable (amendment of Directive 95/18/EC); and
- the allocation of railway infrastructure capacity, the levying of charges for the use of railway infrastructure and safety certification (proposal for a new Directive).

After more than two years of debate, culminating in a conciliation procedure between the Council and the Parliament in autumn 2000, the railway package was formally adopted in February 2001 (OJ L 75 March 15, 2001). It led to the following results:

- by 2003 a Trans European Rail Freight Network (TERFN) will be established, including the main European rail freight corridors as well as their links to ports. All licensed rail undertakings will have the right to provide international freight services on the TERFN, provided that they meet certain security standards;
- by 2008 all licensed rail undertakings should be able to gain access to the entire European rail network for international freight services;
- passenger transport is not included in this package, however the Transport Commissioner Loyola de Palacio has announced the Commission's intention to propose a second package of measures in 2001;

- the decisions on licensing of railway undertakings, charging and train path allocation are taken by a legally and organizationally independent authority, which does not offer rail services; and
- the charging system will be based on the principle of 'social marginal cost pricing' with the possibility of higher charges (up to full cost recovery) in cases where considerable investment in rail infrastructure is necessary. In the long term, a charging system where the user covers the full costs is envisaged. The new charging system should address the barriers thrown up by disparate infrastructure charging schemes in the Member States, which hamper the establishment of international services.

In February 2001 a fourth proposal related to the railway package was finally adopted, namely a Directive on the interoperability of the conventional rail network (2001/16/EC; OJ L 110 March 19, 2001). This should foster the creation and implementation of an integrated and interoperable trans-European conventional rail system based on compulsory Technical Specifications of Interoperability (TSI) along with harmonized standards. A similar Directive for high-speed trains was adopted in 1996 (96/48/EC; OJ L 235 July 23, 1996).

Two major objectives of the initial Commission proposal of the railway package have, however, not been achieved: the entire separation of infrastructure management and transport operations and the creation of a European rail observation system. These issues may be addressed in the second railway package already under preparation in the Commission. At the moment, the following elements are being discussed internally:

- a proposal for a framework Directive on rail safety;
- a proposal for the opening of cabotage (access to intra-Community markets for EU carriers) for rail freight services, ie, the licensed rail undertakings would then have the right to provide national freight services in all Member States; and
- a proposal to extend the scope of the new Directive on interoperability of the conventional rail network.

Furthermore, the idea of the creation of a European rail agency is being further explored in the Commission. Besides the preparation of the second package, which should still be tabled in 2001, the Commission started working on the implementation of the first. A first hearing with large rail freight customers, organized by RAILSERV (European project on rail freight services), was held in Brussels in March 2001. Requirements for improved quality of rail services were defined, for instance: implementation of rail liberalization, improved reliability and information services for European rail freight services and a transparent pricing policy for railway companies. The hearing concluded that a European platform of rail freight customers is needed to ensure that the right actions are taken and to provide the Commission with valuable input for the next legislative steps on the necessary improvement of the quality of rail services.

Business Perspective

Business welcomes the adoption of the rail package, which should increase competition in the European rail sector. This development is very encouraging and an accelerated implementation is supported by business. Special attention has now to be paid to the implementation of the proposed measures, which should lead to better service levels and competitive pricing in the European rail sector thereby increasing overall competitiveness.

However, business remains skeptical of the commitment of all Member States to implement the package uniformly. It remains an important task for the Commission and business stakeholders to encourage Member States to adopt the proposed legislation as soon as possible as a first step towards making the European rail sector a viable transport alternative for European industry.

It is encouraging to see that the rail sector itself has started to realize that it needs to improve its efficiency and effectiveness. This has been demonstrated by the positive reaction of the Community of European Railways (CER) to the adoption of the rail package and by cross-border mergers and alliances between incumbents in the rail sector (eg, the Dutch-German 'Railion'). However business is yet to see the efficiency gains of these developments. Furthermore, business encourages the traditionalist railway companies to engage in innovative ventures with private enterprise in order to improve the services that the rail sector is offering.

3. Liberalization of Postal Services

Background

The European objective of realizing a European single market for postal services while assuring the provision of a basic mail delivery service throughout the EU is the subject of lengthy debates.

The postal market – with a wide variety of services on offer, ranging from basic universal service to very specialized services including express delivery and logistics solutions – is permanently changing and evolving. As a result of this change, the traditional distinction between public post offices and private operators has disappeared.

Although post offices, through acquisitions, have expanded their organization to compete in the open market, private operators are not allowed to operate in the market segment that is fended off and protected by nationally granted monopolies.

There is a considerable risk that public postal operators (ab)use their monopoly revenues to strengthen their place on the open market by investing in commercial activities and financing acquisitions in the commercial sector. Moreover, public postal operators are benefiting from a variety of privileges and preferential treatment over private operators.

Nearly a decade after the Commission's 1988 White Paper on Postal Services, the European Council and Parliament, on December 15, 1997, adopted Directive 97/67/EC (OJ L 15 January 21, 1998), which provides the basic regulatory framework for the postal sector. The Directive includes provisions on the right for users to a universal service at a specified quality and an affordable price; the scope of the national postal administrations' legal monopoly (350g and five times the basic public tariff); the required accounting separation between monopoly and commercial activities; and the required designation of an independent regulator. The Commission's Postal Notice also confirms the application of EC competition rules to the postal sector.

In May 2000, the Commission tabled a proposal for a Directive on the further liberalization of the postal sector (COM (2000) 319 May 30, 2000). This proposal encompasses:

- a reduction of the reserved area for items of domestic correspondence and direct mail to 50 g and 2.5 times the basic public tariff;
- full liberalization of outbound cross-border mail and express mail;
- the prohibition of cross-subsidies, except to the extent necessary to fulfil universal service obligations; and
- foresees, in a new proposal, the further opening of the postal market to be tabled before the end of 2004.

The European Parliament watered down the Commission's proposal stating that it is not in line with a gradual and controlled opening of the market. At the time of writing, the Council was expected to come to a common position on the proposal under the Belgian Presidency, which starts in the second half of 2001, after failing to do so under the French Presidency in the second half of 2000.

EU Member States, in their conclusions at the Lisbon European Council in March 2000, paved the way towards the completion of a true internal market for services, including for postal services. In March 2001, during the Stockholm Summit, Member States renewed this statement by underlining the importance of the internal market and by deciding to put the debate on postal services back on the agenda.

Business Perspective

Business welcomes the Commission's efforts to liberalize the European market for postal services for it is a key element in developing the transport and logistics industry to its full potential. Efficient delivery networks, certainly in this era of e-business, are of paramount importance to business and consumers alike.

The benefits of a free and open market for postal services are huge. Only in a liberalized market with clear competition rules will public postal operators not distort competition. It will eliminate the risk of unfair competition; stimulate business to participate and innovate in this market; and offer consumers wider and more varied choices.

However, business regrets the lack of a final date for full liberalization in the Commission's proposal. Postal operators will now retain a substantial monopoly until 2007 at the very least. It is, therefore, imperative that EU competition rules be respected and rigorously enforced to prevent abuses of a dominant position and stop anti-competitive behavior by monopoly holders.

4. Air Transport & the Environment - Noise & Hushkitted Aircraft

Background

The European Commission's agenda on air transport and the environment for 2001 is mainly driven by developments taking place under the umbrella of the International Civil Aviation Organization (ICAO). The measurement and control of the environmental effects of international aviation have been co-ordinated among countries since 1944, pursuant to Annex 16 of the Chicago Convention on International Civil Aviation. This document, which established the ICAO, classifies aircraft into three levels of noise emissions based on noise characteristics and the size of the aircraft:

- Chapter One: non-certified civil aircraft dating from before 1969, which generate a great amount of noise. Their operation is prohibited in both the EU and the US;
- Chapter Two: older types of subsonic and heavy propeller driven planes. They must meet certain noise parameters at three specific measurement points (sideline, flyover and approach). With a few exceptions for operators from developing countries these aircraft will be phased out in the EU by 2002 (Directive 92/14/EEC). The Boeing 727 and McDonnell Douglas DC-9 are two examples of aircraft that fall into this category; and
- Chapter Three: introduced in 1977, this category applies to all newer types of subsonic aircraft, such as the Boeing 757 and Airbus 320. They are the quietest jet aircraft in service today.

Due to the population density of areas surrounding many European airports, aircraft noise has become an increasingly politicized issue within the EU. The Commission has continued to seek the reduction of noise levels around Community airports. In 1995, the ICAO's environmental task force decided not to consider a new, more stringent noise classification for aircraft (ie, a possible Chapter Four), a decision which was viewed by many European officials as a failure of the international regulatory system. It prompted these officials, supported by environmental organizations and groups from communities located near airports, to consider adoption of Europe-only noise standards for locally-operated aircraft.

After a variety of actions were considered in the framework of the European Civil Aviation Council (ECAC), the Commission finally proposed a Directive on the registration and use within the Community of civil subsonic jet aeroplanes (COM (98) 98 March 9, 1998). This proposed Directive was designed to bar the addition to European fleets, and to limit the operation at European airports of older aircraft which had been modified to meet Chapter Three requirements. This practice, which has been developed and implemented largely in the United States, allows Chapter Two aircraft to be quietened by a variety of technical or operational means to meet the Chapter Three standards, albeit in most cases by small margins. They have been accepted in the US as meeting the international standards retained in Chapter Three and are not selectively restricted at any US airport.

One means of reducing noise is by fitting a muffler, or hushkit, to the Chapter Two aircraft. Although they formally meet the most stringent international standards as explained above, the Commission believes that they still cause more noise pollution around airports than modern state-of-the-art engines. According to the Commission, fewer than 50 hushkitted aircraft are currently in use in the European Union. Yet it also argues that an increasing number of aircraft equipped with hushkits will be registered in third countries in the coming years. For example, the US implemented international agreements on the phase-out of Chapter Two aircraft this year. This implementation means that the number of hushkitted aircraft could rise significantly in the US.

The Commission therefore argued that the proposed 'Hushkit' Directive would act as a protective measure to prevent the deterioration of the noise situation around Community airports. It would affect all aircraft originally manufactured to meet Chapter Two standards, but later recertified because of modifications through any technical measures (hushkits, engine modifications, redesigned nacelles or otherwise - or indirectly through operation restrictions). Additionally, the provisions will also apply to any re-engined aircraft using engines with a bypass ratio of less than 3.0.

Upgraded to a binding Regulation rather than a Directive, the legislation was adopted in its final form by the Transport Council in April 1999 (Regulation EC/925/99 OJ L 115 April 29, 1999), but its implementation was postponed until May 4, 2000, in order to allow for additional consultations between the EU and the US. Those consultations were unsuccessful, and the Regulation is now in effect. The legislation prohibits the addition to European registries of the three targeted types of modified aircraft. For third-country operators (such as US airlines), the Regulation bars operation of such aircraft from April 1, 2002, unless such aircraft have remained on the registry in their homeland since April 1, 1995 and operated within the EU between 1995 and 1999.

US Article 84 Complaint
The failure of US-EU efforts to resolve this dispute and the May 4, 2000 entry into force of the Regulation led the US to formally request intervention by the ICAO Council. On March 14, 2000 the US filed a memorial with the ICAO pursuant to Article 84 of the Chicago Convention, which provides for binding dispute resolution by the Council. That memorial seeks repeal of the EU Regulation. The respondents (the individual EU Member States) initially had a 90-day period in which to respond, but requested and were granted a 30-day extension. The European Commission ultimately filed a response (countermemorial) on behalf of its Member States on December 4, 2000. ICAO Council President Kotaite has since met with the two parties to determine whether there is any basis for a settlement prior to the Council's formal consideration of the substantive issues of the US complaint.

Following the hushkit dispute between the EU and the US, aircraft noise issues have taken precedence over aircraft emission issues in the sphere of air transport and the environment. The Committee on Aviation Environmental Protection of the International Civil Aviation Organization (CAEP) met in January 2001 in Montreal and adopted recommendations aiming at reducing the environmental impact of aircraft noise and emissions. CAEP's main success was the newly agreed noise design standard for jet aircraft which is ten decibels lower ('minus ten'), on a cumulative basis, than the current Chapter Three standards. This new noise standard will apply to new aircraft types submitted for certification as from January 1, 2006.

The CAEP recommendations include a balanced approach to aircraft noise reduction consisting of the following elements:

- reduction of noise at source;
- improved land use planning and control;
- a wider use of noise abatement operational procedures; and
- a proposal for new take-off noise abatement procedures.

These recommendations will be submitted to the ICAO Council (June 2001) for review and further action. CAEP also considered the question of operating restrictions on Chapter Three aircraft but no agreement was reached in that area. Europe has advocated for years a phase-out of the noisier Chapter Three aircraft and it was hoping for an ICAO endorsed European phase-out between now and 2005 of aircraft having a margin of less than five decibels compared to current Chapter Three levels. The European Commission enjoyed tacit support from European carriers on the phase-out of these aircraft (the European Union civil aircraft fleet is approximately half the age of the US civil aircraft fleet).

The matter was further discussed at the ICAO colloquium in April 2001, where Europe appeared very isolated on phase-out. Further negotiations will be required before the 33rd ICAO General Assembly (September-October 2001).

For the US the outcome of CAEP and the April ICAO colloquium was a success, for Europe, it was a set-back. European countries view the outcome of CAEP as a failure because it lacks a meaningful standard for new designs and because no phase-out program was agreed upon. Many countries in Europe regard minus ten (dB) as being no more than a reflection of the status quo throughout most of the manufacturing industry. Environmental problems in Europe are highly political as populations around airports are demanding increasingly stringent measures and politicians cannot ignore these pressures. Any debate on aviation in Europe raises the issue of the environmental impact of aviation. European decision makers believe that the current growth rates of the industry are unsustainable given Europe's infrastructure constraints. This explains to some extent why reducing the environmental impact – and noise in particular – has become Europe's number one priority in the area of air transport.

Business Perspective

Concerning hushkits, US manufacturers, operators and the US Government object to Regulation EC/925/99 for several reasons. The Regulation is inconsistent with international law and ICAO standards because it discriminates on the basis of aircraft nationality and is design-based, as opposed to performance-based. Implementation of the Regulation will place EU Member States in violation of their obligations under the 1944 Chicago Convention to recognize US certificates of airworthiness for aircraft that meet all ICAO standards. The aircraft targeted by the Regulation do, in fact, comply with ICAO's highest noise stringency standard, ie, Chapter Three.

Many European airports are facing severe capacity constraints and their ability to expand is limited by environmental impact assessment inquiries/studies which are now part of any approval for further expansion (see the lengthy Heathrow Terminal five enquiry). Airlines are faced with a proliferation of local operating restrictions, particularly at night, making long term planning difficult. Furthermore, these are increasingly based on the absolute noise levels of aircraft, in contradiction to internationally agreed noise levels. More and more European decision makers perceive maximum noise levels as the key issue and reject the current ICAO noise classification which factors in the weight of the aircraft in the noise equation. This trend to reject international rules creates acute difficulties in an industry which is global by nature.

Business invites the Commission and European decision makers to address aircraft noise and emission issues strictly within the framework of ICAO. The devastating effects of widespread proliferation of local/regional operating restrictions on the functioning of the European single market and on the EU's ability to compete in a 24-hour world economy should also be fully assessed.

5. The Single European Sky

Background

Over recent years, there has been a significant rise in air traffic delays. This has had negative consequences for users and a considerable financial impact for airlines. A large part of these delays may be attributed to the EU's currently fragmented Air Traffic Control (ATC) system.

This situation has prompted Commission President, Romano Prodi, and Transport Commissioner, Loyola de Palacio, to prioritize the creation of a single European sky. This initiative aims to harmonize the organization and management of the air traffic in Europe, including the crucial need to enhance co-operation between civil and military authorities.

In December 1999, the Commission adopted a Communication on the creation of a single European sky (COM (1999) 614 December 1, 1999). This consultation paper analyzed the situation and proposed guidelines for harmonizing ATC systems across the EU.

The Commission then set up a high level group to consider the most appropriate next steps. The group was comprised of civilian and military authorities responsible for air traffic control in the Member States. Eurocontrol (European Organization for the Safety of Air Navigation) also contributed to the work with its technical expertise.

The high level group adopted a final report on the creation of a single European sky. The report put forward the proposed objectives:

- to institute a strong Community regulator of the European airspace;
- to consider airspace a common resource to which all users have access - it should be managed as a continuum, starting with upper airspace;
- to improve co-operation between Eurocontrol and the EU;
- to organize the concrete and operational participation of the military authorities with the Commission in its regulatory tasks;
- to stimulate the introduction of new technologies, whilst respecting the absolute priority of safety, and improve the interoperability of systems and techniques; and
- to develop the involvement of professional and trade union organizations in a social dialogue at the Community level.

The general thrust of these guidelines has been largely supported by both Member States and by industrial and social actors. The Parliament has also expressed a positive opinion on the approach adopted by the Commission.

Following on from the work of the high level group, the Commission is expected, at the time of writing, to adopt a Communication proposing an action plan for the creation of a single European sky by the end of 2004, attached to a framework Regulation specifying the general guidelines for, and fields of, Community intervention. The legislation will be based very closely on the recommendations made by the high level group.

The Communication and proposed Regulation were scheduled for adoption by the Commission in March 2001. However, due to disagreement between the UK and Spain over the airspace over Gibraltar airport, this has been delayed until after the UK general election on June 7, 2001. The future Regulation may include a clause suspending its application with respect to Gibraltar airport until a 1987 agreement between the UK and Spain on the joint use of the airport has been implemented

Business Perspective

The creation of the single European sky will have a number of direct implications for airlines and users.

Firstly, harmonizing the fragmented ATC systems across the EU should lead to a reduction in delays - in 2000, an average of 25.5% of all European flight departures were delayed by more than 15 minutes. It is estimated that around 40% of these delays are caused by the EU's ATC systems.

Secondly, improved air traffic management should have significant environmental benefits. Through reducing the length of time which aircraft have to circle airports before being given permission to land, fuel consumption is estimated to be cut by between 6% and 12% in the next 20 years. This reduction in greenhouse gases will be particularly important in the context of increased pressure being put on industry to reduce emissions through such measures as the EU's Climate Change Program.

Finally, a reduction in air traffic congestion should increase air safety and lower the likelihood of accidents caused by failures in ATC systems.

6. The European Air Safety Agency

Background

The level of aviation safety in Europe is acknowledged to be relatively high. According to ICAO figures, the region accounts for roughly a third of the world's air traffic. Historically, national aviation administrations (through the Joint Aviation Authorities (JAA)) have established their own detailed standards for implementing norms agreed by the International Civil Aviation Authority (ICAO) in accordance with the Chicago Convention. However, this has led to variations in certification procedures and to additional costs for the manufacturing industries which are forced to adhere to various rules.

It is for these reasons that the EU has sought over a long period of time to give Europe a true aviation safety authority, similar to the US's Federal Aviation Administration (FAA). The authority would have the responsibility for drawing up common standards to ensure the highest level of safety, overseeing the uniform application of these standards across Europe and promoting them at world level.

Originally, the air safety agency was planned to be based on an international, rather than Community, model. In 1996, the Commission proposed to transform the JAA into an international organization. Following approval for this suggestion in July 1998, the Commission undertook the task of drafting an international convention to create the air safety authority. However, in autumn 1999, Transport Commissioner Loyola de Palacio revealed that there were problems with the draft founding the convention and some possibly serious constitutional difficulties. It was at this point that the option of a Community agency was examined.

With the Council's backing, the Commission adopted a proposal for a Regulation that would put in place a Community system for air safety and environmental regulation (COM (2000) 595 September 27, 2000).

The task of the future agency will be to define the fundamental principles for the certification and maintenance of aeronautical products, and to ensure that they are implemented. By gradually integrating national certification systems, the European Air Safety Agency (EASA) should avoid the situation whereby manufacturers produce different versions of the same type of aircraft or equipment, depending on the country in which it will be used.

The EASA will ensure uniform implementation throughout the EU by drawing up codes of navigability enabling it to check the conformity of the aircraft with the basic rules, as well as issuing standard certificates for products. The agency will have powers of control and inspection to make sure that these rules are implemented.

The EASA will also provide technical assistance in contacts and negotiations with the aeronautical authorities of third countries and international organizations competent in this area. Expansion of membership will be open to any state which can make the necessary constitutional adjustments to allow them to accept EASA's authority and those which cannot will be encouraged to implement European standards within their own law.

The draft Regulation is now being considered by both the Council and Parliament whose discussions are focusing on the following questions:

- the scope of the agency (safety and environmental approval of civil aviation products);
- the basic principles underlying the agency (such as mutual recognition);
- the tasks of the Commission; and
- the tasks of the agency – its structure and financing.

It is hoped that the EASA will be established and operational by 2003.

Business Perspective

The EASA will have the most direct implications for manufacturers of aircraft and other aeronautical products who will no longer need to undergo re-certification in other countries. Instead they will require certification only by the EASA to be internationally acceptable. Not only will this new process make the certification process quicker and cheaper but it will also facilitate future certification standards.

7. Beyond EU Skies (EU-US Negotiations)

Background

Since 1991, the US has pursued a policy to further liberalize air transport by concluding bilateral open skies air services agreements around the world. It has concluded 18 such agreements with European countries, out of a total of 52 world-wide. The European agreements include the following EU Member States: the Netherlands, Luxembourg, Finland, Austria, Denmark, Sweden, Belgium, Germany, Italy, and Portugal. In cases where full open skies agreements were not possible, the US has sought very liberal arrangements; for example, there is a liberal trans-border agreement with Canada and a near open skies arrangement with France.

United States open skies model agreements provide:

- unrestricted rights to operate between gateways;
- no limits on frequencies of flights or capacity (ie, the number of passengers carried);
- no restrictions on pricing;
- unlimited 'beyond' rights, which include 'fifth freedom' operations (ie, the right to carry passengers and freight between two foreign countries. For example, a US carrier could fly from New York to Amsterdam, pick up passengers in Amsterdam, and fly them to Frankfurt); and
- extensive commercial opportunities, including broad rights to codeshare with the other's airlines.

The Commission has opposed these pro-competitive open skies agreements, alleging that they are not consistent with the EU's single aviation market and that Member States, therefore, did not have jurisdiction to negotiate air service rights with a third country. In 1998, the Commission initiated formal legal proceedings under Article 226 of the EC Treaty against EU Member States who have signed air service agreements with the US since promulgation of the EU's 'third package' aviation liberalization measures in 1993. Member States have rejected the Commission's arguments. The cases are now pending before the European Court of Justice (ECJ), which is expected to render its decision in late 2001 or early 2002.

In 1996, the Commission obtained a limited mandate from the European Council to negotiate so-called 'soft rights' with the US, with the objective of establishing a common regulatory framework. Even though exploratory discussions were held, the US declined to negotiate with the EU in the absence of a Commission mandate to address the core issue of market access (traffic rights and pricing with non-EU states).

In September 1999, the Association of European Airlines (AEA) published a proposal for a so-called Transatlantic Common Aviation Area (TCAA), calling for a US-EU agreement that would go beyond a conventional bilateral air services agreement to address a full range of issues, including competition, safety and the environment. The TCAA proposal also calls for major changes in US legislation or regulations with regard to ownership and control, 'cabotage' (the exclusive right of a country to operate the air traffic within its territory) and the Fly America Act. The Transport Council has endorsed this approach.

Although the US shares the view that it is appropriate to begin exploring options beyond the bilateral structure and welcomes the AEA proposal as a useful contribution to this process, the US has not endorsed the TCAA proposal or committed itself to a single way forward. Rather, the US continues to expand market access through open skies agreements. Most recently, on May 1, 2001 the United States, Chile, New Zealand, Singapore and Brunei signed the Multilateral Agreement on the Liberalization of International Air Transportation in Washington, DC, the first agreement of its kind. In addition to providing a country's air carriers with significant flexibility and access to conclude cooperative agreements such as codeshare arrangements with all parties to the agreement, the Multilateral Agreement eases the ownership requirements traditionally found in bilateral agreements, thereby improving carrier access to international capital markets. The Multilateral Agreement provides a single, streamlined mechanism for the exchange of aviation opportunities on open skies principles between countries worldwide. Once it has entered into force, this agreement will be open to accession by any country that is a party to the four multilateral conventions related to aviation security.

The US has also continued its dialogue with the EU. The US and the Commission held two rounds of informal discussions in 2000 to exchange views on a range of civil aviation issues, including the EU vision of a TCAA, the US view of the expansion of open skies, and cooperation on regulatory matters. The two sides agreed to continue such informal discussions in 2001.

Business Perspective

With its notion of a TCAA, the Commission intends both to complete the internal market and, in its view, increase competition to the benefit of European industry and consumers. Nonetheless, prospects for full bilateral negotiations between the EU and the US remain uncertain in the near future, given key Member States' continuing unwillingness to grant the Commission the mandate to negotiate traffic rights on their behalf. This process is further complicated by the Commission's infringement proceedings against Member States' open skies agreements in the ECJ, which have exacerbated divisions in this area. Changes in the airline industry and market over the last several years, notably the success of international carrier alliances on a global scale, have markedly improved market access, reduced prices, and enhanced competition and consumer choice. Other changes, such as trends toward airline consolidation in both the US and Europe, suggest that continued US-EU dialogue on competition issues is desirable.

8. Galileo: A European Global Navigation Satellite System

Background

The development of a European Global Navigation Satellite System (GNSS) has major strategic, political and commercial implications for Europe's capacity to control positioning, navigation and precision timing services on its own territory. One of the key characteristics of the EU's proposed system is that, unlike the existing American GPS or the Russian GLONASS, Galileo will come with service guarantees and a legal framework to support the full range of civilian uses.

The Commission estimates that the world market potential for applications and equipment will be € 40 billion within a few years, while helping to reduce congestion and contributing to what the Commission calls 'sustainable mobility'.

In its Communication adopted on February 10, 1999 (COM (1999) 54), the Commission called for EU governments to press ahead in the race to develop the next generation of satellite technology.

Satellite signals are already directing international air and sea movements but there is, according to the Commission, growing market potential to help cut traffic congestion by routing cars and trucks more efficiently, as well as for farming, fishing, fraud prevention (tracking and tracing) and infrastructure planning, mineral exploration and land surveys.

However, the present military-based systems fall short of realizing the full potential of satellite technology. In particular, the dual military/civil systems originally designed in the United States (GPS) and the former Soviet Union (GLONASS) are not backed by adequate service guarantees and a legal framework to support the full range of civilian uses. When the national security of these countries makes high demands (periodically, for example, during the Gulf War), the signal becomes unreliable for civilian users.

Ensuring an effective EU role in future developments

The fundamental issues that the Galileo project addresses is how best to ensure that the major strategic, political and commercial interests of the EU are safeguarded, and how Europe can play an effective role in the long-term development of GNSS.

In January 1998, the Commission proposed that the EU should develop its own system, if its main international partners were unwilling or unable to offer:

- firm guarantees that their GNSS service will not be withdrawn or disrupted;
- full European participation in future GNSS design, development, and operation; and
- fair opportunities for European industry to compete in all segments of the market, with equal access to the basic technologies.

The Transport Ministers' Council, in March 1998, asked the Commission to explore the scope for joint development of a system, and asked for proposals by the beginning of 1999. Following extensive discussions, it was clear that, whilst the US would not accept joint ownership and control of the next generation GPS, they do see the potential benefits of a European system that is compatible with GPS. Meanwhile, the Russian Federation has made clear its willingness to consider a joint approach, which could, in principle, have significant advantages for the Union.

Overall approach

Against this background, the shape of Europe's 'best buy' is now clarified:

- It must be an open, global system that is fully compatible (but independent from) GPS, with a significant role for the Russian Federation.
- It should be based on medium Earth orbit (MEO) satellites and will cost between € 2,200 and € 2,900 million;
- It should be developed as a Public Private Partnership (PPP) based on significant funding from the European Union's Trans European Networks (TENs) budget and R&D program, and from the European Space Agency (ESA) - and it should provide for the creation of new revenue streams.

Financing
As long as the US continues to provide its basic GPS signal free of charge, it is clear that European public spending would be needed for the development of Galileo. A financing strategy with three components is proposed:

- substantial financing at European level, through the EU budget, notably the TEN and R&D funds, and through ESA;
- establishment of revenue streams, which is likely to require regulatory action; and
- developing a PPP, to deliver complementary finance and value for money and to ensure that users' needs are met.

The cost of launching the system is estimated at € 2,200-2,900 million. Of this total, about € 750 million of that could come from Community budget lines notably the TEN and the R&D Framework programs. The European Space Agency contribution of around € 500 million could raise European level funding to around € 1,250 million.

With its latest Communication on Galileo adopted on November 22, 2000 (COM (2000) 750), the Commission outlines in detail the financing structure of Galileo which will be totally public for the whole validation phase until 2005 on a 50/50 basis between the Commission and the European Space Agency. After lengthy and controversial discussions within the Council on guarantees as regards the private financing and on the use of Galileo (military or exclusively civil) Member States managed to reach agreement on the continuation of the Galileo programme at the Transport Council meeting on April 4-5, 2001.

A budget of € 100 million will be granted from the Community budget for 2001 (from the trans-European transport network and research budget lines) to fund the development phase of the project. A similar sum is expected from the European Space Agency. The final decision on the continuation of the project will not, however, be made until December 2001 after the Council has considered the results of the upcoming call for tender from the private sector. The tendering process should help identify the commercial and public services to be provided by Galileo and specify the revenue flows that could be generated. The result of the tender evaluation will be available early in November 2001.

Business Perspective

Even without direct US involvement, there is still need for a cooperation agreement, which will ensure that the European system is interoperable and compatible with the US system. In this way, users will have the benefits of the improved service that GPS and Galileo combined will be able to offer (eg, in urban areas, where GPS does not function well).

9. Working Time in the Excluded Sectors

Background

Directive 93/104/EC on certain aspects of the organization of working time (OJ L 307 December 13, 1993) requires Member States to pay particular attention to encouraging improvements, especially in the working environment, as regards the health and safety of workers. It also requires the introduction of a maximum 48-hour working week within the Union, amongst other provisions. When adopting the Directive, the Council of Ministers decided to explicitly exclude air, rail, road, sea and inland waterway transport, sea fishing and off-shore sectors as well as doctors in training. The workers in the sectors excluded from the Directive, including self-employed workers, accounted for about 5.6 million people, of which 3.5 million people work in road transport alone.

Since adoption of Directive 93/104/EC, the Commission began a review of these excluded sectors to determine an appropriate means of regulating working time for all workers, without exception and whether occupied in mobile or sedentary forms of employment. In its 1997 White Paper (COM (97) 334 July 15, 1997) the Commission argued that an exclusion of workers from the Directive should be based on the nature of their work, and not on affiliation to a sector. The Commission expressed its preference for the so-called differentiated approach, which distinguishes between activities which could be accommodated under the general Directive (eg, non-mobile, sedentary tasks) and those which require specific sectoral measures (eg, mobile workers and workers at sea). As regards the latter two groups, the Commission wished to extend to them the provisions of the Working Time Directive concerning: four weeks paid annual leave, health assessments for night workers, adequate rest periods and a maximum of annual working hours. Specific sector-by-sector legislation concerning the working time and rest periods of mobile workers and workers at sea was also envisaged.

After two rounds of consultations, sector specific agreements were reached in both the rail and maritime industries between the respective social partners (employers' and employees' representatives) on September 30, 1998. However, negotiations in the road sector failed to secure an agreement. The Commission nevertheless decided to push ahead and adopt a package of proposals covering working time in all sectors excluded from the 1993 Directive. The Commission proposed amongst other things that the original Directive should include all non-mobile workers (including those in transport-related activities), mobile workers in the rail sector, doctors in training and offshore workers (with necessary derogations) as well as an extension of the basic protection (see above) to other mobile workers, including those in the air sector, on inland waterways and in sea-fishing.

A Communication subsequently outlined the initiatives proposed (COM (98) 662 November 18, 1998):

- a proposal for a horizontal Directive amending Directive 93/104/EC to cover sectors and activities excluded from the latter;
- a proposal concerning the organization of working time for mobile workers performing road transport activities and for self-employed drivers, on which there was no agreement in Council;
- a proposal concerning the agreement on the organization of working time of seafarers; and
- a proposal concerning the enforcement of seafarers' hours of work on board ships using Community ports.

The initiative covering hauliers was criticized by employers federations such as the International Road Transport Union (IRU), which regarded the proposed combination of definitions, working hour limits and derogations as too rigid, and thus unworkable, for the road sector. For example, the definition of working hours was widened to include routine duties such as security checks, customs, as well as loading and cleaning time.

On May 25, 1999, Social Affairs Ministers reached political agreement on three elements of the package, namely the horizontal Directive amending 93/104/EC and the two proposals covering seafarers which were subsequently adopted. Directive 99/63/EC (OJ L 167 July 2, 1999) covers organization of working time of seafarers and Directive 99/95/EC (OJ L 14 January 20, 2000) covers enforcement of seafarers' hours of work on board ships using Community ports. On April 3, 2000 a compromise was finally reached by the Conciliation Committee on the horizontal Directive and subsequently adopted (2000/34/EC; OJ L 195 August 1, 2000). Key features of the agreement were inclusion, in the scope of the 1993 Directive, of doctors in training, offshore workers, railway workers and all non-mobile workers in the previously excluded sectors.

As for the proposal on working hours in the road transport sector, the December 1999 Transport Council called on the Commission to consider an alternative proposal to resolve the issue of self-employed drivers.

In June 2000, the Commission presented a social package on working conditions in road transport, including working time. COM (2000) 754 November 22, 2000 included a legislative proposal which could exclude self-employed workers from the scope of the proposed legislation for three years. The Council adopted a formal common position in March 2001, with Portugal voting against. An assessment of the consequences of the temporary exclusion of self-employed drivers will be made two years after the deadline for transposition of the Directive. According to the proposed Directive, the average weekly working time may not exceed 48 hours. A maximum weekly working time of 60 hours is allowed on condition that, over four months, the average of 48 hours is not exceeded. A night worker may not work more than 8 hours in any 24-hour period, although an extension to ten hours is allowed if an average of eight hours a day is not exceeded within two months. Night work applies when more than two hours of night time work is included in a working period. The Commission has also undertaken to propose an amendment to Regulation 3820/85 on driving time.

Working time of mobile workers in civil aviation was agreed by European employer and employee representatives in March 2000. A Directive was adopted in November 2000 and concerns flying personnel, namely pilots and cabin crews. Working time is restricted to 2000 hours per annum, including waiting time, and reduces flying time to 900 hours.

Business Perspective

As regards the impact of the various proposals on working time in transport and for offshore workers, business has emphasized the need to maintain sufficient flexibility for work patterns in both the transport and offshore work sectors, both of which are exposed to international competition and must be allowed to compete on equivalent terms with their counterparts in other regions of the world. The horizontal Directive, as agreed in conciliation, provides the flexibility to accommodate the very specific work patterns associated with work at sea, through the provision allowing a 12-month reference period for calculation of average working hours. With respect to road transport, business has cautioned against any loss of operational flexibility, which would adversely impact the EU transport sector when firms are looking for efficiencies and timeliness in the movement of goods and wanting to maximize the benefits of the internal market for transport. At a time when traffic congestion and the associated threat to mobility is generating concern among Europe's policy-makers, business wonders whether restricting night-time driving for hauliers is consistent with the goal of improving traffic flows. Increasing day-time goods transport would seem to constitute an aggravating factor rather than taking pressure off peak traffic problems.

Energy
10. Liberalization of the Energy Sector

Background

The first stage of the liberalization process of EU energy markets started with the adoption of Directive 96/92/EC (OJ L 27 January 30, 1997) on the internal market in electricity and Directive 98/30/EC (OJ L 204 July 21, 1998) on the internal market in natural gas. Their essential mechanisms to increase competition in energy production and sales are the same:

- *unbundling accounts* - keeping separate accounts for the production, transmission and distribution activities of integrated energy companies, to prevent cross-subsidization between monopolistic and competitive activities;
- *procedures for access to the electricity and gas networks for new entrants* - conditions for access are set and published *a priori* (regulated access) or agreed on a case-by-case basis with the network operator (negotiated access);
- *construction of new electricity generation capacity* - authorizations must be granted/refused on the basis of objective, transparent and non-discriminatory criteria;
- *gradual market opening* - in three stages, more and more customers are given the right to choose their energy supplier, with a minimum degree of national market opening of 33% in 2003 (last stage of the process); and
- *public service obligations* - must be clearly defined, transparent, non-discriminatory, verifiable and published. They must fall into one of the following categories: security, quality and price of supplies, regularity, and environmental protection.

The Directives were seen as only a first step to open markets to competition. Both Directives left significant freedom to the Member States to choose through which regulatory mechanisms to transpose and implement the Directives. The degree of market opening was in particular left largely to their discretion, and some Member States took advantage of that to shield their state-owned former monopolies from competition. The current situation is that most national markets are still dominated by the former monopolies. The European level playing field is still far from being achieved.

From a strictly legal point, the implementation has been satisfactory: the transposition has been completed on time and in compliance with the provisions of the Directives in most cases, with 'only' three Member States (France, Luxembourg and Germany) being in breach of the Gas Directive and two (France and Belgium) of the Electricity Directive. The Commission has acted vigorously and launched infringement proceedings to force these countries to comply fully.

To complete the internal energy market, the Commission adopted a proposal for a liberalization package in March 2001 (COM (2001) 125 March 13, 2001), which follows co-decision of the European Parliament and Council. The first part of the package consists of amendments to the Electricity and Gas Directives:

- *unbundling* - beyond the mere separation of accounts, the Commission wants transmission system operators (TSOs – the operators of the power grid and gas pipelines) to be legally and functionally separate from the commercial activities of their parent companies, though it does not ask for ownership separation;
- *access to the network* - the Commission proposes that only the regulated access procedure be kept in place and that access tariffs and conditions be objective and non-discriminatory;
- *independent regulatory authorities* - the Commission wants to impose the creation of independent regulators for gas and electricity in each Member State. The regulator would in particular set or approve *a priori* tariffs and conditions for access to the network, define rules for the management and allocation of capacity on interconnectors (the often-congested links between the national transmission systems) and ensure respect for public service obligations;
- *public service obligations* - to ensure that competition is not introduced at the expense of social cohesion and the environment, the Commission wants to grant to all customers [ie, industrial, commercial and households] the right to be supplied with electricity of a specified quality at affordable and reasonable prices (universal service), and oblige Member States to protect vulnerable customers and achieve social and economic cohesion, environmental protection and security of supply; and
- *final market opening* - the proposed Directive aims at full competition in the energy sector, with

all industrial and commercial customers being eligible to choose their supplier by 2003 (electricity) or 2004 (gas), and all customers, including households, by 2005 for electricity and gas.

The second part of the package is a proposed Regulation on cross-border trade in electricity that provides for:

- transit costs - TSOs should be compensated for the costs of hosting electricity transit flows on their systems, according to a complex calculation mechanism that will be applied by the Commission assisted by an advisory committee (ie, comitology - the process whereby committees are consulted before policy is drafted);
- charges for the use of the national power grids should be harmonized, with consumers paying a greater share than generators. They should be cost-reflective, transparent and non-discriminatory. The payments made by TSOs for transit costs should be reflected on all users of the grids, and not just on exporters/importers;
- detailed guidelines for the harmonization of network charges will be laid down by the Commission, assisted by a Regulatory committee; and
- mechanisms to ensure that interconnection capacity is efficiently allocated.

The great majority of Member States are broadly supportive of the liberalization package. France however is fervidly resisting the proposal to accelerate full market opening, and by doing so has brought upon itself the anger of some of the other Member States. Germany for its part opposes the mandatory creation of national energy regulators (it is the only Member State without a regulator at the moment, relying instead on a self-regulatory system enforced by the *Bundeskartellamt* – the Federal Office for Monopolies). The two countries asserted that the draft conclusions of the Stockholm European Council of March 2001 be toned down and are expected to ally together to fight the most challenging aspects of the new proposal.

Business Perspective

The Commission's March 2001 proposal for a Liberalization Directive, if implemented as such, would allow new entrants to carve out market shares from the former monopolies. This is true at least for, broadly speaking, the northern part of the EU (the UK, Finland and Sweden) where Member States have already gone beyond the minimum requirements set out in the existing Gas and Electricity Directives and sought to open their markets widely to competition. France, Greece, Portugal, The Netherlands and Austria however are lagging behind in the degree of market opening. Agreement on the Directive will probably require concessions from pro-competition Member States and should not be expected before 2003 at the latest. Consequently, the way things look now, it will take some time before the single European energy market will take place.

The proposed Regulation on cross-border electricity trade is a key to integrating the fifteen electricity markets into one, bringing electricity prices down and allowing power companies to grow across borders organically, rather than through mergers and acquisitions.

Chapter XII
References

THE EU COMMITTEE
OF THE AMERICAN CHAMBER OF COMMERCE IN BELGIUM

A

ACP	Africa, Caribbean & Pacific countries
ADR	Alternative Dispute Resolution
AEA	Association of European Airlines
APEC	Asia Pacific Economic Cooperation Forum
ASEAN	Association of South East Asian Nations
ARM	Alternative Regulatory Models
ASEM	Asia-Europe Ministerial Meeting
ATS	Alternative Trading System

B

BIAC	Business and Industry Advisory Committee
BITs	Bilateral Investment Treaties
BSE	Bovine Spongiform Encephalopathy
B2B	Business-to-Business
B2C	Business-to-Consumer

C

CAA	Conformity Assessment Agreement
CAD	Capital Adequacy Directive
CAP	Common Agricultural Policy
CARDS	Community Assistance for Reconstruction, Democratization & Stabilization
CCC	Community Customs Code
CCT	Common Customs Tariff
CDM	Clean Development Mechanisms
CEECs	Central & Eastern European Countries
CEN	European Committee for Standardization
CENELEC	European Committee for Electro-Technical Standardization
CEO	Chief Executive Officer
CEPT	European Conference of Postal & Telecommunications Administrations
CERCLA	Comprehensive Environmental Response Compensation and Liability Act
CESDP	Common European Security and Defense Policy
CFSP	Common Foreign and Security Policy
CJD	Creutzfeldt Jacob Disease
COCOM	Co-ordinating Committee on Multilateral Export Controls
COM DOC	Communications Document (Commission publication)
COP	Conference of Parties
CoR	Committee of Regions
CORE	Council of Registrars
CPC	Community Patent Convention
CSE	Council of Ministers document
CSR	Corporate Social Responsibility
CTG	Council for Trade in Goods

D

DG	Directorate General
DNS	Domain Name System
DSL	Digital Subscriber Line
DSP	Dispute Settlement Panel

E

EAP	Environmental Action Program
EASA	European Air Safety Agency
EBRD	European Bank for Reconstruction & Development
ECAC	European Civil Aviation Council
ECB	European Central Bank
ECBS	European Committee on Banking Standards
ECCP	European Climate Change Program
ECJ	European Court of Justice
ECN	Electronic Clearing Network
ECOFIN	EU Economic and Finance Ministers
ECS	European Company Statute
EEA	European Environmental Agency
EEC	European Economic Communities
EEE	Electrical & Electronic Equipment
EFA	European Food Authority
EFTA	European Free Trade Association
EHMC	European Health Co-ordination Monitoring Center
EIB	European Investment Bank
EIDHR	European Initiative for Democracy and Human Rights
EINECS	European Inventory of Existing Commercial Chemical Substances
EIORP	European Institution for Occupational Retirement Provision
ELV	End-of-Life Vehicles
EMAC	Economic & Monetary Affairs & Industrial Policy
EPA	Economic Partnership Agreement
EP	European Parliament
EPC	European Patent Convention
EPER	European Pollutant Emission Register
EPO	European Patent Office
EPRD	European Program for Reconstruction & Development
EQS	Environmental Quality Standards
ERC	European Radio Communications
ERTMS	European Rail Traffic Management System
ESC	Economic & Social Committee
ETSI	European Telecommunications Standards Institute
ETUC	European Confederation of Trade

	Unions
EU	European Union
EURES	European Employment Services
EUROPOL	European Police Office
EUROSTAT	European Statistical Office
EWC	European Works Council

F

FCCC	Framework Convention on Climate Change
FDI	Foreign Direct Investment
FESCO	Federation of European Securities Commissions
FRY	Federal Republic of Yugoslavia
FSCs	Foreign Sales Corporations
FTA	Free Trade Area
FTTA	Free Trade Area of the Americas
FYROM	Former Yugoslav Republic of Macedonia

G

GATS	General Agreement on Trade in Services
GATT	General Agreement on Tariffs & Trade
GDP	Gross Domestic Product
GHGs	Green house gases
GMMs	Genetically Modified Micro-organisms
GMO	Genetically Modified Organisms
GPA	Government Procurement Agreement
GPSD	General Product Safety Directive
GPS	General Product Safety
GSM	Global System for Mobile Communications
GSP	Generalized System of Preferences
gTLD	generic Top-Level Domain Names

H

HGV	Heavy Goods Vehicles
HPV	High Production Volume

I

IANA	Internet Assigned Numbers Authority
ICANN	Internet Corporation for Assigned Names & Numbers
ICAO	International Civil Aviation Organization
IEF	Information Exchange Forum
IEPCE	Initiative for Ethical Production and Consumption in Europe
IET	International Emissions Trading
IGC	Intergovernmental Conference
ILO	International Labor Organization
IMF	International Monetary Fund
IMO	International Maritime Organization
IMT	International Mobile Telecommunication
IOPC	International Oil Pollution Compensation Funds
IPP	Integrated Product Policy
IPPC	Integrated Pollution Prevention and Control
IPR	Intellectual Property Rights
IPTS	Institute for Prospective Technological Studies
ISD	Investment Services Directive
ISDN	Integrated Services Digital Network
ISP	Internet Service Provider
ISPA	Instrument for Structural Policies for pre-Accession
IT	Information Technology
ITA	Information Technology Agreement
ITU	International Telecommunications Union

J

JHA	Justice & Home Affairs
JI	Joint Implementation
JCC	Joint Cooperation Committee

L

LCA	Life Cycle Approach
LDCs	Less Developed Countries

M

MEA	Multilateral Environment Agreement
MEP	Member of the European Parliament
MFN	Most Favored Nation
MNE	Multinational Enterprises
MNEPR	Multilateral Nuclear Environmental Program
MoU	Memorandum of Understanding
MTO	Mutual Trade Organization
MVNO	Mobile Virtual Network Operator

N

NAFTA	North American Free Trade Agreement
NAP	National Action Plan
NATO	North Atlantic Treaty Organization
NCTS	New Computerized Transit System
NERA	National Economic Research Associates
NCAs	National Competition Authorities
NGO	Non-Governmental Organization
NIS	New Independent State
NME	Non-Market Economy
NRA	National Regulatory Authorities
NTA	New Transatlantic Agenda
NTMA	New Transatlantic Marketplace

O

OCIMF	Oil Companies International Marine Forum
OECD	Organization for Economic Cooperation & Development
OJ	Official Journal of the European Communities
OHG	Global Operators Harmonization Group
ONP	Open Network Provision

P

PCA	Partnership & Cooperation Agreements
PCS	Personal Communications Services
PHARE	Poland and Hungary Assistance for the Reconstruction of the Economy
PICS	Platform for Internet Content Selection
PPM	Process & Production Method
PSTN	Public Switched Telecommunications Network
PVC	Polyvinyl chloride

Q

QMV	Qualified Majority Voting

R

RAPEX	Rapid Alert System
RoHS	Restriction of Use of Certain Hazardous Substances
R&TD	Research and Technological Development
RSA	Republic of South Africa

S

SAA	Stabilization & Association Agreement
SANCO (DG)	Health & Consumer Affairs
SAPARD	Special Accession Program for Agricultural and Rural Developments
SEA	Single European Act
SEA	Single European Authorization
SEC	Commission internal document
SEE	South East Europe
SHP	Safe Harbor Principles
SLIM	Simpler Legislation for the Internal Market
SMAP	Single Market Action Plan
SME	Small & Medium-Sized Enterprise
SMP	Significant Market Power
SSC	Scientific Steering Comittee

T

TABD	Transatlantic Business Dialogue
TACD	Transatlantic Consumer Dialogue
TACIS	Technical Assistance for the CIS
TAED	Transatlantic Environment Dialogue
TASBI	Transatlantic Small Business Initiative
TBT	Technical Barriers to Trade
TCAA	Transatlantic Common Aviation Area
TDCA	Trade, Development & Cooperation Agreement
TEC	Treaty of the European Communities
TENs	Trans-European Networks
TEP	Transatlantic Economic Partnership
TEU	Treaty on European Union
TIES	Transatlantic Information Exchange Service
ToA	Treaty of Amsterdam
TRIMS	Trade-Related Investment Measures
TRIPS	Trade-Related Intellectual Property

U

UCITS	Collective Investment in Transferable Securities
UNCTAD	United Nations Conference on Trade & Development
UMTS	Universal Mobile Telecommunications System
UN	United Nations
UNICE	Union of Industrial & Employers' Confederations of Europe
UNFCCC	United Nations Framework Convention on Climate Change

V

VAT	Value Added Tax
VHS	Video Home System
VIES	VAT Information Exchange System
VIEW	Institut für Europäisches Wirtschafts und Verbraucherrecht

W

W-CDMA	Wideband Code Division
WCO	World Customs Organization
WEEE	Waste from Electrical and Electronic Equipment
WEU	West European Union
WIPO	World Intellectual Property Organization
WRC	World Radio Conference
WTO	World Trade Organization
WWW	World Wide Web

X

XDSL	Generic Digital Subscribers Lines

A

B

C

D

E

F

G

H

I

J

K

L

M

N

O

P

Y

Abbott Laboratories
Adamson BSMG
Accenture
Agilent Technologies
A.I.G.
Akin, Gump, Strauss, Hauer & Feld
Alcan
Alcoa Europe
American Express
AOL Europe
AOL Time Warner
Amway
Andersen
Ashurst Morris Crisp
AT&T
Avon Products

Baker & McKenzie
Baxter World Trade
Becton Dickinson
Bellsouth
Black & Decker
Boeing International
Bristol-Myers Squibb
British American Tobacco

Cargill
Caterpillar
Chiquita
Chiron
Chubb Insurance Company
Citibank
Cleary Gottlieb Steen & Hamilton
Clifford Chance Pünder
Coca-Cola
Compaq
Concert
Corning
Coudert Brothers, Coppens, Van Ommeslaghe & Faure
Covington & Burling

DaimlerChrysler
Dechert Price & Rhoads
Dell
DHL Worldwide Network
Dorsey & Whitney LLP
Dow Corning
Dow Europe
Dun & Bradstreet
Du Pont de Nemours

Eamonn Bates Europe
Edelman
EDS
Eli Lilly
Emerson Electric Co.
EPPA
Ernst & Young
ExxonMobil Chemical
ExxonMobil

Federal Express
Foley & Lardner
Ford of Europe
Freshfields Deringer Bruckhaus

General Electric
General Motors
Gillette
GlaxoSmithKline
Goldman Sachs
GPC
Grayling Political Strategy
Guardian Europe

Hewlett Packard
Hill & Knowlton
Hogan & Hartson
Honeywell
Hunton & Williams

Intergraph
IBM
Instinet
Intel
International Paper

Johnson & Johnson
Jones, Day, Reavis & Pogue

Keller & Heckman
Kellogg's
Kimberly Clark
Kodak
KPMG
Kraft Foods

LeBoeuf Lamb, Greene & Macrae
Levi Strauss
Linklaters & Alliance
Lovells Boesebeck Droste
Lucent Technologies

3M
Masterfoods
Mastercard
Mattel
McDonald's
McKinsey & Co.
Merck Sharp & Dohme
Merial
Microsoft
Monsanto
Morgan, Lewis & Bockius
Morgan Stanley
Motorola

Nalco
NCR
Nike
Nortel Networks

Oppenheimer, Wolff & Donnelly
Oracle

Pennzoil
Pfizer
Pharmacia
Philip Morris
PriceWaterhouseCoopers
Procter & Gamble

Qualcomm

Reebok
Reliant Energy
Rohm & Haas

SBC Communications
Skadden, Arps, Slate, Meagher & Flom
Solutia
Squire, Sanders & Dempsey
Standard & Poor's
Sun Microsystems

Texaco

United Parcel Service
United Technologies Corporation

Van Bael & Bellis
Verizon Communications
Viacom
VNU World Directories
Vodafone

Walt Disney Company
Weber Shandwick
Weil Gotshal & Manges LLP
Western Union
White & Case
Wilmer, Cutler & Pickering
W. L. Gore & Associates
Worldcom

The EU Committee
The American Chamber of Commerce
avenue des Arts, 50 box 5
1000 Brussels, Belgium
Tel: 02 513 68 92 Fax: 02 513 79 28
EUC@post1.amcham.be
http://www.eucommittee.be

I wish to order:

__ copy(ies) of the **Business Guide to EU Initiatives 2001/2002 - NEW!**
__ copy(ies) of the **EU Guide to Consumer Affairs 2001 - NEW!**
__ copy(ies) of the **Guide to the European Parliament 1999-2004 (updated edition) - NEW!**
__ copy(ies) of the **EU Environment Guide 2000**
__ copy(ies) of the **EU Transport & Logistics Guide 1999**
__ copy(ies) of the **Guide to the Enlargement of the EU**
__ copy(ies) of the **EU Information Society Guide 1998**
€ 50 (2,017 BEF) non-members;
€ 40 (1,614 BEF) AmCham Belgium members;
€ 25 (1,009 BEF) EU Committee members

__ copy(ies) of the **EU Information Handbook 2001**
€ 60 (2,420 BEF) non-members;
€ 45 (1,815 BEF) AmCham Belgium members;
€ 30 (1,210 BEF) EU Committee members

__ annual subscription(s) to **Business Guide Supplement** (ten issues per year)
€ 250 (10,085 BEF) non-members;
€ 210 (8,471 BEF) AmCham Belgium members;
€ 160 (4,437 BEF) EU Committee members

__ annual subscription to **Business Guide Supplement On-Line** (ten updates a year)
€ 200 (8,068 BEF) non-members;
€ 160 (6,454 BEF) AmCham Belgium members;
€ 110 (6,454 BEF) EU Committee members

Name:
Organization:
Address:

Tel: **Fax:** **E-mail:**

PAYMENT

For credit card orders, please call the Communications Department on (32 2) 513 68 92

I enclose a check for ___________ € / BEF*

I have transferred the sum of ___________ € / BEF* to the EU Committee's Office account No. BBL 310-0823099-43 Banque Bruxelles Lambert, ave. des Arts 26, B-1000 Brussels

* Please add € 10 (403 BEF) for bank transactions if payment is made outside Belgium
* Please also add € 5 (202 BEF) for postage & packaging per book for Belgium and EU countries and € 10 (403 BEF) for the rest of the world
* For the Business Guide Supplement, please add € 25 (1,009 BEF) for postage & packaging for Belgium, € 35 (1,412 BEF) for EU countries and € 40 (1,614 BEF) for the rest of the world

Complete this form and return by mail or fax, with appropriate payment, to the above address.

Signature:___________________________ **Date:**___________________________